Complete CAT

Clare Gibson and Maria Costantino

Published by SILVERDALE BOOKS
An imprint of Bookmart Ltd
Registered number 2372865
Trading as Bookmart Ltd
Blaby Road
Wigston
Leicester LE18 4SE

D&S Books Ltd
Kerswell,
Parkham Ash, Bideford
Devon, England
EX39 5PR

e-mail us at:- enquiries@d-sbooks.co.uk

This edition printed 2007

ISBN 13: 9-781-84509-371-6

DS0075. Complete Cat

Creative Director: Sarah King
Editor: Judith Millidge
Project Editor: Anna Southgate
Designer: Debbie Fisher & Co.
Photographer: Paul Forrester

Fonts: Futura and Times New Roman

Material from this book previously appeared in *The Cat Care Handbook* and *The
Handbook of Cat Breeds*.

Printed in Thailand

3 5 7 9 10 8 6 4 2

CONTENTS

Introduction		6
	Out of Africa	7
	Cats of the Orient	10
	Feline superstitions	11
	Raining cats and dogs	13
	Introducing Caspar and Melchior	14
	Of crossped and purebreds	15
1	The feline world	18
	A hunter's build	21
	A tooth-and-claw fighter	25
	An acrobat's skills	26
	The feline senses	28
	The cat's social life	36
	The cat's powers of communication	39
	Feline self-maintenance	43
2	Adopting a cat	48
	Cat or kitten?	50
	Male or female?	52
	One cat or more?	53
	Moggie or pedigree?	54
	Cat sources	57
	What to look for in a kitten or cat	58
	Basic cat-care equipment	60
	Making your home safe for your cat	75
	The big day: bringing your cat home	77
	Handling your cat	80
	Your cat and children	81
	Your cat and other household pets	82
3	Cat-care fundamentals	84
	Registering with a vet	85
	Vital vaccinations	86
	Worms and worming	91
	Fleas and de-fleaing	93

	Cat identification	95
	Neutering your cat	96
	Having kittens	97
	Caring for growing kittens	99
	Feeding dos and don'ts	101
	Feline-related hygiene measures	103
	Grooming your cat	104
	Fostering feline fitness	108
	Training your cat	111
	When the human's away . . .	114
	Felines on the move	116
	Caring for an older cat	118
4	Feline afflictions and their treatment	121
	Afflictions of the skin and coat	122
	Afflictions of the ears	126
	Afflictions of the eyes	129
	Afflictions of the nose	132
	Afflictions of the mouth	133
	Monitoring a cat's vital signs	135
	Giving a cat medication	136
	Caring for an injured or sick cat	138
5	Symptom diagnosis and emergency action	142
	Symptom diagnosis	143
	Emergency action	147
6	Cat Breeds	155
	Glossary	251
	Index	253
	Addresses	255
	Bibliography	256
	Dedicaton, credits and acknowledgements	256

I, born of a race of strange things,

Of deserts, great temples, great kings,

In the hot sands where the nightingale never sings!

Ford Madox Ford, from The cat of the house.

INTRODUCTION

The ambivalence with which it is regarded has elevated the cat to a unique position among domestic animals. Since it first chose to co-exist with humans around four millennia ago, the cat has appeared as a home-loving creature of comfort by day that transforms itself into a wild hunter by night. An enigmatic character, it has become an object of admiration and worship on the one hand, and a victim of suspicion and persecution on the other. Perhaps the key to unlocking the paradox of the cat is that it made a pragmatic choice to throw in its lot with humankind, without ever forfeiting the streak of wildness that earns it the respect of those who appreciate its independent character and the vilification of those who are unsettled by its inscrutability. And, as Ford Madox Brown observed, every cat of the house, be it a humble moggie or pampered pedigree, exudes an air of exotic mystery, its cool, self-contained gaze taking us back in time to the 'hot sands' and 'strange things' of its ancient Egyptian ancestors.

OUT OF AFRICA

The domestic cat, Felis catus or Felis domesticus, can trace its lineage back 50 million years, to the Miacis from which the Dinictis, Machairodus and eventually today's cat family, the Felidae (which comprises Acinonyx, cheetahs; Panthera, big cats; and Felis, small cats), evolved. And although the specific ancestry of the domestic cat has been veiled by the mists of time, and further clouded by the interbreeding of various species of wildcat the world over, genetic analysis indicates that most European domestic cats are descended from the African wildcat, Felis sylvestris lybica.

The history of the African wildcat's domestication is depicted in ancient Egyptian art, the world's earliest feline image being seen in an Egyptian tomb painting dating from around 2600 bc. Although the subject of this portrait is probably an African wildcat, the house cats that are immortalised in the tomb paintings found at Dier el Medina show that by 1600 bc certain members of the Felis sylvestris lybica family had become domesticated. The most likely reason why these cats initially consented to exchange their wildcat lifestyle for one of domestication – and why the ancient Egyptians welcomed them into their homes – is that of mutual benefit, the cats finding plentiful prey around the Egyptians' grain stores and the Egyptians in turn valuing their efficiency as pest-controllers. A practical relationship of mutual advantage was established, and cats eventually came to be prized as far more than just skilled mousers and keen-eyed killers of the snakes that slithered into Egyptian homes.

ALL CATS HAVE ANCIENT EGYPTIAN ANCESTRY.

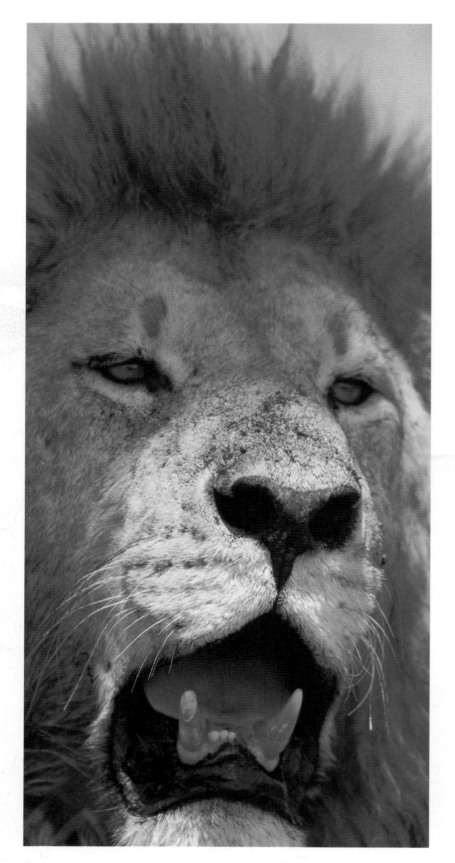

LIONS WERE SAID TO PULL CYBELE'S CHARIOT, AND SMALLER EUROPEAN WILDCATS THAT OF FREYA.

Cats feature largely in the mythology of ancient Egypt, and always as protectors: the cat-headed goddess Mafdet, for example, being venerated for her role in protecting the pharaoh's palace from venomous snakes. The goddess who was primarily responsible for elevating the cat to its sacred status, however, was Bast, or Bastet, the cat-headed sister of Sekhmet (the lion-headed war goddess) and either the wife or sister of Ra (the Egyptians' sun god and supreme deity), who slayed the underworld serpent Apep before it could capsize the boat in which Ra traversed the sky by day. Worshipped as the vigilant guardian of the sun god, as well as the home, Bast was especially revered as a moon goddess who had the power to bestow the gift of fertility upon her worshippers. Along with their snake-killing prowess, another reason why cats were so closely identified with Bast can be seen in their waxing and waning pupils, for, as Edward Topsell reported in 1607, in his Historie of Foure-footed Beasts,

The Egyptians have observed in the eyes of a Cat, the encrease of the Moonlight for with the Moone, they shine more fully at the full, and more dimly in the change and wain, and the male Cat doth also vary his eyes with the Sunne; for when the Sunne ariseth, the apple of his eye is long; towards noone it is round, and at the evening it cannot be seene at all, but the whole eye sheweth alike.

While female cats were associated with the moon goddess, and toms with the sun god, all cats were sacred to Bast, the 'mother' of cats whose centre of worship was the city of Bubastis. Cats led a pampered existence at Bast's temple in Bubastis, being embalmed and mummified when they died before being interned in a vast feline necropolis. It was certainly a cat's life in Egypt, particularly after Bast became the national deity in around 950 bc. The Greek historian Herodotus, writing in about 450 bc, tells us that when a house cat died, the whole family shaved off their eyebrows as a sign of mourning, Diodorus Siculus adding during the first century bc that killing a cat was a crime punishable by death.

Cats were jealously guarded against abduction from Egypt by unworthy foreigners (although a few were probably smuggled out by Phoenician traders), but things changed when the rule of the pharaoh was replaced by that of the Roman emperor in 30 bc. By ad 390 Bast's worship had been banned, and with Egypt's star in decline and Rome's in the ascendant, some of the deposed goddess's sacred creatures travelled to the outposts of the Roman Empire with the legions (who, no doubt, valued their rodent-killing services aboard their galley ships), others following the Silk Road to the Far East.

Although they were never venerated to the exalted degree enjoyed by the sacred cats of Egypt, their Graeco-Roman descendants were nevertheless accorded respect through their association with the Greek moon goddess Artemis and her Roman counterpart Diana, both of whom were equated with Bast. And with the spreading of the Graeco-Roman influence throughout Europe, cats were said to pull the vehicle of Freya, the goddess of fertility whose appearance in Norse mythology may have been inspired by the prototypical figure of Cybele, the fierce

Phrygian mother goddess who travelled in a lion-drawn chariot (the feline discrepancy being due to the prevalence of wildcats, and not lions, throughout Northern Europe). And if their religious associations won them some honour, their vermin-suppressing prowess covered them with glory, cats forcing the mongoose, ferret and stone marten to concede their combined title of Rome's champion rat-killers during the fourth century ad. Wherever they lived, cats were highly valued for their hunting skills, as was reflected by a decree made in 948 by the Welsh prince Howel the Good, that anyone who killed or stole one of his granary's cats would be made to forfeit a sheep, lamb or a considerable quantity of grain.

IT WAS THE ANCIENT EGYPTIANS WHO FIRST DOMESTICATED THE CAT.

CATS OF THE ORIENT

At the same time as cats were hard at work controlling European rodents, their Oriental brethren were providing a similar service in the paddy fields and silk farms of China and Japan. In the Far East, however, cats were as much admired for their sleek feline beauty as for their hunting skills. The Cat Book Poems of medieval Siam (Thailand), for example, praised the Korat for its 'hairs so smooth, with tips like clouds and roots like silver, with eyes that shine like dewdrops on a lotus leaf'. In contrast to Europe's workaday felines, the ancestors of such sacred cats as the Korat, Siamese and Burmese were cherished for their elegant appearance and were therefore prevented from crossbreeding, with the result that most Oriental purebreds have unbroken pedigrees that stretch back for centuries.

There are many stories attached to Oriental cats, some connected to their physical characteristics and others explaining why they are worthy of honour. In the Buddhist belief of Thailand, for example, when an extremely rarefied human spirit dies, their soul enters a Siamese cat and only attains nirvana when the cat in turn passes away. Indeed, during the twentieth century, it was still the custom for

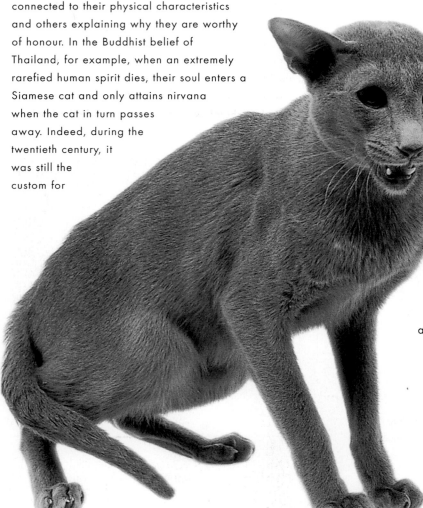

a Siamese cat, into which, it was believed, the recently deceased king of Siam's soul had passed, to attend the coronation of his successor. Another tale speaks of how the Birman, Burma's sacred cat, gained its golden fur and blue eyes when a priest of the Khmer temple at Lao-Tsun died while invoking the aid of the goddess Tsun-Kyan-Kse to repel a Siamese raid on her temple, his prayers being answered after his spirit left his body and entered his favourite cat, who also assumed the goddess's colouring.

Other Oriental beliefs concerning cats are, however, less complimentary, it being said, for instance, that the cat is cursed because it did not mourn the death of Buddha. And Chinese and Japanese folk belief swings from regarding the cat as a bringer of prosperity (probably because it is the enemy of destructive rodents) to fearing it as a malevolent shape-shifter that heralds misfortune. Although the Maneki-Neko, the effigy of a cat that beckons with its left paw, is a symbol of good luck in Japan that is kept in many homes, many felines are thought to be the bringers of death and destruction. Considered a yin creature of the night in China, white cats are said to be turned into demons by the moon's rays, while in Japan, a race of vampire cats (whose forked tails fortunately make them instantly recognisable) are furthermore said to murder women, take on their appearance and, thus disguised, suck the life-blood out of their sleeping bedfellows. Similarly, cases of cot death in Europe were once blamed on vampire cats that allegedly fed on the breath of babies.

THE SMOOTH FUR AND SLEEK APPEARANCE OF CATS WAS HIGHLY VALUED IN THE FAR EAST.

FELINE SUPERSTITIONS

Despite such Far Eastern reservations about the cat's exact intentions towards humanity, it is considered wise to hedge one's bets and to treat cats with respect, as in Persia (Iran), where black cats are said to be jinns (spirits that assume feline form) or hemzads (individuals' guardian 'angels'). The world over, the cat's mysterious, far-seeing eyes are considered to reveal its clairvoyant powers, as well as its agility and cunning ingenuity, just some of the characteristics for which it is respected as a totemic animal by many African and Native American peoples.

FELINE EYES HAVE PROMPTED MANY SUPERSTITIONS.

Two charming stories from Islamic tradition reveal why the cat is regarded with affection by many Muslims. The first tells that when a pair of rats multiplied and over-ran Noah's ark, Noah stroked the lion's nose, its reflexive sneeze producing two cats who swiftly solved Noah's vermin problem. The second relates that the 'M' that can be seen on many cats' foreheads is the mark that was made by the Prophet Mohammed when he stroked his favourite cat. Interestingly, this explanation for the cat's 'M' has a parallel in a long-forgotten Christian tradition, it being said that it is evidence of the Virgin Mary's gratitude to the cat who kept the baby Jesus warm in his manger in Bethlehem. Echoing the tale of Dick Whittington, sometime mayor of London, certain Western European folk beliefs furthermore tell of cats (called matagots in southern France) that typically repay their owners' kindness with riches and other life-transforming rewards.

Such positive feline associations are sadly rare in Christianity, however, whose influence decimated the feline population of Europe (with the result that, as some social historians believe,

rats flourished, enabling the bubonic plague, or Black Death, to sweep in deadly swathes across Europe). Long before they were converted to Christianity, the Celts, who told of terrible giant cats that did battle with their heroes, sacrificed their 'evil' feline representatives on earth in religious rites. Whether or not such old beliefs simply persisted or newer anti-feline sentiments replaced them, from medieval times until the last of the vicious witch hunts that infected Europe until the age of Enlightenment, the Roman Catholic Church branded cats – especially black ones – the servants of Satan.

They were regarded as the nocturnal (in itself considered suspicious, along with their eerily glowing eyes) 'familiars', or demonic helpers, of witches, who were, of course, in league with the devil. Part of the cat's association with witchcraft dates back to its link with the Roman goddess Diana, whom the Church accused medieval 'witches' of invoking in their sinister satanic rituals, as well as with Hekate, or Hecate, the fearsome Graeco-Roman goddess of the underworld who transformed the maiden Galinthias into a cat to serve as her priestess. A more prosaic explanation, however, is that the lonely old women who were accused of witchcraft were often outcasts who had only their pet cats for companionship.

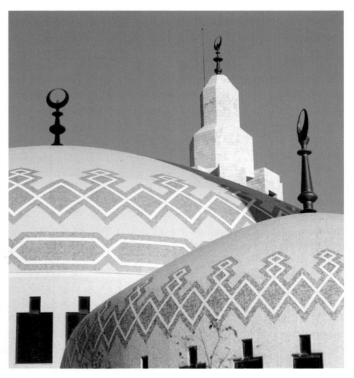

CATS ARE REGARDED WITH AFFECTION IN ISLAMIC TRADITION.

WITCHES

A vital justification of the Church's attempt to stamp out any beliefs that it regarded as being heretical was the damning 'evidence' that those accused of being heretics carried out satanic rites in which the devil was worshipped in the form of a black cat. (The satanic symbolism of the black cat was potent: the epidemic of Sydenham's chorea, or St Vitus's dance, that raged through what is now the French town of Metz in 1344 was said to have been caused by Satan in the form of a black cat, and for centuries thereafter cats were publicly burned in the spirit of commemorative revenge.) And when Europe's mass 'heresies' had been all but eradicated, the Church turned to smaller fry – 'witches' and their 'familiars'.

**BLACK CATS SIGNIFY BOTH GOOD
AND BAD LUCK.**

In his instructions to the Inquisition, for example, Pope Innocent VIII (who reigned from 1484 to 1492) ordering the hunting-down of cat-idolaters.

In England, the ascent to the throne of James VI of Scotland as James I in 1603 heralded a virulent period of anti-witch hysteria, fuelled by the new king's authorship of a treatise on witchcraft, Daemologie (1597), and compounded by the Witchcraft Act of 1604. The salacious transcriptions of the trials of the unfortunates accused of witchcraft, such as Agnes and Joan Waterhouse and Elizabeth Francis at Chelmsford in 1566, are strewn with references to feline familiars, in this case 'Sathan' (unusually, a white-spotted cat, albeit supposedly a blood-sucking one), whom Agnes Waterhouse, it was said, once 'toke . . . in her lap and put hym in the wood before her door, and wylled him to kyll three of the Father Kersyes hogges'. Agnes Waterhouse was hanged, and if Sathan was captured, it is likely that he suffered an agonising death. (Perhaps cats have ancestral memories of those terrible times, and maybe it is no quirk of nature that domestic cats can adapt to the feral lifestyle so readily.)

Vestiges of such irrational anti-feline prejudices survived long after the last 'witch' swung from the gibbet. Dead cats were often laid in the foundations of buildings to ward off evil (or rodents: Bohemian farmers believed, for instance, that burying a cat in a field would protect their crops from mice). A black cat crossing one's path was said by some to be a harbinger of bad luck (although British superstition stipulates the reverse), while spiteful women were sometimes described as being 'catty'. And if that wasn't enough, cats are said to cause bad weather, too.

RAINING CATS AND DOGS

King James's interest in witchcraft had been kindled in 1590 by the trial of Dr John Fian, who was accused of having used sorcery to try to kill the king himself as he returned from Denmark to Scotland by sea. It was alleged that Fian and his coven had thrown cats into the sea in a murderous attempt to whip up a ship-wrecking storm, an expedient that would not have sounded so ridiculous to the sixteenth-century ear as it does to us today. Indeed, nautical lore holds that throwing the ship's cat overboard will result in a storm (but presumably disposing of the ship's vermin-killer-in-chief should only be done in the most desperate of circumstances), while trapping one in a barrel can produce a contrary wind. (Conversely, Japanese sailors believe that the tortoiseshell Mi-Ke cats that they welcome aboard have the power to repel storm devils.)

WHILE THE CAT IS ASSOCIATED WITH RAIN, STORM WINDS ARE THE DOG'S PROVINCE.

BAD WEATHER

Folk belief has long credited felines and canines with the ability to influence the weather – hence the expression 'raining cats and dogs', with cats denoting torrential rain and dogs storm winds – an attribution that probably stems in part from the powers and characteristics of the Norse gods and their attendant creatures and in part to both animals' acute sensitivity to changes in the weather and the cat's to water in particular.

A further traditional belief is that cats can act as feline weather-forecasters if you know how to read the signs, as Jonathan Swift, the author of Gulliver's Travels (1726), explained in verse:

> Careful observers may foretell the hour
> (By sure prognostics) when to dread a shower;
> While rain depends, the pensive cat gives o'er
> Her frolics, and pursues her tail no more.

Swift's reference to tail-pursuing echoes the nautical expression 'the cat has a gale of wind in her tail', describing a cat's agitation when it senses a stiff following wind, as well as the belief that rain is imminent when a cat settles down to enjoy a thorough ear-washing session.

INTRODUCING CASPAR AND MELCHIOR

Despite the devoted attention that they pay to ear-washing, sadly neither of our two cats seem to possess the power — or, perhaps, the inclination — to save us the bother of watering the garden on a sultry summer's night. Caspar and Melchior will be putting in an occasional appearance in the pages of this book to illustrate some of the choices and problems — as well as the pleasures — that all cat-owners inevitably face. I hope that sharing our experience of their habits and idiosyncrasies, as well as of the ailments that have afflicted them during the past twelve years and the care strategies that we have used (some successful, others less so), will prove useful to you.

Caspar and Melchior have been constant — if often mutually intolerant — companions for most of their lives. Born a couple of weeks apart at the same cat-rescue sanctuary, Caspar is a dark-silver tabby (a crosspedigree, or 'crossped' for short, a name that describes both his parentage and sometimes also his mood when food doesn't materialise fast enough), while Melchior is a light-silver Somali, although, having no pedigree certificate, I cannot vouch for the purity of his lineage. Neither cat's parentage matters to us, but pedigree is of vital importance to many cat-owners. (And 'owner' is not really an accurate description of those who live with cats, most of whom know that if anyone can be said to be 'owned' in a human–feline relationship, it is the human. The intractability of the cat is reflected in British law, which holds that because it is a wild animal that cannot be controlled, its 'owner' cannot be held responsible for its actions, in contrast to a dog, whose owner must both licence it and be prepared to be held to account for any damage or nuisance that it causes.)

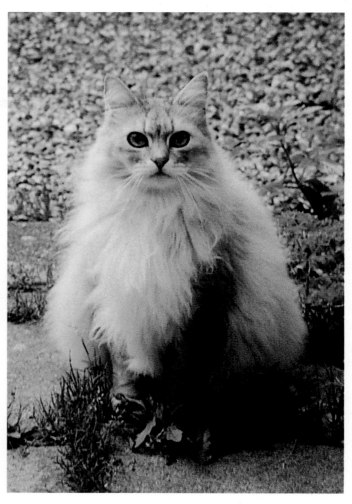

CASPAR, THE CROSSPED

MY OWN CATS: CASPAR, THE DARK-SILVER TABBY, AND MELCHIOR, THE LIGHT-SILVER SOMALI.

OF CROSSBREDS AND PUREBREDS

As we have seen, although European domestic cats were largely left to fend for themselves and to breed unchecked, their Oriental cousins often led a more sheltered existence and were subjected to controlled breeding to ensure that the characteristics that were so prized in their particular breed remained untainted. Thus while medieval depictions of European cats reveal how the leggy elegance of their Egyptian ancestors gradually gave way to stocky sturdiness (probably as a result of interbreeding with the European wildcat, Felis sylvestris), the physical characteristics of Orientals have remained remarkably unchanged throughout the course of history.

THE TYPICAL TABBY COAT PATTERN IS EITHER BLOTCHED OR STRIPED.

The predominant type of European domestic cat is the shorthair, of which the tabby is one of the most common examples. The name 'tabby' is ultimately derived from the al-'attabiya area of Baghdad, in Iraq, where the watered silk that resembles the blotched pattern of some tabbies' coats was first manufactured, another characteristic pattern being Caspar's striped, or mackerel, coat configuration. Longhaired cats are not indigenous to Europe, but were introduced from the East by smitten European travellers during the sixteenth century, the first breed to arrive being the Angora, from Turkey – the French statesman Cardinal Richelieu (1585–1642) owned one, which he rather provocatively, especially in view of his rank in the Catholic Church, named Lucifer – followed by the Persian, from Iran. Such exotic Eastern felines were initially 'luxury' pets, feline status symbols that belonged exclusively to the most privileged members of society, a situation that would, however, change during the nineteenth century with the advent of the 'cat fancier', of whom Harrison Weir was the most notable.

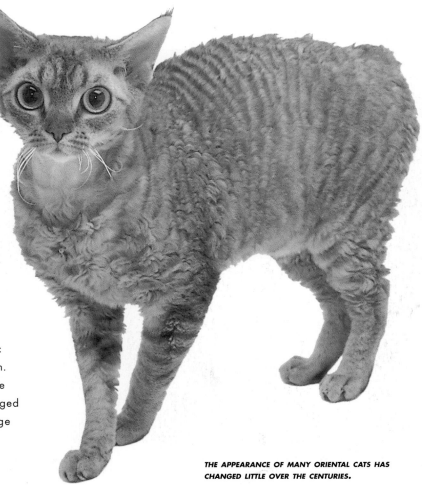

THE APPEARANCE OF MANY ORIENTAL CATS HAS CHANGED LITTLE OVER THE CENTURIES.

Although dog shows had become commonplace during the nineteenth century, no such dedicated arena existed in which to admire the feline's inimitable qualities, a deficiency that the cat-loving Weir decided to remedy 'so that different breeds, colours, markings, etc, might be more carefully attended to, and the domestic cat sitting in front of the fire would then possess a beauty and an attractiveness to its owner unobserved and unknown because uncultivated heretofore'. As a result of Weir's energy and determination, the first formal cat show, at which 160 felines were exhibited in 25 classes, was held in London's Crystal Palace in 1871. A resounding success with its Victorian visitors, the show was responsible for launching the phenomenon of the 'cat fancy', and with it a plethora of new breeds.

Whereas cats once exhibited only a handful of coat colours, today they are resplendent in more than fifty, while their eye colouring ranges from yellow to blue to green, and, in the case of the odd-eyed white Persian, one even being blue and the other orange. The coat can be either the tabby's agouti (striped or ticked with different-coloured bands along the length of each hair), self-coloured (plain),

SIAMESE CAT

two-toned (as seen in smoke, shell, shaded or tortoiseshell fur) or pointed (with the extremities displaying a contrasting shade to the body), as well as shorthaired, semi-longhaired or longhaired, while the somewhat controversial Sphynx has no hair at all. Build and character vary widely between the breeds, too, from the lithe, highly sociable Siamese, to the bushy-tailed, ultra-laid-back Ragdoll.

CAT SHOWS ARE TODAY AMONG THE HIGHLIGHTS OF THE 'CAT-FANCIER'S' YEAR.

The number of cat breeds continues to grow, and to describe them all would require another book. To take just one example, the Somali breed evolved about twenty years ago in North America from longhaired mutations born to shorthaired Abyssinians. Defying the sceptics, some romantics believe that Abyssinians (and thus also Somalis) originated in Ethiopia, to the south-east of Egypt, and that because they so closely resemble the cats of ancient Egyptian art they are descended from Bast's sacred cats (a theory that, I suspect, our Somali, Melchior, would promote if he thought that it would win him extra food and cosseting).

Be they pedigrees or moggies, Somalis or crosspeds, however, every cat, to cannibalise the words of the poet Graham R Tomson, are sphinxes of our quiet hearths, whose lore is that of the ancient Egyptian gods Ra and Rameses. I hope that this book will answer any questions that you may have about how to understand and care for your own house sphinx.

SPHYNX CAT

OWNING A CAT OR TWO WILL PROVIDE YOU WITH A SOURCE OF ENDLESS ENTERTAINMENT.

chapter 1

THE FELINE WORLD

Appearances can be deceptive: however innocent and harmless your cat may appear, its genetic software has programmed it to be a hunter of the kind who shows no mercy and takes no prisoners. Its ancestors may have found it convenient to trade their wild existence for the relative ease of a domesticated lifestyle, but make no mistake: your cat will revert to its roots in an instant if its hunting instinct is aroused or its home conditions no longer suit it. Even the most indolent of house cats remains essentially wild, with a body and mentality that evolution has honed to focus above all on the pursuit and capture of prey.

THE FELINE WORLD

While domestication has to some extent altered the way in which the cat views its world (in the human–feline household regarding its owners as having assumed its mother's role, for example), scratch the surface of the feline psyche and evidence of its deeply embedded ancestral inheritance immediately becomes apparent. As the zoologist Desmond Morris puts it in his book Catwatching (1992), 'As it crosses the threshold [to go outside] the cat becomes transformed. The kitten-of-man brain is switched off and the wild-cat brain is clicked on'. Do not try to reprogramme your house feline's wildcat brain – not only will you be fighting a losing battle, but you will at best only succeed in confusing your cat, resulting in all sorts of behavioural problems, and, in the worst-case scenario, even forcing it to leave home to try its luck in more cat-congenial surroundings. And if you cannot stomach the thought of disposing of the corpses of small creatures that may occasionally materialise on your kitchen floor – the natural conclusion of the feline hunting instinct – think twice before adopting a cat.

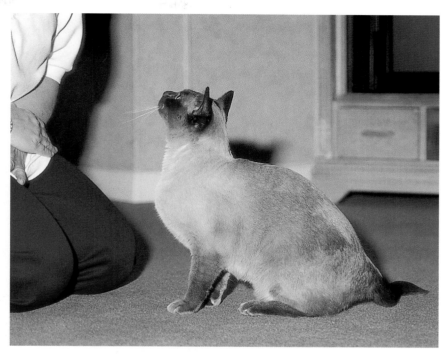

HOWEVER DOMESTICATED THEY MAY APPEAR, ALL CATS ARE WILDCATS BY NATURE.

CATS START TO LEARN AND PRACTISE
THEIR HUNTING SKILLS IN KITTENHOOD.

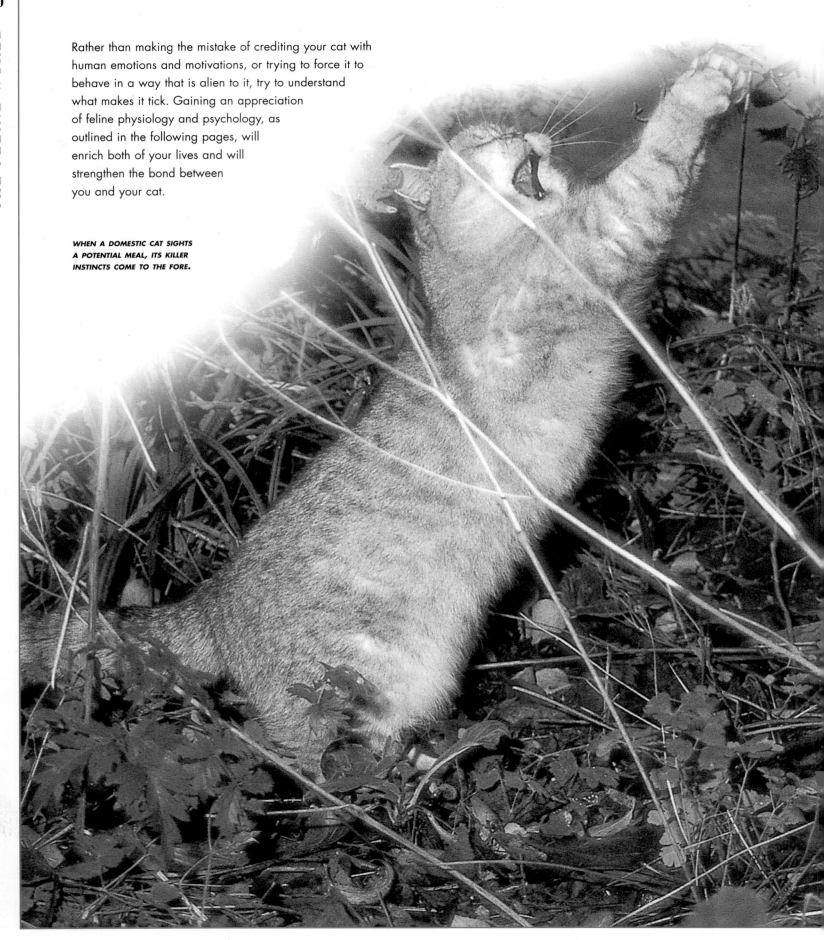

Rather than making the mistake of crediting your cat with human emotions and motivations, or trying to force it to behave in a way that is alien to it, try to understand what makes it tick. Gaining an appreciation of feline physiology and psychology, as outlined in the following pages, will enrich both of your lives and will strengthen the bond between you and your cat.

WHEN A DOMESTIC CAT SIGHTS A POTENTIAL MEAL, ITS KILLER INSTINCTS COME TO THE FORE.

A HUNTER'S BUILD

Evolution having fine-tuned every fibre, nerve and cell of the feline body many millennia ago, the domestic cat of the twenty-first century closely resembles its wildcat ancestors in both build and mentality. Like every other species – Homo sapiens included – the cat's ultimate raison d'être is the constant search for, and acquisition of, food, a mission for which nature has equipped it superbly.

Reflecting its wildcat pedigree, the cat is a predatory carnivore whose natural diet consists exclusively of small mammals, typically rodents, such as mice and rats, that are small enough for it to pounce on and dispatch without incurring serious injury. Contrary to the popular view of cats as bird-killers, although cats will often stalk birds, the avian talent for vertical take-off make them harder to catch than ground-hugging rodents.

Similarly, despite the specialised piscine-preying prowess of the wild fishing cat of southern Asia, fish do not form part of the cat's staple diet.) And because rodents are largely nocturnal, cats prowl our gardens at night in search of easy pickings,

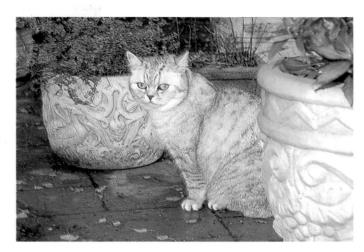

EVEN RELAXED CATS REMAIN ALERT.

much as their ancestors would have stalked the dusty terrain of Egypt. Nor is its night vision the only example of the physical traits that make it a hunting specialist, for from the tips of its whiskers to the end of its tail the cat is a hunting machine par excellence.

CATS ON THE PROWL ARE CONSTANTLY ON THE ALERT FOR PREY.

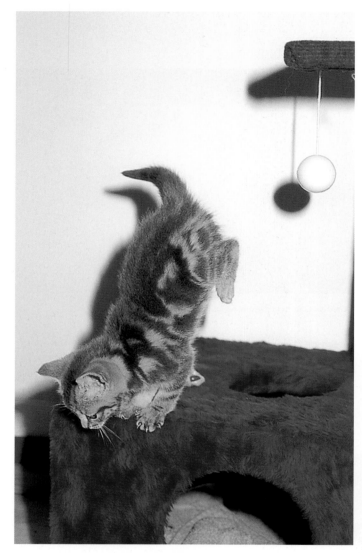

CATS HAVE A REMARKABLE TALENT FOR ACROBATICS.

Combine a narrow physique, a head that can rotate more than 180 degrees, forelimbs whose length of stride can be greatly varied, a fluid backbone, highly muscled, springboard-like hindquarters and a tail whose position aids balance with an extraordinarily developed muscular system, all covered with loosely attached fur, and the result is both a formidable predator and a master of escapology.

Among the cat's most celebrated attributes are its remarkable agility and innate talent for acrobatics – which must surely make it the envy of any circus entertainer – both of which enable it to get into, and out of, the tightest and most awkward of spots.

Complementing the cat's sure sense of balance (see pages 26 to 27) are its flexible spine and strong muscles, along with the looseness of its skin and skeleton compared to ours. These features endow it with markedly more accomplished gymnastic skills than most humans can boast of. Some of the most notable differences between the feline and human skeleton are the forty extra bones that the feline's contains (mainly in the backbone and tail), along with the less rigid arrangement of the cat's vertebrae and the marked reduction in clavicle (collarbone) size, which is compensated for by powerful muscles.

FELINE WHISKERS ARE VITAL SENSORY TOOLS.

As well as offering considerable advantages, the cat's body does, however, have its drawbacks, the inevitable consequence of the compromises that nature was forced to make when designing Felis catus. Because the wildcat was – and remains – an opportunistic predator that could not rely on a regular supply of food, for example, the stomach that its descendants have inherited takes up a disproportionately large amount of room at the expense of its heart and lungs. This means that although the cat has mastered the pouncing dash, its heart and lungs do not have the capacity to power any sustained form of exercise. It also explains why a well-fed house cat will frequently go off hunting virtually as soon as it has had its post-prandial wash and brush-up: it may not have digested its supper yet, but its ancestral programming tells it that it must be on the constant search for prey as an insurance against the lean times that could strike at any moment. Whether or not it actually eats its prey does, however, depend on how hungry it is.

Its physical inability to stalk its victims for long periods of time means that the cat has developed a less energy-consuming hunting strategy, that of lurking and waiting for prey, be it during the day or the night, according to when it has discovered that the locality's food supply is the most plentiful. Typically having taken up a covert position under a shrub – and preferably one that blends seamlessly with its coat to provide maximum camouflage – the cat will then patiently wait for a tasty morsel to cross its path.

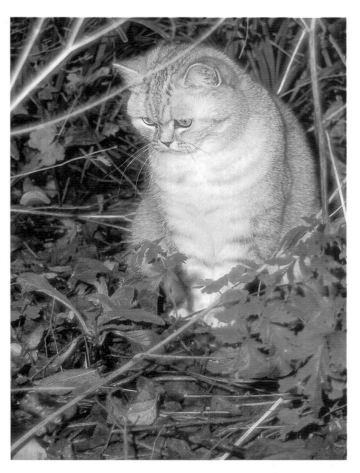

AFTER ITS EARS HAVE SIGNALLED THE PROXIMITY OF POSSIBLE PREY, A CAT BRINGS ITS EYESIGHT INTO PLAY.

FEW HUMANS WOULD DARE TO TREAD IN THE FOOTSTEPS OF A SURE-FOOTED FELINE.

As soon as it hears a tell-tale rustle or espies a sudden movement out of the corner of its eye, the cat's ears and eyes (see pages 28 to 29) spring into full-alert mode to monitor its quarry's progress as it prepares to pounce. Quivering with suppressed tension, the crouching cat fixes its eyes on its potential meal as it inches slowly towards it, sometimes freezing in mid-slink if it thinks that it may have been spotted. Once within pouncing distance, the cat springs forward for the kill, its hindquarters powering the leap while its front paws, razor-sharp claws unsheathed, reach out to pinion its prey to the ground before the deadly feline jaws close around the hapless victim's neck. If all goes smoothly, the cat's canine teeth (see page 25) deliver the neck-breaking killing bite by dislocating its quarry's vertebrae, but if the execution proves problematic, it may rake the claws of its hindlegs along its prey's body, simultaneously gripping and maiming as it seeks to administer the coup de grâce with its teeth.

Having won the life-or-death battle, before settling down to the feast, the cat will carry its quarry's corpse to a place that offers protective cover from other predators that may try to snatch its meal away from it. The reason why a cat will often proudly present its kills to its unappreciative owner is due to a number of factors, including how hungry it is. If it is ravenous, it will eat its prey, starting from the head. If its appetite is already sated, however, it may make a gift of its victim to its owner, probably because this is what a mother cat does when her kittens have been weaned. The house cat is thus providing both food and education for its human family: food, in that the fresh

A SUDDEN MOVEMENT CAUSES A CAT TO SNAP INTO FULL-ALERT MODE.

kill constitutes a 'proper' feline meal that it rarely – if ever – receives from its owners; and education, in that if its prey is still clinging on to life, the cat will often demonstrate to its owners how to dispatch it, just as a mother cat would instruct her kittens by example. (Although many people believe that when a cat 'toys' with a half-dead mouse it is being gratuitously cruel, this isn't so: it is simply practising its deadly skills in order to become a more proficient hunter.) So if you find yourself the recipient of such an unwanted gift and don't want to hurt your cat's feelings, first praise it profusely for its largesse and then discreetly dispose of your 'meal' when it isn't looking.

KITTENS LEARN FROM THEIR MOTHERS

A TOOTH AND CLAW FIGHTER

As we have seen, in the final stages of the hunt the cat uses its claws to pin down its prey and its teeth to administer the killing bite. In non-aggressive mode, the cat's claws are retracted – or, more properly, sheathed – into the tips of its toe bones (the phalanges), both to prevent them from injuring itself or its friends and to preserve the sharpness of their points for, as every successful hunter or warrior knows, if you look after your weapons, when it comes to the crunch they'll look after you. The cat's eighteen claws (four on each hind paw and five on each front paw, the fifth, called the dew claw, being higher up the paw) are made of a protein called keratin, the same substance that forms human nails. Like our nails, the feline's claws are constantly growing, the difference being that they are doing so beneath the existing set, so that when an elderly claw has outlived its usefulness, the cat will strop it off to reveal its fighting-fit replacement. (The process can loosely be compared to the way in which a snake sloughs off its old skin.) Anchored firmly into the phalanges by rubbery ligaments, when the feline brain deems it prudent to unsheathe its primary weapons, further ligaments push the phalanges forward, and with them the claws, the process being performed at lightning speed,

A CAT USUALLY KEEPS ITS CLAWS SHEATHED.

STROPPING KEEPS FELINE CLAWS FIGHTING FIT.

similar to the way in which a flick knife is activated. Once in contact with its prey, the claws relay positional information regarding how effectively the cat is twisting them, as well as the suitability of the pressure that it is using, enabling it to readjust its clawhold if necessary.

If the cat's claws can be roughly equated with human nails, the padded cushions of hairless skin at the bottom of its paws can be described as being equivalent to the palms of our hands and the soles of our feet. The softness of the paw pads in comparison to, for example, the hooves of non-predatory creatures like the horse, muffles the cat's approach, giving it the advantage of surprise when stalking. Only when its paws have carried the cat close enough to pounce are the claws unsheathed in readiness for their deadly mission.

Perhaps rather insultingly to the feline community's pride, the teeth that close in for the kill are termed the canines, the fangs that can be seen on either side of the cat's miniature incisors. Being sensitive to pressure, as well as extremely sharp, they enable the cat to judge exactly where to sink them in order to dislocate its victim's vertebrae and cause its instantaneous death. Once it has dispatched its quarry using this swift and effective method, the same teeth are used to tear at the corpse to expose the warm flesh beneath the fur or feathers, the more delicate scraping and ripping work being done by the incisors. The molars, and particularly the sideways-slicing carnassials, at the back of the cat's mouth now come into their own by reducing the flesh to bite-sized chunks. Unlike our flattened molars, the cat's back teeth have sharp tips that speed up the food-preparation process (another legacy of its wildcat heritage, in that felines are programmed to eat as quickly as possible in case their meal is snatched away by another predator that has been attracted by the smell of the kill). And, again in contrast to human eating patterns, the cat does not pre-digest its food by chewing it thoroughly before swallowing, instead leaving most of the digestive process to its stomach's gastric juices.

AN ACROBAT'S SKILLS

A cat climbs like a monkey, walks as gracefully as a ballerina and balances with the effortless ease of a champion tightrope-walker. As we have seen, when a cat is hunting, its powerful back legs provide the momentum that launches it into a leap or pounce, while its front legs stretch out to grasp its prey. This pattern is repeated when a cat climbs a vertical object like a tree or fence, its hindquarters propelling it upwards – sometimes up to five times the cat's height – and the hooked claws of its front paws sinking into the surface to act as grappling irons, thereby enabling the cat to get a firm enough hold to pull itself upwards with its strong front legs.

The delicate elegance of the cat's walk is the result of the configuration of its leg and paw bones, which differs from the way in which human legs and feet are constructed. Your leg consists of a thighbone (femur), knee and, beneath that, a parallel shinbone (tibia) and fibula, then comes the ankle joint above the heelbone (calcaneus), in front of which is the large talus bone, followed by a series of smaller bones that culminate in the metatarsals and finally the phalanges, the toe bones. In contrast to us, the cat walks on the tips of its phalanges, which are far longer than human toe bones, while its leg bones are shorter. Not only does this 'digitigrade' arrangement allow a longer stride, it enables the cat to run far faster than if its feet were 'plantigrade' like ours. Balancing on the tips of its toes, the cat walks in a diagonal fashion by putting forward its left hindleg first, followed by its right foreleg, its right hindleg and finally its left foreleg, before stepping out with its left hindleg again, positioning each front or back paw directly in front of

the previous one on the same side so that if you examined its tracks in the snow (that is, if you could persuade it to consent to having its feet frozen in the first place), they would form two straight lines. Again, it is the cat's powerful hindquarters that provide the ambulatory momentum, while its front legs support the weight of its head. This way of walking can be varied to enable the cat to break out into a trot or gallop, and it has been estimated that the cat can attain a top speed of around 30 miles (48 km) an hour.

The precise, economical feline gait is of considerable help when it comes to performing an intricate balancing act along a wall or fence, as is the tail in correcting potential imbalances, but that's only part of the story. Having scrambled onto the wall, once it is again moving horizontally, the cat's brain is guided by its vestibular organ, which relays positional information that enables the cat to adjust its movements if necessary to forestall a tumble. Although the cat's vestibular organ is situated in the inner ear, as in the human body, its performance is remarkably superior to its human counterpart, and not only as regards balance: unlike many people, cats never suffer from motion sickness, for instance. The vestibular organ comprises three hair-lined, fluid-filled, semi-circular canals that are arranged at right angles to each other. When the cat moves its head, the fluid in one canal responds to up-and-down motions, another to left-and-right movements and the third to oblique positions, the movement of the fluid being detected by the adjacent hairs and reported to the brain. The crystalline saccular and utricular otolith organs represent further refinements of the vestibular organ that register gravity on the one hand and speed of movement on the other. Each of the vestibular system's components works instantaneously, together sending an array of reflexive signals to the feline brain, as well as to the muscles that are instrumental in maintaining balance, that report the position of the cat's head in relation to the ground and therefore enable it to correct any false move. If the cat does fall, however, the workings of this system allow it to recover in mid-air, to correct the position of its head and to prepare itself for a safe landing by twisting its body so that its shock-absorbing legs will be the first to hit the ground, also arching its back to minimise the shock of the impact and stretching out its tail to act as a counterbalance. The cat's ability to right itself is amazing in itself, but what is perhaps even more astonishing is that this complex set of manouevres is performed in less than the blink of an eye.

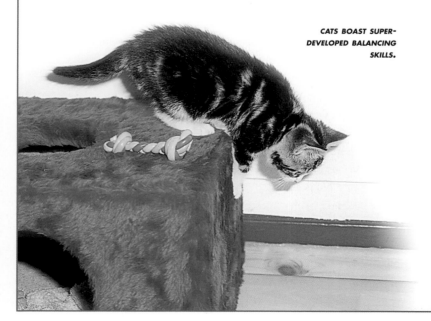

CATS BOAST SUPER-DEVELOPED BALANCING SKILLS.

HAVING DECIDED THAT IT'S TIME TO MOVE FROM ITS COMFORTABLE POSITION, THE SEATED CAT BEGINS THE DESCENT, ITS FRONT LEGS LEADING THE WAY, WITH ITS HINDQUARTERS PROVIDING THE AMBULATORY MOMENTUM.

THE FELINE SENSES

Apart from its sense of taste (and as a carnivore it has no need for the luxury of a gourmet's appreciation of the delicacies of flavour – fresh meat is, after all, fresh meat, although shrews must taste really disgusting because it appears that only the most ravenous cat will consume them), the functioning and powers of the feline's senses are generally far superior to ours. They need to be, for in its natural state the cat relies on them for its very life.

Citing the saying that cats have nine lives (and, indeed, many stroll away from hair-raising scrapes virtually unscathed), some people believe that the cat is guided through life by a sixth sense, also known as extra-sensory perception. Although there is, as yet, no compelling scientific evidence to confirm this, it is thought that cats, in common with many animals, are far more sensitive both to electrical changes in the atmosphere and the earth's magnetic field. This may explain on the one hand why many cats become uneasy at the approach of an electrical storm or earthquake and, on the other, why some cats who have been forcibly relocated, perhaps because their human family has moved house, have an uncanny ability to find their way back to their old home. Generally, however, their conventional sensory perceptions are more than adequate to enable them to survive and thrive.

SEEING AND THE CAT'S EYES

Once the exact location of an interesting sound has been identified by its ears, the cat directs its eyes in that direction to try to identify its source. This may take a little time if the culprit rodent, for example, has spotted the cat and has frozen, or else is moving slowly, because feline eyes are genetically programmed to respond primarily to sudden movements and to focus on objects that are moving either quickly or erratically, as would its prey when trying to outmanoeuvre and escape it. (To observe the cause and effect of this instinct, all you need to do is watch a cat trying to catch a butterfly.)

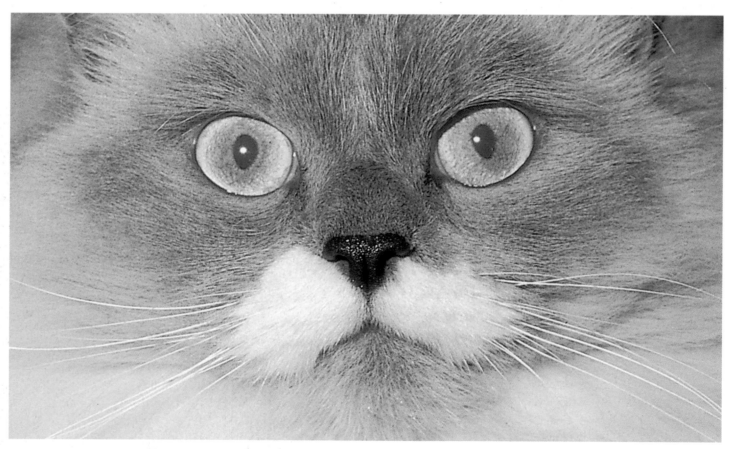

SAUCER EYES EQUAL SUPERIOR SIGHT.

Indeed, the cat's eyes are in every respect those of a predator, being both extremely large in comparison to the size of its skull, in order to maximise its visual capabilities, and set at the front of the head, facing forwards. In contrast to the eyes of creatures that are typically preyed upon, such as rabbits, which are positioned on either side of the head, giving them sideways monocular (one-eyed) vision in each direction, the better to scan a wide area for potential predators, the cat's binocular (two-eyed) vision is designed to enable it to focus intently on a tasty-looking victim, the image registered by each eye overlapping with the other to give a detailed, stereoscopic view that results in a three-dimensional image. While the size and generous curve of the cat's eyes give them a visual scope of up to 285 degrees, their range is further extended by the impressive swivelling capability of the neck, which means that the cat's eyes can cover a wide area without its body having to move to any great extent – an invaluable asset when operating under cover.

No cover is more effective than that of darkness and, its African ancestors having bequeathed Felis catus the gift of night vision, most cats will go out to hunt at night if they can. Although they can't actually discern objects in total darkness (for, as every photographer knows, an image cannot be recorded in the total absence of light), and it takes some time for their eyes to adjust to the dark, they can still see at least six times better than humans in dusky conditions. This is due to three factors: firstly, their ability to vary the size of their pupils to a considerable degree; secondly, the teeming population of rods (three times greater in number than in the human eye) that the feline eye contains; and, thirdly, the tapetum lucidum that is located at the back of the eye. In response to the dark of night, the cat's pupils widen enormously to form a full circle (during the day they can be narrowed from slits to pinpricks to protect the eye from dangerous dazzle, the nictitating membrane, also known as the haw, or 'third eyelid', being enlisted in extreme conditions), which maximises the amount of available light that enters the eye. Once the light has passed into the eye, it is focused by the lens to form an image on the retina, which is picked up by receptor cells called rods (whose job is to 'switch on' the cat's night vision by registering the intensity of light), which then transmit it to the brain via the optic nerve. Some light may have eluded the rods, however, in which case it continues to travel forward, beyond the retina to the tapetum lucidum (the Latin for 'bright mirror'), fifteen layers of flat, reflective cells that deflect the light the way it came, giving the rods another chance to register it and send it on to the brain. (It is light bouncing off the tapetum lucidum that gives the luminous shine to the eyes of

creatures of the night that in 1934 inspired Percy Shaw to invent the cat's-eyes that today guide drivers along the roads at night by reflecting the light emitted by their headlights.)

There are a few disadvantages inherent in the feline night-stalker's vision, however. One is that the cat's eyes contain fewer cones (the receptor cells responsible for sending messages to the brain to enable the eyes to focus in daylight) than ours, which means that it does not see as clearly as we do during the day. And because it is also cones that are responsible for distinguishing colours, although cats are not colour blind, it is thought that they do not discern different shades and hues as well as we do. However, neither ability is particularly important when Felis catus is out hunting at night. Another drawback is the difficulty that cats have in focusing on objects that are less than 15 centimetres (6 inches) away. Caspar, for example, who is partial to the occasional peanut, cannot see where one has fallen when it is tossed in front of his nose onto our similarly coloured floor because he cannot distinguish between nuances of shade and there is insufficient contrast for him to be able to identify the peanut's shape. This is not, however, a major handicap, for Caspar, like every cat, is able to call on his senses of touch and smell to lead him directly to the peanut.

BINOCULAR VISION AIDS A CAT'S FOCUSING POWER.

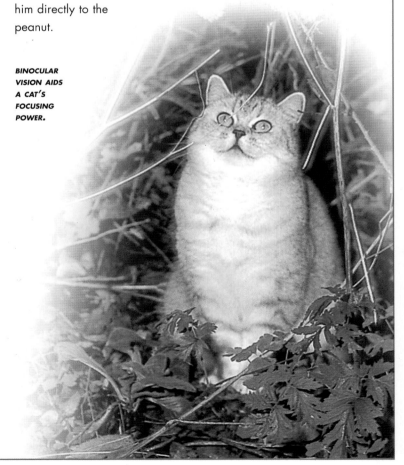

TOUCHING AND THE CAT'S TACTILE RECEPTORS

Whether it be an immobile peanut, a living victim or any other object that the cat considers worthy of more detailed exploration, the feline has an armoury of sensitive touch receptors at its clawtips – and not only there. You may have seen a curious cat tentatively patting an object – perhaps a new toy mouse – with its paw. Although it may look comical, the cat isn't playing, but is instead conducting a serious investigation. After all, it doesn't yet know that this alien object is a toy – it doesn't show signs of life, but that doesn't mean that it won't jump up and bite the cat on the nose. With caution being the watchword, the cat therefore extends a forepaw, keeping its vulnerable nose well away from the potential danger, and delicately touches the toy mouse. The instant it does so, a barrage of messages is relayed to the brain by the touch

WHEN FACED WITH AN UNFAMILIAR OBJECT, A CAT WILL USUALLY FIRST INVESTIGATE IT WITH A TENTATIVE PAW.

NOT EVEN A COMPUTER MOUSE CAN ESCAPE THIS CAT'S CURIOSITY.

receptors – nerve endings – in the hairless pads of its paw, which are activated by sideways, brushing movements similar to those that the cat is generating as it pats and strokes. (So sensitive are the paw pads that many cats hate having them stroked – Melchior certainly does, although Caspar tolerates it – presumably because it elicits a tickling sensation that is too excruciating to stand.) Only when the feline brain has ascertained that the toy mouse doesn't present a threat will the cat draw closer to investigate it with its nose, which is equally chock-a-block with touch receptors, both touching and smelling the mouse to garner as much information as it can. If the toy were a real mouse, this closeness of contact would trigger an innate set of killer reactions in which further touch receptors under the skin of the mouth and lips play a vital role in prompting the cat to bare its fangs ready for the killing bite, the final information that seals the mouse's fate being relayed by nerve endings within the mouth and pressure-sensitive receptors at the base of the canine teeth.

Beneath its fur the feline skin is packed with touch receptors (which is one of the reasons why cats are so responsive to being stroked), but certain areas are more sensitive than others – around the cat's mouth, for example. Among the most responsive to touch are the vibrissae: the whiskers and stiff, whisker-like hairs that sprout from above a cat's eyes, from its chin and the sides of its head, as well as from the 'wrists' of its paws. Not only do the vibrissae register touch when they come into contact with a solid object, thereby acting as feelers, they also identify changes in air pressure, even the most imperceptible (to humans) movement causing the vibrissae to bend and triggering a brain-signalling response in the touch receptors at their base, within the skin. Because solid objects affect the air flow or pressure around them, the cat is alerted to their presence and can therefore avoid them. As well as enabling it to map out the size and shape of any object that the cat encounters (including the prey that it holds in a death grip), the vibrissae provide an invaluable navigational aid, giving the cat the ability to ascertain with remarkable accuracy, particularly during its night-time sorties, whether it can squeeze through a prohibitively small-looking gap.

RECEPTORS AT THE BASE OF THE CANINE TEETH RELAY DATA TO THE FELINE PREDATOR'S BRAIN.

THE CAT'S WHISKERS TRIGGER TOUCH RECEPTORS.

CATS ADORE BEING STROKED.

Never cut off a cat's whiskers, for if you do, you will be inflicting a considerable handicap on it by removing its ability to make accurate spatial judgments and will also probably be condemning any future prey to a lingering death as a result of the cat's impaired ability to judge exactly where to administer the coup de grâce.

TASTING AND THE CAT'S TONGUE

The feline senses are generally far more sensitive than those of humans, but there is one that compares relatively badly to ours: the cat's sense of taste. Although some cats are said to be fussy eaters, this has less to do with their ability to distinguish subtle nuances of flavour and is more concerned with the freshness of the food offered to them: they distrust the smell of stale, or even rotting, food, having the instinctive knowledge that it could make them ill. Another reason for the refusal on the part of Felis catus – a creature of habit – to countenance any food to which it is not accustomed is the legacy of its usually unvarying carnivorous diet in the wild. Indeed, many owners find that a cat that turns its nose up at a certain type of proprietary canned cat food will not be able to resist a morsel of fresh flesh of any type, be it meat, fish or poultry.

Its innate preference for fresh meat aside, there are also certain biological explanations for the cat's likes and dislikes when it comes to food. The human palate, which boasts eighteen times more taste buds than the feline's, is not only far more sensitive to different tastes, but more tolerant of the four cardinal flavours: sour, bitter, salt and sweet. This is because humans are omnivores and have therefore become accustomed over the course of many millennia to eating plants and other food stuffs, as well as meat. The carnivorous cat, by contrast, will shrink from the acidity of a sour citrus fruit and will wrinkle its nose at the bitterness of a particular herb – and neither flavour occurs naturally in meat – in addition appearing indifferent to salt, presumably because meat contains all of this nutrient that its body needs, and hardly seeming to register sweetness because sugar does not form part of a feline's nutritional requirements.

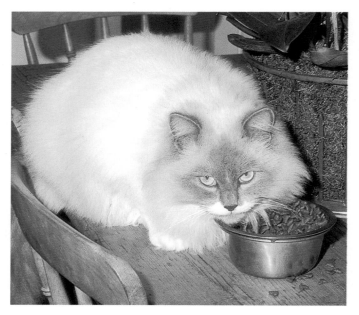

THE ONLY TASTES THAT A CAT TRULY APPRECIATES ARE THOSE OF MEAT AND FAT.

Indeed, the only flavours that are pertinent to a feline's nutritional needs are those of meat and fat, which supply it with tissue-maintaining protein and storable energy, and these are the ones that are registered by the cat's taste buds, which are mainly located on the edges of the tongue. The centre of the tongue contains the papillae (tiny, backward-pointing hooks) that trap the water that the cat drinks when it is moderately thirsty or when only a thin layer of water is available. When a feline has a powerful thirst, however, or the water source is deep, it will form its tongue into a shape resembling a spoon, thus enabling it to ladle larger quantities of water down its throat.

FEW CATS CAN RESIST A MEAT-BASED MEAL, AS LONG AS IT IS FRESH AND DOESN'T SMELL STALE.

HEARING AND THE CAT'S EARS

Its hearing is the first sense that alerts the cat to potential prey when it is out hunting and, due to its genetic inheritance, the sounds that are most likely to signal the proximity of rodents, its favourite meal, are the ones to which it is the most attuned. And because rodents utter high-pitched squeaks, the upper frequencies of the sound range are those that the cat's ears are especially adept at detecting, exceeding both dogs and humans in their sensitivity. Indeed, when you think that our detection of acoustic vibrations rises to around 20,000 hertz, and a cat's to 50,000, we must be deaf to a cacophony of interesting sounds.

Watch any cat, whether it is lurking with murderous intent or deeply relaxed, and you will often see its ears suddenly spring into action, whether or not you can hear the noise that prompted them to go into a state of full alert. Initially you may see its funnel-shaped ear 'lobes' (pinnae), which, with their sweeping range of 180 degrees are remarkably mobile, as well as designed to amplify sound, swivelling (often independently of each other) in much the same way as a radar detector as they attempt to pinpoint the precise location of the trigger sound. This process is accomplished within the middle and inner ears, which vibrate in reaction to the frequency of the sound that has been picked up, causing the nerve cells within the ears to relay the information detected to the cat's brain. Having received differing messages from each ear, their subsequent comparison enables the feline brain to calculate the positional source of the tantalising noise. Corresponding to the frequencies of sound emitted by rodents, this direction-finding method is usually more successful with higher registers than with lower ones (and explains why cats are typically more responsive to women's voices than to men's), when the cat will be forced to bring its eyesight into play.

MOBILE FELINE EARS RESEMBLE RADAR DETECTORS.

SMELLING AND THE CAT'S NOSE

Although how its food smells determines whether or not a cat will eat it, the feline nose is a far more versatile organ of smell than simply a food-identifier. Indeed, it plays a crucial role in feline relationships – both sexual and social – and if a cat's sense of smell is impaired for any reason, it may start to behave in a most unfeline way.

Because their noses contain twice as large an area containing smell receptors (hosting around 19 million nerve endings) than humans (our noses contain about 5 million), cats are significantly more sensitive to smell than we are. The reason why many cats, to their owners' despair, prefer drinking from unhygienic-looking puddles to the water bowl that has been provided for them, for example, is because they are repelled by the smell of the chemicals with which many water companies treat tap water (although they are barely detectable to us, if at all), and may also dislike the lingering odour of the washing-up liquid – another unnatural-smelling substance – that may have been used to clean the bowl.

And it is not just to the odours emitted by food and water that cats react strongly, the scent of a female cat on heat, for instance, attracting toms from quite some distance away, with the toms increasing their spraying rate in response. It is thought to be primarily sexual scent signals that are responsible for the peculiar face that cats of both sexes occasionally pull, whereby

A CAT SWAPS SCENT SIGNALS WITH ITS OWNER.

they raise their upper lip and open their mouths to expose their incisors, their eyes all the while displaying a distant, dreamy expression. Known as 'flehming', this unmistakable grimace enables a particularly tantalising scent to pass through a duct in the roof of the mouth behind the incisors to the Jacobson's organ, which consists of two sacs, opened by the cat's flehming, that contain receptors that pick up the odour and report it to the cat's brain for analysis.

THE FELINE NOSE IS CHOCK-A-BLOCK WITH BOTH TOUCH RECEPTORS AND SMELL RECEPTORS.

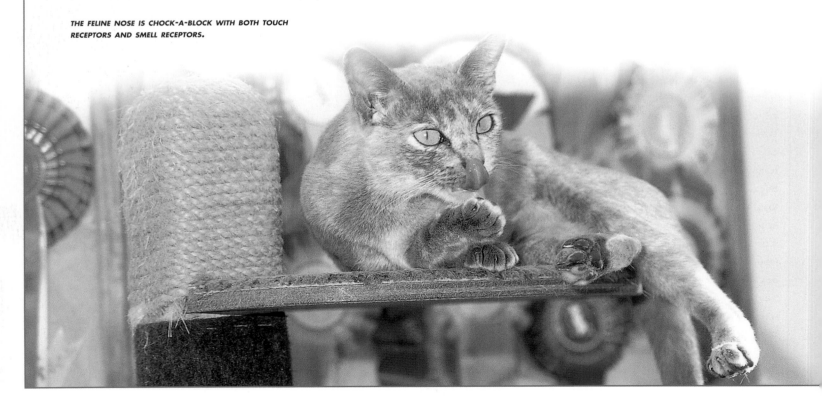

When a cat rubs its head or chin against your leg or hand, it is not simply demonstrating how much it loves you, but is both marking you as its property and exchanging scent signals with you. Along with those situated on the feline's temples, chin and at the corners of its lips, there are sebaceous glands at the base of its tail and around its anus that produce the cat's own, unique smell. In rubbing against you, it is transferring its individual scent to your skin or clothing, and when it pulls away and embarks on a vigorous washing session, it is not insulting

SEBACEOUS GLANDS EMIT A CAT'S UNIQUE SCENT.

A CARPET MAY HAVE A FASCINATING STORY TO TELL.

of the cat's vocabulary of scent and, indeed, find it difficult to imagine the extent to which a feline's life is both regulated and enhanced by smell.

THE FELINE NOSE IS AN INSTRUMENT OF DETECTION.

you by trying to remove all traces of your body odour from its fur as fast as it can – although it may certainly be trying to restore its own fragrant status quo – but is enabling the taste buds on its tongue to savour your personal taste. Such exchanges of scent are crucial in reinforcing the shared 'family' smell that makes a cat feel at home. Similarly, when a cat insists on sniffing your hand or clothes with rapt fascination, it is 'reading' scent messages that tell it where you have been, what you have been doing, and with whom. Sadly, we are largely oblivious to the richness

THE CAT'S SOCIAL LIFE

As well as controlling the essential functions of eating, drinking and breeding, in many respects the feline sense of smell can be said to be the engine that keeps cat society running smoothly, defining as it does the individual cat's place within its feline (or feline-human) community, its relationship with other cats (or, in the case of a human household, surrogate cats) and the boundaries of its personal territory.

Despite the prevalent belief that cats prefer a solitary existence (and they certainly don't hunt in packs as wolves do, for example), observers of feral felines – cats that have reverted to a wild lifestyle – have noted that they tend to live in groups, mainly consisting of females and their offspring. Such cat communes operate along communist lines, with the females often sharing out the job of nurturing and raising kittens. Toms, however, are usually conspicuous by their absence, partly because they are polygamous by habit and rarely stay with one family group for long before moving on to bestow their favours upon another, and partly because much of their time is spent securing and defending their territory from other male marauders. Every cat has its place within the feline community, largely determined by the powerfulness of the scent of its sex hormones: the tom, who has fought and vanquished another tom to establish his status, is the top cat; queens, or actively breeding females, rank next, followed by other females; while

THIS CAT IS IN THE PROCESS OF SCENT-MARKING ITS TERRITORY.

the kittens' place is at the bottom of the heap. A good part of a cat's kittenhood is spent scrapping with its littermates in an attempt to gain precedence, and when young males have become sexually mature they will either challenge the dominant tom for control of the group or leave the community in search of their own territory. Neutering, which results in a decrease in sex hormones and therefore their odour, heralds a dramatic loss of status for cats, neutered cats being immediately relegated to the bottom of the social ladder.

THE BATTLE FOR PRECEDENCE IS AN IMPORTANT PART OF KITTENHOOD.

The cat's two most vital requirements are food and shelter, and once it has found a place, or household, that offers both it will come to regard both it and its immediate environs, such as a garden, as its personal territory that it must defend against interlopers at all costs. Because this strict territorial division isn't always practical or possible in densely populated localities, there may be some areas, such as streets, that the neighbourhood's cats deem neutral zones (although they usually avoid coming into contact with other felines there), while others will be designated feline meeting places, rather like human cafés. Generally, however, every cat regards its core living space as its kingdom and will not tolerate it being threatened by any cat that is not part of its immediate feline or human family. Just as we enclose our gardens with gates and fences,

the cat does much the same around its home turf, although its 'Keep out!' notices are the intangible ones of scent, which you will often see a tom depositing by spraying his urine, tail aquiver as he directs it backwards, on certain points around his realm's boundaries. (And if even we, with our inferior sense of smell, recoil from the pungent odour of a tom's urine, imagine what effect it has on a fellow feline.) All cats mark their territory with their smell, be it via their urine or their scent glands (by rubbing their heads against trees, for example), refreshing their personal fragrance regularly as it fades. You will often see a cat pausing and reflectively sniffing a plant or garden feature as it 'reads' another feline's message, occasionally adding a fragrant footnote of its own so that a subsequent visitor will know that it has been there.

THE GREAT OUTDOORS IS TEEMING WITH THE FELINE SCENT SIGNALS THAT MARK THE BOUNDARIES OF A CAT'S KINGDOM.

Although a cat will unhesitatingly defend its territory against feline intruders (and it prefers to do this by means of deterrence rather than direct confrontation), its relationship with those that it lives with – its family, be they blood relations or not, fellow cats or humans – is far less aggressive. Having left behind kittenhood, when playing games with other kittens served both as an education in hunting skills and established each kitten's place in the feline pecking order, cats become increasing aloof from one another as they mature. Certain feline interactions remain important, however, in maintaining the bond between cats that live together. One is mutual rubbing and grooming sessions, in which scents are exchanged and feelings of trust are reinforced. And when one cat returns to its home base from a border patrol, its curious housemates will often sniff its head and tail avidly to ascertain from its scent what it has been up to while it was away. Usually it is an inferior cat who initiates rubbing, sniffing and grooming sessions, probably as a way of ensuring that it retains the superior cat's friendship, or at least tolerance, and this may also explain why cats prefer to approach their owners (whom they regard as boss cats) for some affectionate interaction rather than the other way round, which breaches feline etiquette.

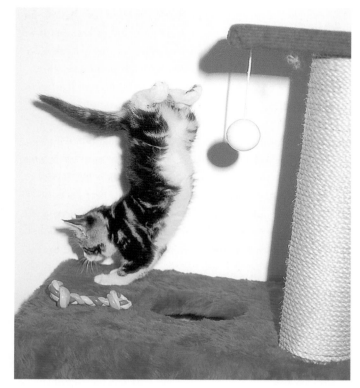

A KITTEN PRACTISES LEAPING AND POUNCING.

A DOMINANT CAT INITIATES A SCRAP, PROMPTING ITS HOUSEMATE TO BEAT A HASTY RETREAT.

THE CAT'S POWERS OF COMMUNICATION

As well as transmitting and receiving scent messages, cats communicate volumes by means of their body language and vocalisation.

The feline body – particularly the ears and tail – is a highly expressive instrument that instantly communicates how a cat is feeling within its skin if only you know how to interpret the keynotes. The emotional signal that is perhaps the easiest for humans to recognise is fear. When threatened by a more dominant cat with hostile intent which it has no desire to fight, the undercat will nevertheless stand its ground, albeit flattening its body, fur and ears in an attempt to make itself look as small and inoffensive as it can, shortly thereafter beginning to creep slowly backwards as it tries to remove itself from danger. All the while, the more aggressive cat, its pupils contracted into slits, will be trying to stare down the other feline with unblinking concentration – an aggressive action in cat language – while the other cat, pupils dilated and blinking in response, will be trying to convey the message, through its avoidance of eye contact, that it means no harm. These gestures signal submission, and if all goes well and the aggressor decides not to pursue the undercat, it will be able to slink away, all the while keeping a wary eye on its tormentor. If, on the other hand, the felines are evenly matched, a staring match may take place that may last for a considerable time, with, to the human eye, very little happening apart from some hisses and growls. A battle of wills is, in fact, taking place, which, if neither feline gives in, may well escalate and end either with them swiping at each other with their forepaws or in a claw-flashing, fur-flying fight, during which the losing cat may be forced to roll onto its back, both to protect its neck from the killing bite and to enable it to lash out with its powerful hindlegs. The end of the scrap is signalled with the loser lying flat on

MAKING ITSELF LOOK SMALLER SIGNIFIES SUBMISSION.

A CAT'S BODY LANGUAGE BETRAYS ITS INTENTION TO POUNCE.

the ground and the victor apparently losing interest, perhaps turning away and sniffing raptly at a nearby spot, a contemptuous gesture intended to convey the message that its vanquished opponent no longer poses any sort of threat.

FLATTENED EARS DENOTE A REALLY RATTLED CAT.

backwards and its hindlegs forwards, and raising its tail to increase its height, also fluffing up the fur on its body and tail (which it may sometimes curve into a hooped shape) to make itself appear wider and more substantial. If the situation is looking really desperate, it may furthermore resort to the diversionary tactic of hissing, growling and making explosive spitting sounds in an attempt to startle the dog and thus break its concentration, giving the cat a breathing space in which to escape. (Most animals are at the very least wary of snakes, if not terrified of them, and it is probably no coincidence that a cornered cat's hiss, followed by spitting, resembles the warning sounds made by a serpent. This association may also explain why many cats flee when an aerosol can is squirted and why Melchior makes himself scarce when the steam iron's switched on.)

Cats usually prefer to resolve their differences by means of psychological warfare than risk being injured, and you will probably have seen many variations on the aggressive–submissive body-language theme. Another defensive message, for instance, is signalled by what is known as the 'arched-back' posture beloved of cartoonists, which is typically enacted in response to the danger of an imminent attack by a truly dangerous foe – a dog, for example. The cat's primary intention in assuming this position is to make itself look larger and more formidable, thereby trying to trick the dog into believing that it would be no pushover in a fight. It accordingly arches its back by stiffening its limbs, pointing its forelegs

Actual feline fisticuffs aside, signs of aggression or confidence are less easy for human observers to spot, that is, unless they are versed in the vocabulary of the feline body language. If a cat is in the mood to initiate a showdown, it signals its intent by stalking stiffly towards its chosen opponent. Once it has come within staring distance, it will concentrate every part of its body on its victim. The tip of its tail may twitch, betraying the tension that it is experiencing, but its ears will be pricked, albeit protectively pulled back, as it stares intently at its rival. With luck, that will be enough to cow the other cat into submission, and off the boss cat will then strut, with its tail held high, looking inordinately pleased with itself.

FELINE CONFRONTATION TACTICS INCLUDE MANY VARIATIONS ON THE AGGRESSIVE–SUBMISSIVE THEME.

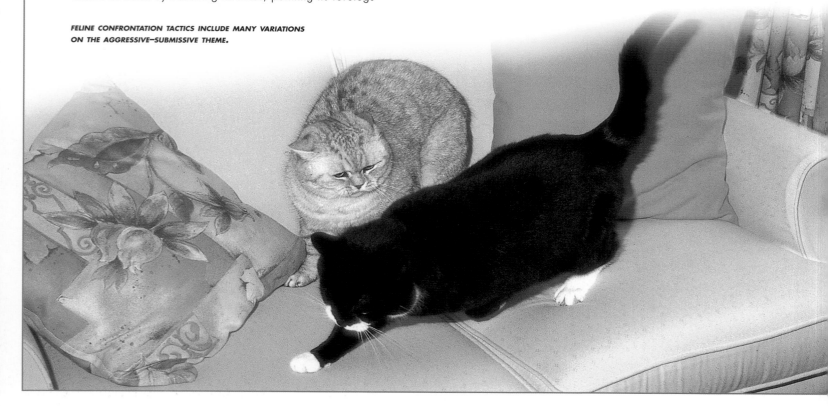

Indeed, you can tell a lot by looking at a cat's tail and ears: if its tail is vertical and its ears are pricked, the cat is feeling confident, and if the tip of its erect tail is kinked, it's offering you a tentative greeting. When a cat turns its back on you and quivers its tail, it's sending an unreserved, 'Please acknowledge me' plea that may well hark back to a kittenhood invitation to its mother to clean its nether regions. If a cat is becoming annoyed, however, it often indicates its frustration by swishing its tail from side to side and drawing back its ears, and if it becomes really irate, it will lash its tail as fast as it can and flatten its ears completely.

The final chapter in the beginner's guide to feline communication consists of the various sounds that a cat makes. As we have seen, cats that find themselves in situations of potential conflict often resort to issuing warning growls, hisses and explosive spits, signals that are often interspersed with low wails and harsh snarls. If the conflict escalates, a torrent of ear-splitting yowls and caterwauls may be unleashed, as well as the occasional shriek of pain if a sharp claw sinks into soft flesh. Such unfriendly noises signify both aggression and deterrence, the intention being to make the foe think that the cat will prove such a formidable opponent that it would be wiser not to attempt an attack. At night especially, loud, unearthly wails may rend the air – these are the call-and-response yowls initiated by the vocal invitations of females on heat and the toms' answering 'mowls', although because all of the neighbourhood's toms are likely to have hot-footed it in the female's direction, some will be the aggressive noises made by a tom facing down a rival.

CONFIDENCE IS SIGNALLED BY ERECT EARS AND A STEADY GAZE.

A MOTHER CAT USES A RANGE OF GENTLE SOUNDS TO COMMUNICATE WITH HER BROOD.

The conversational sounds that a cat makes are far quieter, as well as more musical, than those that it produces in response to the crises of warfare or sex. A queen communicates with her kittens using a variety of coos, trills and chirrups, all of which quickly become part of a kitten's vocal repertoire that it retains when it grows into adulthood. Be it to greet, encourage, chivvy, make a request or simply to express how a cat is feeling, these gentle sounds have many purposes, and each cat's use of them is unique. To the human ear, the cat's most familiar sound is, of course, the miaow, or mew, a feline word that has entered the vocabulary of many human languages: mau in Egyptian, naoua in Arabic, myaus in India, mio in China, miaou in France and Miau in Germany, to give just a few examples. Interestingly, most cats miaow more at humans than at fellow felines, which has led some researchers to believe that the miaow and its various nuances may be the cat's attempt to imitate human speech and therefore to initiate a conversation that humans are more likely to understand than the feline language, in which humans are, of course, near-illiterates.

The feline sounds discussed above are all made consciously, unlike purring, which is an involuntary response. Typically made when a cat is feeling relaxed and contented – while being stroked, for instance – the low, rumbling sound that is characteristic of the purr is generally thought to be produced as the air that the cat breathes in and out passes over a pair of vestibular folds (false vocal cords) in the throat, the sound thereby generated being amplified by the vibration of the larynx as its muscles relax and contract. Despite its general association with contentment, a cat may also purr frantically when it finds itself in an uncomfortable plight, a paradoxical response that may be a feline attempt either to reassure or distract itself from its fear of being a situation over which it has no control. (Caspar, for example, often does this when he's being examined by the vet, who is not his favourite person, despite the vet's gentle hands and demeanour, when it could also be interpreted as a plea for kindly treatment.)

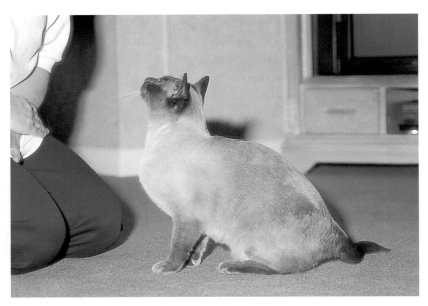

BY MIAOWING, IS A CAT TRYING TO SPEAK 'HUMAN'?

A CONTENTED CAT PURRS AUTOMATICALLY.

FELINE SELF-MAINTENANCE

A successful hunter needs to be fit, and cats keep themselves trim by strolling the perimeters of their territory on their regular inspection tours, climbing trees or other lofty vantage points from which they can monitor any interesting goings-on and, of course, pouncing at potential prey. (The reason why many indoor cats occasionally career around the house at top speed is both to let off steam and to indulge in the type of hunting exercise that outdoor cats more regularly enjoy.) Exploratory or deadly mission having been accomplished, it's then time for the cat to give itself a thorough wash and brush-up before settling down to enjoy a well-earned snooze.

All animals, humans included, need to keep themselves clean if they are to remain healthy, and cats are particularly scrupulous when it comes to personal hygiene. Unlike humans, cats don't have sweat glands (apart from some in their paw pads), which means that it is difficult for them to keep cool in hot weather. (Although they generally like to bask in a sunny spot, their preferred response to soaring temperatures is to find the coolest available spot to lie in and then to stay prone, declining to participate in any heat-generating, energetic pursuits. If heatstroke threatens, they will either lick their fur, the saliva cooling their bodies as it evaporates, or, in extreme cases, pant.)

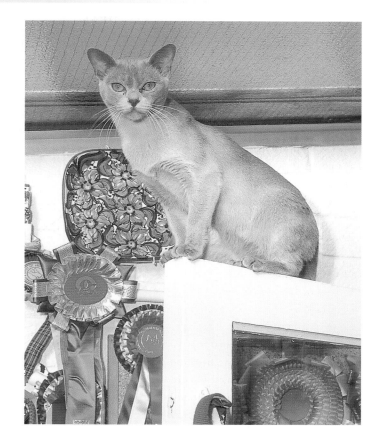

A LOFTY VANTAGE POINT GIVES AN INQUISITIVE CAT A BIRD'S-EYE VIEW OF ITS SURROUNDINGS.

ITS REGULAR BOUNDARY PATROLS HELP TO KEEP AN OUTDOOR CAT FIT AND TRIM.

The absence of sweat glands, however, means that their personal ablutions are less concerned with cleansing than with grooming; excising their body odour – their personal hallmark – is anathema to felines. Cats also wash as a displacement activity. If a cat finds itself in an agony of confusion, or feels that it has suffered a loss of dignity, it will often lick its flanks vigorously, partly to give itself time to recover its self-composure and partly to save face and make it appear purposeful instead of baffled.

HEAD DEALT WITH, THE FORELIMBS ARE NEXT UP . . .

. . . FOLLOWED BY THE FLANKS . . .

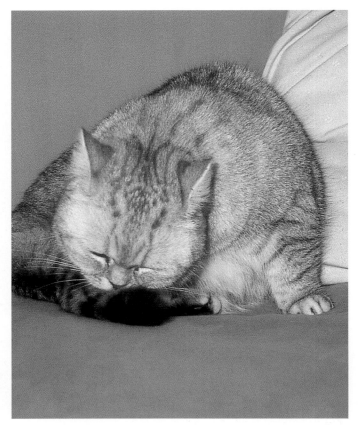

. . . AND, FINALLY, THE TAIL.

What the feline tongue lacks in the way of taste buds, it more than makes up for with its plethora of hooked papillae (see page 32) that serve as an essential grooming aid. Although you may think that a cat is washing in the human sense when you see it licking its fur, it is actually combing its coat, which, depending on its breed, generally consists of three layers: the short, soft down hairs nearest the skin, then the slightly longer and thicker awn hairs (both types insulating the feline body against the cold) and finally the even longer and coarser guard hairs that make up the protective topcoat. Working from the head to the tail, as the barbed papillae move over the surface of the coat, they remove any superficial tangles, as well as hairs that are no longer firmly embedded within the skin – dead hairs – thereby encouraging new growth. More stubborn clumps of tangled fur are nibbled out with the incisor teeth, which a cat also uses to pull off its old 'toenails' which, unlike its front claws, it cannot strop away against a tree. Despite the impressive revolving capability of the feline neck, which allows it to take care of its back, it can't give a feline tongue access to its nape or head, and cats therefore give these areas a good scrub by rubbing them with a pre-licked forepaw, following a precise routine. And when it comes to gaining access to the feline nether regions, cats demonstrate an innate talent for yoga with their ability to raise an obstructive hindleg to the vertical position.

A CAT MOISTENS A FOREPAW AS IT PREPARES TO WASH ITS FACE.

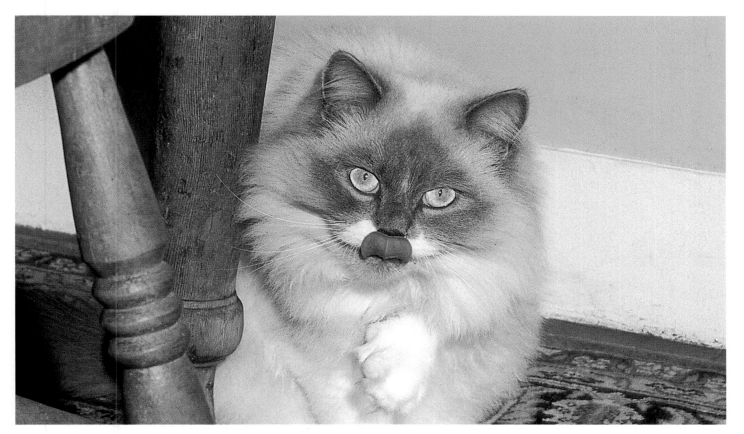

CATS TAKE CLEANLINESS VERY SERIOUSLY.

Because cats spend so much time washing and bury their faeces, too, many people approvingly regard them as being fastidiously clean creatures. Although this is undeniably so, there are more reasons underlying the feline's fetish for hygiene than simply the desire to keep itself, as well as its surroundings, spick and span.

Covering over faeces with earth does, of course, prevent the spread of disease, but perhaps a more important benefit to the feline is that this procedure reduces the likelihood of the faeces' smell either guiding an enemy to its whereabouts, especially the home in which it feels safe, or alerting potential prey to its presence and sending them scuttling away. Studies have provided support for this theory, it having been observed that immature and neutered cats, who are at the bottom of the feline social stratum, are more rigorous faeces-buriers than toms and queens, who have a better chance of successfully defending themselves against hostile interlopers and of catching elusive quarry.

SLEEP IS SO IMPORTANT FOR A FELINE THAT MOST CATS SPEND TWO-THIRDS OF THE DAY SNOOZING.

IT IS NOT ONLY FOR REASONS OF HYGIENE THAT CATS, UNLIKE DOGS, BURY THEIR FAECES.

As for any animal, sleep is vital for the cat, this down-time enabling it to recharge its batteries and giving its body the necessary peace and quiet in which to digest food and carry out tissue maintenance without the distraction of external stimuli. And the reason why cats sleep so much – typically for around 16 hours out of every 24 – is to conserve energy in preparation for their intense, night-time forays. Like ours, the cat's sleep is divided into two distinct phases: light and deep. You can tell when a cat is sleeping lightly – having a catnap – because it will have curled up in a comfortable spot, with its tail curved around its body and its head tucked in neatly. Despite appearances, it is still in a state of alertness, ready to respond to any interesting sound (try giving a high whistle and see its ears prick up in response) and to spring into action if necessary.

A disconcerting sight to the human observer, sometimes a cat will sleep with its eyes open, with its third eyelids pulled across the surface of its eyes to seal in moisture. When its body is lying at full stretch and has become completely floppy, the cat has entered a deep sleep. And if you see a paw, ear or whisker twitch, your feline friend is in all likelihood enjoying an action-packed dream in which it is reliving hunting triumphs, analysis of the brainwaves of sleeping cats having shown marked similarities to those of humans during the dream state.

chapter 2

ADOPTING A CAT

Making the decision to adopt a cat – or cats – should not be taken lightly, so think long and hard before impulsively taking home an irresistibly appealing kitten who has melted your heart at first sight. If you and your cat are to enjoy a long and happy future together, there are a number of factors that you will have to take into consideration before welcoming it into your home. Cats are increasingly living to ripe old ages – often up to twenty years – years during which you will have to be prepared to be a responsible owner. So before taking the plunge, ask yourself the following questions.

CAN I AFFORD TO KEEP A CAT?

Although a cat's maintenance costs are relatively low, there are certain unavoidable expenses that cat-ownership will incur over the years. These include providing your feline with the minimum of two meals a day of a nutritious proprietary cat food; buying cat litter for an indoor cat; settling an annual veterinary bill for vaccinations; and funding any additional veterinary treatment that a cat may need as a result of an accident or illness. Investigate these costs by paying a visit to your local pet shop or supermarket and veterinary surgery, noting down prices and asking for information.

CAN YOU AFFORD TO FEED YOUR CAT A PROPRIETARY CAT FOOD TWICE A DAY?

THIS MONTH-OLD KITTEN COULD NOTCH UP TWENTY YEARS.

ARE MY FAMILY CIRCUMSTANCES SUITABLE?

A cat's primary requirements are a regular supply of food and water, along with a safe and comfortable place of shelter: potentially your home. Can you guarantee to able to feed and water it every day, ideally twice a day, at the same time? Would your home suit the feline lifestyle? Although some cats do live in one-bedroom flats, most would prefer more space to

LIKE ALL BABIES, KITTENS NEED LOTS OF AFFECTION AND ATTENTION.

roam around in, although a garden isn't necessary if you can supply alternative opportunities for exercise within your home. Despite the legendary feline independence, a cat will pin without some affection and attention – could you provide this if

you are out working all day and partying at night? How would a cat fit in with any existing family members, children and other pets, for example? And what arrangements would you need to make to ensure that it would be well looked after when you go away on holiday? Could you call on a neighbour to cat-sit, or would you need to arrange for it to stay in a cattery? If, having considered these issues, you feel that you could give a cat a good home, there are still more decisions to be made.

CAT OR KITTEN?

The essential question to ask yourself when deciding whether to adopt a cat or a kitten is whether you have sufficient time to devote to a young animal's needs. Although you should in any

KITTENS ARE BOTH CAPTIVATING . . .

case never take a kitten from its mother before it has been weaned (usually when it is between eight and twelve weeks old), which makes feeding it easier, a kitten still requires a considerable amount of attention. Will you have the time to bond with it, to play with it (a vital part of kittenhood), to guide it as it becomes acquainted with its new household, to teach it human- and furniture-friendly habits, to rescue it from the scrapes that it will inevitably get itself into, and, above all, to make it feel a loved and valued member of your family?

THINK LONG AND HARD BEFORE WELCOMING A CAT INTO YOUR HOME.

VERY YOUNG KITTENS NEED THEIR MOTHER'S MILK.

. . . AND HIGHLY ENTERTAINING.

There are also certain practical and financial considerations to be taken into account. You will probably have to take a kitten to the vet's for its first set of immunisation vaccinations (see pages 86 to 88), for example, and should also be prepared to foot the bill for medication, as well as provide nursing care, should it develop any ailments that you hadn't bargained for (in Caspar and Melchior's case, ear mites and ringworm). In addition, you may find yourself having to wean it from a diet to which it has become accustomed. All of these non-negotiable responsibilities take time and cost money. That having been said, kittens are fun-filled, captivating creatures, who are more

tolerant of boisterous children than older cats, and it is fascinating to watch their personalities develop as they grow into adulthood. And when a cat has lived with you for most of its life, and you have years of shared companionship behind you, life simply wouldn't be the same without it. Although it may require more patience to make it feel at home, adopting an older cat brings its own rewards. Certain aspects of its care will be easier: it will almost certainly be house-trained, for instance, and won't demand as much of your time and attention. The main difficulties will probably be educating it in the ways of your household and gently dissuading it from persisting with old habits – and you may even have to learn to live with them – as well as winning its trust and affection. If you persevere and forge a strong bond with it, however, even the most wary of adopted older cats will offer you their friendship, thereby enriching your life immeasurably.

**FEEDING TIME IS OFTEN A ROUGH-AND-TUMBLE
AFFAIR WHEN KITTENS ARE INVOLVED.**

MALE OR FEMALE?

If, like the majority of responsible cat owners, you would prefer your cat not to breed, a simple neutering operation (see page 96) will iron out the most significant behavioural differences between male and female felines. With the removal of the organs that pump sex hormones – testosterone in males, and oestrogen in females – into the cat's body, both sexes will become less likely to roam or spray (particularly males), less temperamental and, most importantly, incapable of adding to an already teeming feline population. (Unchecked breeding has resulted in many unwanted kittens and cats, who, if they are lucky enough to survive in the first place, may be forced to become strays or to adopt a feral lifestyle.)Unless you are prepared to keep, or find homes for, any kittens that she may have (and in her prime she may be capable of producing four or five three times a year), you should pre-empt the arrival of a litter of kittens by having any female cat that you adopt spayed as soon as your vet recommends it. Similarly, your male cat may sire numerous offspring – although the likelihood is that you'll be blissfully unaware of them – unless you take him to the vet to be castrated.

If, however, you would prefer your cat to remain entire, it's important that you're aware of the behavioural differences

SITTING ON SHOULDER

between male and female cats. A tom is unlikely to be at home much because his hormones will be urging him to patrol his territory to ward off trespassers, as well as to respond to the calls and scent of any local females on heat. In the laying-down of territorial markers, he will be an assiduous sprayer of pungent urine and may require frequent trips to the vet as a result of the wounds that he'll inevitably sustain in his scraps with other toms.

An entire female is usually more home-loving, apart from when she's on heat, when her sex hormones kick in and she'll begin to invite the attention of toms. If she becomes pregnant, her kittens will be born nine weeks later, her maternal duties then keeping her fully occupied for two to three months.

A SINGLE FEMALE WILL HAVE MANY OFFSPRING.

ONE CAT OR MORE?

The fact that we both went out to work during the day was at the forefront of our minds when we decided to adopt two kittens rather than one. When they are young, cats require a great deal of company and stimulation, and we felt that it would be unfair to leave a single kitten alone in our home for around ten hours a day during the working week. In this respect, letting ourselves in for double trouble was certainly the right decision for Caspar and Melchior, who, according to our downstairs neighbour, played a kitten's version of football all day while we were away. The downside is that keeping two cats well fed, healthy and happy does, of course, cost twice as much.

When weighing up the pros and cons of how many cats to welcome into your home, you should first ask yourself what would be in the best interests of the cat or cats. Although cats are remarkably self-sufficient, a solitary kitten (but less so an older cat, who requires less active mutual interaction) could become lonely if it has to spend most of its time on its own. But if two are company, would three or more be too much of a crowd in a small home? Would you be able to provide each of your cats with sufficient food and a comfortable home, both of which top the list of cat priorities?

Don't forget to take your existing family into consideration, too. If your house is already packed with children, pets or both, how would they react to one or more cats joining them? Because it's far easier for kittens to learn to get along with both children and other household pets – even dogs – and vice versa, a single kitten would probably fit in better than either two or an older cat or cats. If you're tempted to adopt more than one kitten or cat, ask yourself whether it would be wise to take on the commitment of caring for them if space, time and money are already tight.

A single cat is a good choice if you live on your own. Because you won't have to spread your attention thinly between two or more felines, the likelihood is that you'll forge a strong, companionable bond with your feline friend.

One or more? You'll probably already instinctively know the answer to that conundrum.

TWO CATS WILL PROVIDE COMPANY FOR EACH OTHER.

MOGGIE OR PEDIGREE?

Unless you intend to breed from, or show, your cat, there is little that a pedigree feline can offer that a mongrel moggie can't match. Just like people, every cat is a unique character, whether their lineage is uncertain or you can trace it back for many generations. Probably the only significant difference between purebreds like our Somali, Melchior, and crosspeds like his companion, Caspar, is that you can predict with reasonable accuracy how any kittens that a pedigree cat may have will look, especially if the other parent is of the same breed. And although it is often said that because moggies, unlike many pedigrees, aren't inbred, their mixed gene pool makes them more resistant to disease and generally tougher, this claim hasn't been scientifically substantiated (and in any case, many moggies are born into close-knit family groups).

When deciding whether to adopt a moggie or pedigree, the first consideration to be taken into account is cost. If you are charged for it at all – and many human surrogate parents of moggie kittens simply require the assurance that they will go to a good home – it is unlikely that you will be asked to pay more than a token sum for a crossped and, depending on its age, perhaps the cost of any initial immunisation vaccinations that it has been given. A carefully controlled parentage, on the other hand, commands a premium, and, depending on the breed, you may be asked to pay the equivalent of a washing machine or even a car for the privilege of becoming the owner of a purebred cat.

LONGHAIRED CATS NEED HUMAN HELP TO KEEP THEIR MAGNIFICENT MANES TANGLE-FREE.

Both moggies and pedigrees come in a vast array of coat colours and fur lengths and, your personal preferences aside, you would be wise to take some of these into consideration. Cats with white coats, for example, are susceptible to sunburn and hence skin cancer, so, as ridiculous as it may sound, you should apply sunblock to their vulnerable noses and ears before allowing them outside to bask in the sunshine. Be warned, too, that white cats, especially if they have blue eyes, may be congenitally deaf.

While longhaired cats often look magnificent, bear in mind that most will need help with grooming and that you will therefore have to comb them regularly, often daily in the case of Persians. Their long, fine hairs may furthermore exacerbate an allergy to cat fur in humans, which may not be triggered by a

shorthaired cat. Shorthairs usually manage to keep their coats sleek without human assistance, although it's still advisable to comb them once a week. All cats, be they long- or shorthairs, moult, so you should be prepared constantly to have to remove dead hairs from your clothing and furniture, but note that longhairs' soft awn hairs are particularly clingy (Melchior's light-silver fur, for example, seems to be magnetically attracted to dark clothing). Another disadvantage of owning a longhaired cat is that its self-grooming process can result in a build-up of fur in its stomach, resulting in the production of more furballs (see page 105) than in its shorthaired counterparts.

Despite every cat's individuality of personality, certain pedigree breeds are noted for their peculiarities of temperament.

FELINE CHARACTERISTICS CAN VARY GREATLY.

BRITISH SHORT HAIRED – RED SILVER SPOTTED

docile characters, as are the Ragdolls that are descended, the story goes, from a Persian female who had been injured in a road traffic accident. When handled, Ragdolls relax their bodies so that they become as floppy as the doll after which they are named, and it is also claimed that they have an extremely high pain threshold (which, of course, is no excuse to maltreat them).

Longhaired breeds that evolved from Oriental shorthairs tend to have retained the characteristics of their Oriental lineage. Being a Somali (a longhaired Abyssinian), Melchior, for example, is a vocal, lively personality who is very human-oriented and likes to keep a constant eye on what we are doing, as well as join in

phone conversations, in contrast to Caspar, our self-sufficient shorthaired crossped, who prefers to snooze the day away in peace. British and European shorthaired breeds are usually quiet, even-tempered and relatively undemanding, unlike many of their Oriental shorthaired cousins, who are both incessant conversationalists and insist on playing an active role in any household pursuit. Siamese and Burmese cats are especially renowned for their irrepressible curiosity and craving for close companionship and will frequently make their own entertainment if left to their own devices (curtain-climbing is a particular favourite, as is wool-sucking). All in all, think hard about adopting a hyperactive feline!

SNOWSHOE (MALE) SEAL AND WHITE POINT

MAINE COON, RED, SILVER & WHITE

ABYSSINIAN, BLUE

PERSIAN, BLUE TABBY

CAT SOURCES

Unless you have already reserved a kitten from the litter of a mother cat whose owner you know, your first port of call when looking for a cat to adopt should be your local vet's. Most veterinary surgeries display notice boards on which people whose cats have produced kittens, or those who sadly can no longer keep their older cats, can 'advertise' felines in need of a good home. Many veterinary nurses are in any case founts of knowledge and advice, both regarding reputable cat sources and aspects of feline care. Never buy a kitten from a pet shop: not only may it have been traumatised by its noisy surroundings, but it will in all likelihood have been exposed to a host of germs. And if a stray cat decides to adopt you, before giving it a permanent home, make every effort to ensure that it is not already part of a loving family, particularly if it looks well fed.

A vet's notice board may also display the details of cat-rescue organisations, which is how, having first called to make an appointment, we found ourselves in the feline nursery of a suburban cat sanctuary where we were introduced to, among other kittens, Melchior and Caspar. Before making our choice, we were vetted to assess our suitability for cat-ownership and were also asked to sign an agreement undertaking to have the cats neutered; to take full responsibility for their welfare and to

TINY KITTENS ARE VULNERABLE TO DISEASE.

give them a happy and loving home; to obtain veterinary treatment in case of illness or injury; and to ensure that they wore identity tags when outside the home. In addition, we undertook to allow a member of the cat sanctuary to visit our home to check that the cats were happily settled; to return the cats to the sanctuary if we could no longer keep them; and, in the event of them going missing, to report their loss so that a search could be instigated. All of these stipulations had the cats' welfare at heart, and we were happy to go along with them, as well as make a modest donation towards the upkeep of the cat sanctuary.

Finally, if you are looking for a specific breed of pedigree cat, a good starting point is the pages of specialist cat magazines, which contain the contact details of societies and breeders.

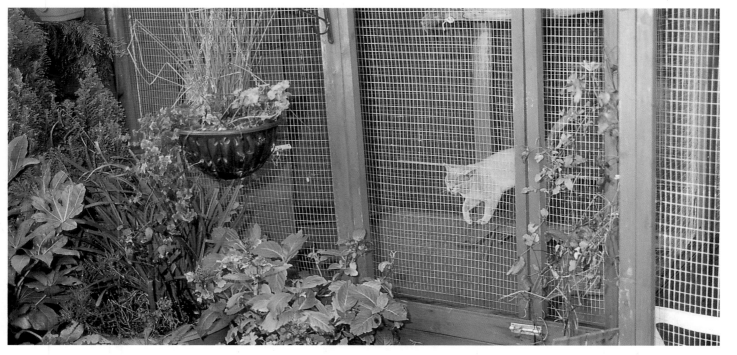

REPUTABLE CAT SANCTUARIES TRY TO ENSURE THAT THEIR FELINE CHARGES GO TO GOOD HOMES.

WHAT TO LOOK FOR IN A KITTEN OR CAT

When meeting a prospective feline member of your family for the first time, be it a kitten or a cat, a crossped or a purebred, the essential question to ask yourself is whether it looks healthy. If you have any doubts, it would be wiser not to adopt it: not only could you be condemning yourself to exorbitant veterinary bills and a new career as a feline nurse, but you could even have to suffer the premature death of your feline charge.

In the case of kittens, remember that they should not leave their mother until they have been weaned, usually when they are between eight and twelve weeks old (although you can always reserve one earlier). If possible, ask to see the mother cat with her litter so that you can assess the cleanliness of their surroundings and also how the kittens interact, which should give you some idea of their respective personalities, as well as of their mother's temperament.

Because you're likely to be charmed and distracted when you come face to face with a delightful heap of fluffy kittens, before leaving home it's best to write down a checklist of things to look out for to consult while carefully inspecting each kitten in turn.

ASK TO SEE THE FELINE FAMILY INTERACTING.

A CAT'S EYES SHOULD BE CLEAR AND BRIGHT.

On taking charge of Caspar and Melchior, the owner of the cat sanctuary warned us that they had ear mites (and Caspar must have been incubating ringworm, too, although there was no indication of that when we first met him). Both conditions cleared up completely after the appropriate treatment, but many of the symptoms listed above may not be so easily dealt with. If you have any concerns, discuss them with the kitten's breeder or owner and don't allow your worries to be brushed aside. If you are really torn between what your head and heart – or the owner – are telling you, ask if you can take the kitten to a vet for an expert opinion; most responsible breeders or owners should have no objection to this, that is, as long as you pay the bill!

Personality-wise, look for friendly curiosity in a kitten. Some kittens may appear bossy and others more timid – you will know better than anyone else which personality traits will suit you and your home best, so be guided by your instincts, but nevertheless try to make an informed choice. Note that an older cat will often be wary of strangers, so don't be put off if it appears a little aloof.

Finally, remember that if a kitten or cat has been immunised you will need its vaccination certificate so that your vet knows which brand to use when it's time for its boosters. Along with a purebred, you should also be given a pedigree certificate stretching back four generations as proof of its lineage should you wish to show it or breed it with another pedigree.

The following checklist is as applicable in most respects to older cats as to kittens.

- Does the kitten look generally healthy and alert? If so, it has probably not contracted any life-endangering viruses or illnesses from its mother or environment.

- Any juvenile wobbliness aside, do the kitten's legs appear to be functioning normally? If it seems lame, it may be suffering from a non-reversible birth defect, have a broken limb or be showing the first signs of a serious illness.

- Do its ears look clean? Look out for head-shaking, ear-scratching, specks of dark grit or a profuse, brown, waxy discharge, all of which could be signs of ear mites (see page 126). These aren't disastrous, but the kitten's ears will need treating with eardrops to get rid of them.

- Do its eyes look clear and bright? Danger signs include soreness, weepiness, discharge and the third eyelid partially pulled across the eye, all of which indicate the presence of a potentially serious infection.

- Does its nose look clean and is it healthily damp? A runny nose may indicate cat flu (see page 90).

- Do its gums look rosy pink and its teeth white and healthy? Red, inflamed gums could be a sign of gingivitis (see pages 133 to 134) and pale ones a sign of illness.

- Is it sneezing, wheezing or coughing? All of these symptoms are potentially very serious.

- Does its fur look springy and in good condition? Are there any tiny black specks in it? A dirty, greasy, matted or bedraggled coat could indicate illness, and black specks a flea infestation (which, although not life-threatening, will require combating, see pages 93 to 94).

- Are there any bald spots in the fur? If so, the kitten, may have ringworm (see page 123), a fungal infection that will need to be treated with ointment and medication.

- Does it have a pronounced pot belly? If it does, it may be suffering from worms (see pages 91 to 92), which must be banished with medication.

- Does its bottom look clean? If you see any worms, these are relatively easily dealt with, but chronic-looking diarrhoea may signify a grave illness.

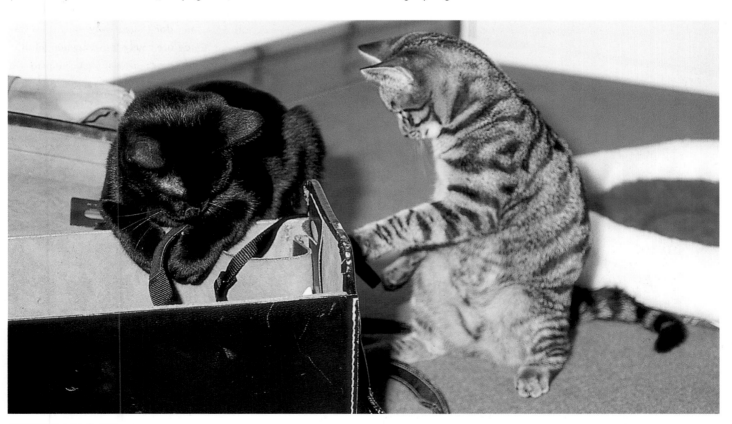

CURIOSITY IS A GOOD SIGN.

BASIC CAT-CARE EQUIPMENT

Before you welcome your cat or kitten into your home, you will need to prepare for its arrival by assembling the following cat-care basics.

A CARRYING BASKET

The first item that you'll need is a carrying basket in which to transfer your cat or kitten from its existing home to yours. Don't imagine that you will be able to carry it home in your arms: your feline is a creature of habit who will regard its previous place of residence as a safe haven, so as soon as you – after all, someone whom it doesn't know, and doesn't know means well – remove it from its familiar surroundings, it will panic and will start to lash out in an attempt to bolt away. If the feelings of high anxiety caused by its displacement weren't bad enough, it's more than likely that its journey to your home will necessitate an introduction to motorised transport, be it a car or a bus, the sounds and motion of which it will find so terrifyingly alien that it will freak out. The last thing you want is a frightened cat running amok under seats and foot pedals, so invest in a carrying basket, which you'll in any case need for future trips with your feline, such as to the veterinary surgery.

A CAT-CARRIER SHOULD BE WELL VENTILATED.

You'll find a selection of carrying baskets in your local pet shop, including traditional wicker baskets or fibreglass boxes with a grille-like front opening and plastic-covered, wire-mesh 'cages' that open at the top. Both types will do an efficient job of transporting a cat safely, but the wire-mesh carriers are probably more practical, being both more quickly cleaned should any panic-induced mishaps occur and easier to place a recalcitrant feline into (you can just drop them in, while you'll have to lift and push a cat into a front-opening carrier).

Whichever you choose, line the bottom with newspaper (or, after your cat has lost its fear and has become resigned to being incarcerated in its carrier, a piece of fabric), which will make the carrier more comfortable, as well as mopping up the mess if your petrified cat loses control of its bladder or bowels. If the weather's cold, line the sides with newspaper, too. Cardboard carriers may be cheaper, but they won't last long, and resist the temptation to place a cat in a zipped carrier or overnight bag – it simply won't give the cat enough air.

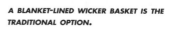

A BLANKET-LINED WICKER BASKET IS THE TRADITIONAL OPTION.

FOOD AND DISHES

In the interests of maintaining good hygiene, it's important that your cat has its own food and water bowls (separate ones are more practical than combined versions) rather than borrowing a saucer or dish from its human family. These are available from pet shops and should have a heavy base so that they won't tip over when your cat is eating or drinking. Battery-operated, covered food bowls are another option, many of which contain a type of cooling system that keeps food fresh in hot weather or over extended periods and may also incorporate a timer that you can set so that the lid springs open at a certain time when you're not around to feed your cat. If you have more than one cat, each should still be provided with its own pair of bowls to ensure that one doesn't hog them at feeding and watering times. (After their initial feeding frenzy, our cats tend to swap bowls midway through their meal, possibly, I suspect, to check whether they've been missing out on something more interesting.)

YELLOW PLASTIC BOWL

CAT FOOD BOWL

CERAMIC BOWL

TO AVOID TEARS AT TEATIME, PROVIDE EACH CAT WITH ITS OWN FOOD BOWL.

complete CAT

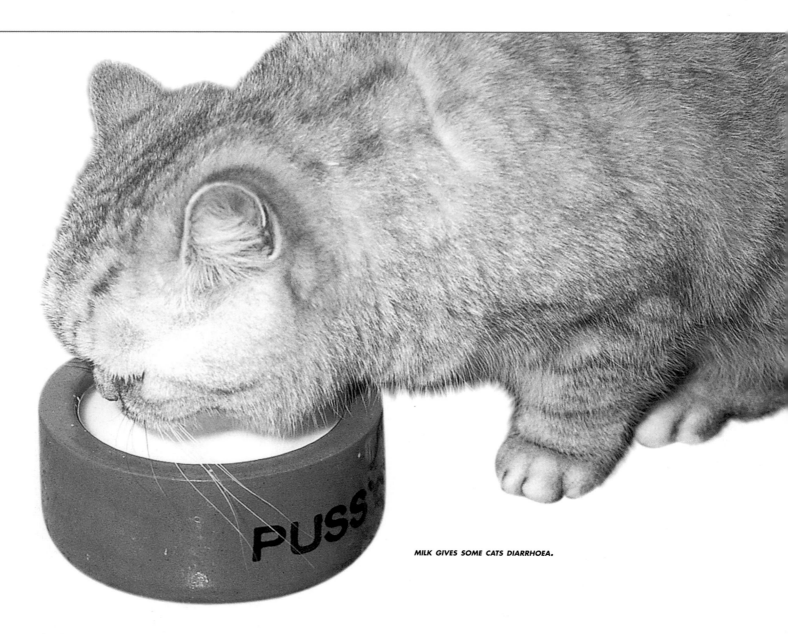

MILK GIVES SOME CATS DIARRHOEA.

The best place to feed a cat is in the kitchen, where any spillages can be easily wiped away and bowls washed. A cat's sense of security is increased if it is always fed in the same spot, so pick a quiet corner where it can eat undisturbed by other members of your family and where you won't trip over its bowls.

If the litter tray is also situated in the kitchen (and, for the purposes of hygiene, try to keep it as far away from food-preparation areas as possible), it's best not to set the cat's bowls next to it as it will find the proximity of its food and lavatory most off-putting. If you – or your cat's – preferred food is fresh, tinned or semi-moist, its bowl should be washed after every meal, separately from the human family's dishes. Bowls that contain dried food can be washed less frequently, but nevertheless at least once a week, along with water bowls. Use hot water and washing-up liquid to clean food and water

bowls, but make sure that you rinse them thoroughly because the cat's sensitive noise doesn't find the smell of household detergents appetising.

You should change the water in your cat's water bowl twice a day (you'll find it easy to remember to do this if you get into the habit of emptying and refilling it just before feeding time). It's vital that a bowl of water is always available to your cat (this is especially crucial if you feed your cat dried food), but note that many cats won't drink from a freshly replenished water bowl until the smell of the chemicals with which the water has almost inevitably been treated has subsided to tolerable levels. Do not substitute milk for water: contrary to popular belief, cow's milk is not a feline staple (although many enjoy it) and, indeed, many cats find the lactose that it contains difficult to digest, the result being diarrhoea.

WHAT, AND WHEN, SHOULD YOU FEED YOUR FELINE?

The first thing to note is that a cat's nutritional requirements will change throughout the course of its life. Their mother's milk contains all of the nutrients that kittens need for the first month or two of their lives, after which, in the wild, they would be weaned on mice and other sources of fresh flesh. Your kitten should have been weaned before it moves in with you, but because its nose and stomach will probably have become accustomed to a particular diet, you will probably have to wean it off this gradually before switching to your preferred alternative full-time. Remember to ask its previous owner for details of what it's been used to eating (this precaution also applies to older cats, who dislike change), and, if necessary, a diet sheet.

Just like human babies, kittens have small stomachs and will therefore need to be fed more often than adult cats, so aim to give them four small meals a day. By the time that your cat is six months old, you should have reduced its meals to two a day (one in the morning and one in the evening), thereby instituting a feeding regime that will remain the same for the rest of its life, that is, as long as it remains healthy. Your vet will be able to advise you when, and what, to feed an ill, convalescent or old cat, but see also pages 101 to 102.

ITS MOTHER'S MILK PROVIDES ALL OF THE NOURISHMENT THAT A YOUNG KITTEN NEEDS.

Gone are the days when domestic cats procured their own food, supplemented by a few scraps from their household's kitchen. And although you can certainly give your cat the occasional treat of a morsel of cooked fish, meat or poultry or cheese (see pages 101 to 102) to spice up its diet, providing it exclusively with home-cooked food, day in, day out, is not only extremely impractical, but could also result in your cat's body becoming deficient in some of the essential nutrients that are vital for the maintenance of feline health. Just as the make-up of a cat's body is specific to a cat, so its body needs the correct balance of feline-fuelling nutrients to avoid malnourishment and to enable every part of its body to function efficiently. The bodies, and hence nutritional needs, of human omnivores, as well as of dogs, differ from those of felines, so don't think that a cat will thrive on a human or canine diet – it won't. Protein, for example, which is required to maintain organs, muscles and tissues, should make up 30 to 40 per cent of a cat's diet, around three times the level recommended for a dog, and it also needs fat (at least 10 to 15 per cent) for energy, along with fibre (around 7 per cent) for roughage and trace amounts of vitamins and minerals.

MOST PROPRIETARY CAT FOODS HAVE BEEN FORMULATED TO MEET A FELINE'S NUTRITIONAL NEEDS.

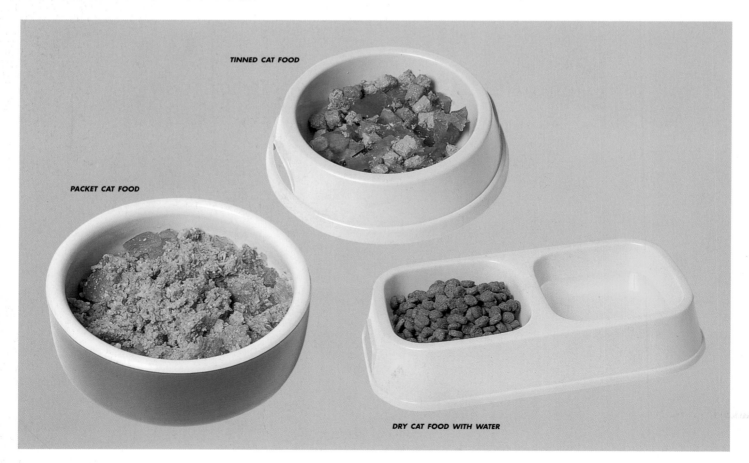

TINNED CAT FOOD

PACKET CAT FOOD

DRY CAT FOOD WITH WATER

To ensure that your kitten or cat consumes all of the nutrients that it needs, and thus remains fit and healthy, the safest option is to base its diet on a 'complete' (not 'complementary', 'treat', 'incomplete', 'varietal' or any similar euphemism, so check the label carefully) proprietary cat food, be it tinned, foil-packed or dry. You'll then be secure in the knowledge that the cat-food industry's experts in feline nutrition have ensured that their products contain exactly the right proportions of the nutrients that are essential for the maintenance of feline health. Some cats find tinned or foil-packed food more appetising than dry, although the disadvantages to humans include their powerful smell and speedy rate of spoilage. Dry food generally works out cheaper than its tinned or foil-packed counterparts and has the further advantage of offering less wastage, also giving the cat's teeth and gums a thorough work-out (remember that feline teeth were designed to crunch on bones). Most reputable manufacturers of cat food offer a range of products that have been specially formulated to suit every cat's age and condition, and their labels usually contain guidelines advising you how much of the product to feed your cat a day. If you have any doubts about what, and when, to feed your feline, ask your vet for advice.

KITTENS SHOULD BE WEANED WHEN THEY ARE BETWEEN EIGHT AND TWELVE WEEKS OLD.

A LITTER TRAY AND ACCOUTREMENTS

Even if your new feline is going to be an outdoor cat, you'll still need to buy a litter tray for it to use while it settles into your household, when you should keep it house-bound until you

YOU'LL NEED A LITTER SCOOP . . .

are certain that it knows where home is (see page 79). Once you have given it permission to roam, your cat will regard your garden as a giant litter tray, but there will nevertheless be occasions when you'll have to resurrect the real thing: if your cat becomes ill and can't stray too far from its sickbed, for example, or if you have to disbar it from going outside for a day or two. A litter tray is essential for indoor cats, along with cat litter and a litter scoop with which to carry out ad hoc waste removal. See page 103 for details on how often to change cat litter and clean a litter tray. Visit your pet shop to see what kind of litter trays, cat litter and scoops they stock. Basic litter trays consist of a shallow, toughened-plastic tray, but if you can afford it I'd recommend that you buy a covered one (the lid is easily detachable for cleaning the tray) because it gives the user more privacy and also limits the amount of cat litter that inevitably ends up being scattered around the floor. Some covered litter trays incorporate a cat-flap-type swing door, but many suspicious cats (ours included) refuse to enter this lavatorial portal.

A COVERED LITTER TRAY GIVES A LITTLE PRIVACY.

You'll also need cat litter, and if your cat or kitten is already trained to use a litter tray, remember to ask its breeder or owner which type of litter it has been used to. We neglected to do this, and although we'd shown the new arrivals the litter tray, they weren't keen to enter it, after a day of leg-crossing finally leaving a deposit or two overnight on the earthy surface of a large plant pot. Flummoxed, we contacted the owner of the cat sanctuary for advice, and it transpired that they'd been used to a granule-type litter, whereas we'd provided them with an alien, fuller's-earth-based product. The litter was changed and the problem was solved.

. . . A LITTER TRAY AND CAT LITTER.

If they aren't already familiar with a litter tray, most kittens and cats instinctively understand their purpose and need only to be shown its location, although as an educative measure you could always lift your feline into the tray, gently hold its front paws and then make a scratching motion with them.

CATS UNDERSTAND THE LITTER-TRAY CONCEPT.

EQUIPMENT FOR THE INDOOR AND OUTDOOR CAT

If you intend your feline to be an outdoor cat, think about how it is going to gain access to the great outdoors.

With your special skill as a door-opener, are you prepared to be miaowed at every time, day or night, that your cat wants to be let in or out? If not, and you don't want to restrict your cat's movements, fitting a cat flap into a wall or door (for which some DIY expertise will be required) is probably the answer. Many types of cat flap are sold by pet shops, all of which operate on the hinged-flap principle, with most featuring a catch that shuts the flap should you wish to keep your cat inside. Some variants are magnet-operated, with a magnet in the cat flap whose polarity corresponds to one that the cat wears on its collar, giving it its personal pass key and preventing strange cats from invading the house. For easy feline access, a cat flap should be situated no higher than 6 centimetres (around 2 1/2 inches) above ground level.

A CAT FLAP WILL GIVE YOUR CAT INDEPENDENCE.

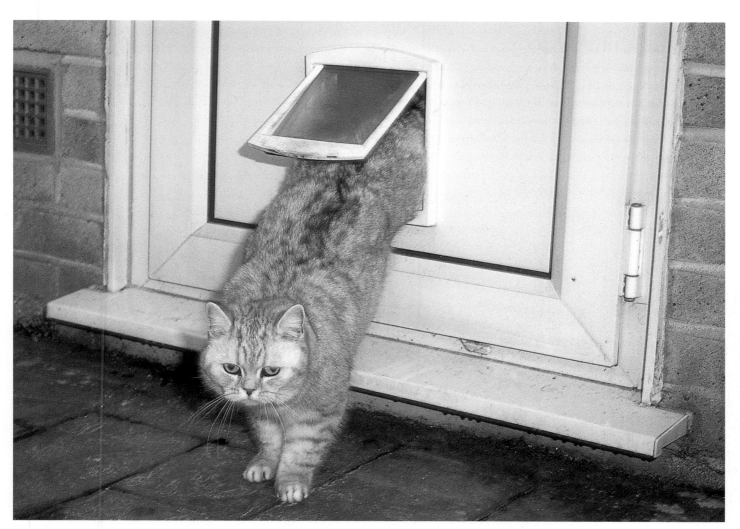

WHEN INSTALLING A CAT FLAP, REMEMBER TO POSITION IT AT A FELINE-FRIENDLY HEIGHT.

Outdoor cats can strop their claws on fences and trees, but unless you provide an indoor cat with a scratching post, it will be forced to turn its attention to your cherished furniture. Your options are either to improvise, by, perhaps, giving your cat a log of wood (one that won't splinter) to scratch at, or to buy a scratching post (or a wall-mounted scratching panel) from a pet shop. Most consist of a wooden pole around which rope is tightly coiled, fixed into a wooden base that is usually covered with carpet fabric (which I personally think may confuse a cat: if it's encouraged to scratch the base of the scratching post, why not also your expensive Axminster?) Some incorporate a

PROVIDE AN INDOOR CAT WITH A SCRATCHING POST.

TAKE STEPS TO SAFEGUARD YOUR FURNITURE.

horizontal spur from which a ball on a string dangles, temptingly inviting play, and others support a platform on the top (ideal for kittens to leap on in play, although there is a risk that an older cat's weight won't be spread across it evenly,

OPINION VARIES AS TO WHY FELINES NIBBLE AT GRASS AND FOLIAGE, BUT THEY DO.

causing the apparatus to topple over). Note that a scratching post will become well worn from constant use and will therefore eventually have to be replaced, and also that when your cat is adult a scratching post should be as tall as possible to enable your feline to stretch up to enhance the stropping experience.

Finally, although theories vary as to why, all cats like to eat grass. In the absence of the real thing, an indoor cat may nibble at a house plant (which could poison it, see page 76), so be a considerate owner and grow it a pot of indoor grass; grass seeds specifically recommended for feline consumption are stocked by many gardening outlets.

GROOMING EQUIPMENT

Unless you are about to become the proud owner of a Sphynx, which has no hair at all, if you buy nothing else in the way of grooming equipment, you should at least invest in a comb that has been specially designed for felines (not a human one) to help your cat to keep its coat tangle-free. Human-assisted grooming is vital for longhaired cats to prevent their coats from becoming so drastically matted that the only solution is a trip to the vet's to have the solid clumps of fur shaved away. Grooming your cat will lessen the frequency with which it vomits up furballs, too, as well as giving you the opportunity regularly to check for fleas and skin problems. Two types of cat comb are typically sold by pet shops: ones with short teeth of identical length for shorthairs and others with long teeth interspersed with shorter ones for longhairs.

MANY CATS ENJOY THE SENSATION OF BEING MASSAGED AS THEY ARE BEING GROOMED.

coat a final smoothing, while an old toothbrush is ideal for brushing its facial fur. (See pages 104 to 106 for guidance on how to groom both long- and shorthaired cats.)

Claw-clippers are usually a prerequisite for an indoor cat, who, unlike a freely wandering feline, will not have the opportunity to keep its front claws in trim (although it will pull off its back claws with its incisor teeth once they have outlived their usefulness) by walking on hard surfaces or stropping them against wooden objects.

GROOMING PROVIDES AN OPPORTUNITY FOR YOU TO BOND WITH YOUR CAT.

Both normally have plastic handles with fingerholds moulded into them to give the human groomer a good grip. In addition, if you are anticipating the arrival of a longhaired feline, you may like to invest in a soft-bristled cat brush with which to give your cat's

AS A FINISHING TOUCH, YOU COULD USE A SLICKER BRUSH TO GIVE YOUR CAT'S COAT A GLOSSY SHEEN.

Even if you provide your indoor cat with a scratching post, it still may not indulge in regular enough stropping sessions to shorten its claws adequately, which is when a human wielding a pair of clippers – either ones designed specifically for felines or human toenail-clippers – should step in to provide assistance. (See pages 106 to 107 on how to cut your cat's claws.)

Finally, consult your vet about maintaining your feline's dental health. Depending on your cat's age and diet, you may be advised to clean its teeth regularly, using a plastic finger brush and toothpaste that has been specially formulated for cats (human toothpaste is unsuitable). Although you may scoff at the notion, the alternative may be that your cat's teeth become decayed (having paid a vast sum to have two of

CAT TOOTH BRUSHES

Melchior's teeth extracted by the vet under general anaesthetic, I have now become an assiduous brusher of our cats' teeth).

PET SHOPS STOCK MANY FELINE GROOMING AIDS, AND, IF NOTHING ELSE, AT LEAST INVEST IN A CAT COMB.

YOU'D BE ADVISED TO CLEAN YOUR CAT'S TEETH, BUT MAY PREFER TO USE A FINGER BRUSH.

A CAT BED

Unless you welcome the idea of sharing your bed with your cat and suffering the consequences in terms of sleep-deprivation (a cat will rarely stay co-operatively prone at the bottom of the bed all night), start as you mean to go on and prepare a bed for it. The day on which it arrives in its new home will be bewildering and tiring for your kitten or cat, and after the adrenaline rush has subsided it will welcome a comfortable bed in which to sleep to enable it to recover from the upheaval that it has experienced.

Pet shops stock an array of feline beds, from traditional wicker baskets to washable oversized cushions and bean-bags to fake-fur nests and igloos. If you buy a basket-type bed, your comfort-loving cat will appreciate some extra padding and insulation in the form of an old blanket, which should be washed regularly, just as the bed itself should be kept clean. A cheaper provisional alternative is to make a cat bed from a sturdy cardboard box by cutting off any flaps, placing it on its base (cut out a section at the front to act as a doorway) or side and lining it with newspaper topped with a blanket. As an extra welcoming touch, particularly for a kitten, who may miss its

A KITTEN'S FIRST BED

mother and littermates' body heat, you could slip an electric heating pad (for safety's sake, one designed specially for felines) or hot-water bottle filled with warm, but not boiling, water under the blanket, but place it at the side, rather than centrally, so that the cat has a choice of a warm or cold spot to curl up on.

A PLASTIC CAT BED HAS THE ADVANTAGE OF BEING EASY TO CLEAN.

Think carefully about where to place your prospective feline's bed: you may be tempted to position it at the hub of family life so that it feels included and you can continue to admire it while it sleeps, but this will probably not suit the cat's need to feel private and safe when it abandons itself to unconsciousness. It is usually better to position the bed in a quiet corner where it can sleep undisturbed. In addition, try to choose a draught-free spot so that your cat won't become chilly – test for cat-level draughts by getting down on your hands and knees – and if this is by a radiator or gets some sun during the day, so much the better: cats adore luxuriating in comforting warmth as they sleep.

PROVIDE YOUR CAT WITH SOME EXTRA INSULATION.

Be warned, however, that as your cat gains in confidence, it may ignore the bed that you have so considerately provided, instead preferring a snoozing place of its own choice, such as an armchair or your own bed.

A BED WILL MAKE YOUR CAT FEEL MORE AT HOME.

TOYS FOR FELINE GIRLS AND BOYS

If you are bringing home a kitten, it is important that you provide it with some toys to play with: play is a vital part of a kitten's development, whereby it practises its chasing and pouncing skills. Playing with your kitten will also strengthen the bond between you, as well as being great fun for all of the game's participants, be they human or feline. The imaginations of older cats, too, are often stimulated by a toy mouse to 'hunt', particularly if they are indoor cats who neither have access to the real thing nor much opportunity to exercise. Although, for example, our pair of twelve-year-olds have reached the age when they no longer always spring into action when a thing-on-a-string is dangled in front of their noses, toy mice materialise overnight in spots where once there were none, evidence that our felines are not too old to indulge in nocturnal games of cat and mouse.

HUMAN–FELINE GAMES ARE GREAT FUN.

ENSURE THAT A MOUSE'S 'EYES' ARE FIRMLY ATTACHED.

NOTHING IS SACRED AT PLAYTIME.

The manufacturers of cat toys are constantly supplying pet shops with ever-more ingenious products, from mice on strings and springs to balls containing bells. Many fabric mice are stuffed with dried catnip (Nepeta cataria), a plant that sends many cats into paroxysms of ecstasy, making such mice irresistibly attractive playthings. There's no need to spend money on your feline's entertainment, however: a table-tennis ball will provide many fun-packed sessions of high-octane exercise and excitement, as will a crumpled-up paper bag, while a cotton reel tied to a piece of string – with you attached to the other end to jerk it into action and pull around – for your cat to stalk and pounce on will provide it with all of the exhilarating thrill of the chase. Before introducing any new toy to your cat, first ensure that it is an object with which a cat can safely play. Make sure that any mouse 'eyes', for example, are securely attached, that there are no protruding pins or staples that could cause injury, that a rubber toy isn't small enough to be swallowed and also be vigilant about preventing your cat from ingesting lengths of string or wool. Note, too, that most cats are terrified, rather than intrigued by, clockwork or motorised toys.

PLAY PROVIDES HUNTING PRACTICE.

MAKING YOUR HOME SAFE FOR YOUR CAT

Within a few hours of his arrival in his new home, Caspar the kitten went missing. Certain that he couldn't have ventured outside, but baffled as to what sort of hiding place he could have found in a modestly sized flat, we searched high and low, to no avail. Something eventually led us into the kitchen, and then to the upright fridge-freezer. There was a small gap between the back of the appliance and the wall . . . he couldn't have, could he? Sure enough, on pulling out the unit, we discovered our new kitten curled up in a space within the backless freezer, its electrical innards all the while buzzing away ominously. This cautionary tale goes to show that you should take the same stringent precautions to make your home safe for a new kitten or cat that you would for a toddler – even more so, since toddlers lack the advanced escapology skills of a cat.

The tale of Caspar the kitten also highlights the advisability of introducing a kitten or cat to only one room of your home for the first day or so, although this strategy may not always be practical if its food and water bowls, as well as its litter tray, are in a different room. However many rooms you decide to give your new feline access to on its arrival, you should at least

ELECTRICAL APPLIANCES AND THREAD SPELL 'DANGER'!

pre-empt it streaking off through windows and doors by making sure that they are firmly shut. Another chapter from the annals of Caspar's kittenhood tells of how he managed to push up, by squeezing under, a first-floor sash window that was open at the bottom by about an inch. Having startled him as he was sitting on the windowsill enjoying the view, he reacted by leaping down into the garden, 5 metres (around 16 feet) below.

AN OPEN WINDOW: AN OPPORTUNITY TO ESCAPE?

MANY SUBSTANCES PRESENT A DANGER TO YOUR CAT.

Thankfully, apart from everyone concerned having had a fright, no damage was done, but many cats who suffer similar falls are not so lucky: because they may have been snoozing peacefully when they slipped off a windowsill, they may not be able to alert their senses in time to ensure that they land on their feet. Alternatively, even if they manage to land on all four paws, the force of their impact on landing may be so great that their legs buckle and break and their jaw may hit the ground and be smashed. It's therefore crucial that you're especially vigilant about your cat's safety if you live in a high-rise flat or if your home has a balcony and, if your cat persists on sleeping on a windowsill, it would be wise to fit some sort of barrier – perhaps a trellis – along it to prevent a fall.

Because it is not unusual for panicked kittens to shoot up fireplaces, if there are any open ones in your house, either place a fireguard around them or stuff the chimney flues with newspaper. In addition, try to tuck any trailing electrical cables out of the way of a cat, who may be tempted to exercise its teeth and gums by gnawing on them. When it is feeling brave enough to explore every inch of your home, a kitten in particular will leap onto any available surface, so it would be sensible to take the precaution of temporarily stowing any breakable objects, such as vases, out of harm's way. Don't leave threaded sewing needles where a cat could gain access to them either: it could be tempted to chew, or play with, the dangling thread, presenting the real danger that it may swallow the needle; rubber bands can

also wreak internal havoc if ingested. Remember, too, that a decorated Christmas tree represents a challenging activity centre to a cat. Speaking from rueful experience, unless you shut the door on your Christmas tree at night, you may wake up to a scene of devastation, with glass decorations smashed to smithereens (and a cat with bleeding feet), sodden piles of regurgitated lametta strewn all over the floor and possibly also widespread damage caused by a toppled tree.

Try to scrutinise your kitchen from your cat's vantage point: if a saucepan or kettle boils over, for example, your feline could be splashed and scalded by the boiling liquid. Another danger to cats lies in common household chemicals like bleach, which could burn or poison them, so keep them out of your cat's way, preferably in a cupboard. The same goes for any caustic or corrosive liquids, such as paint-thinners, paraffin, creosote and pesticides. But be warned: although he cannot rival Caspar's talent for getting himself into hair-raising scrapes, the ever-inquisitive Melchior has perfected the art of opening the doors of certain cupboards with his paw and nose, so make sure that any cupboards which you don't want your cat rooting around in have firmly sprung hinges or magnetic catches and always keep the doors of washing machines and tumble-driers shut. Note, too, that certain plants, including mistletoe, ivy, poinsettia, rhododendrons and azaleas, oleander, Philodendron, Caladium, Dieffenbachia, Prunus laurocerasus and Solanum capiscastrum, can poison cats, so don't grow any of these inside and reduce the risk of a house plant being nibbled by providing an indoor cat with its own pot of grass (see page 68).

BLOCK YOUR CAT'S ACCESS TO AN OPEN FIREPLACE.

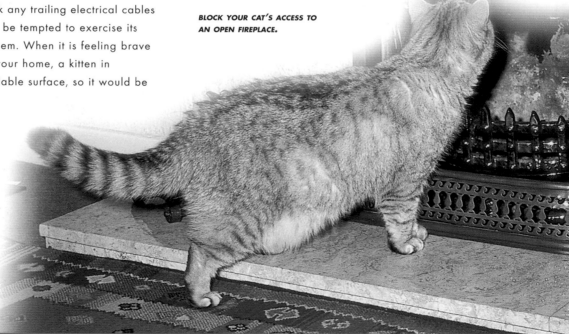

THE BIG DAY: BRINGING YOUR CAT HOME

As the great day dawns, you'll awake to the realisation that life will never be quite the same again. Ideally, you will have arranged to collect your cat or kitten on a day when you will be at home so that you can reassure it and get to know each other, and also when your household will be as quiet as possible. Before collecting the new feline addition to the family, check that you have all of the food and equipment that you'll need to take care of your cat and also that you have positioned its food and water bowls, bed and litter tray in suitable spots – as a temporary measure, perhaps in the room to which you'll first introduce it (when your cat feels at home, you can move them to more permanent places). Finally, before picking up your cat-carrier (don't forget to line it with newspaper) and heading out through the door, ensure that all doors and windows are firmly shut.

A HEATED BED ESPECIALLY DESIGNED FOR FELINES.

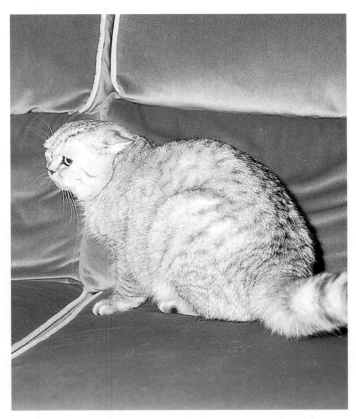

YOUR NEW CAT WILL INEVITABLY BE FRIGHTENED.

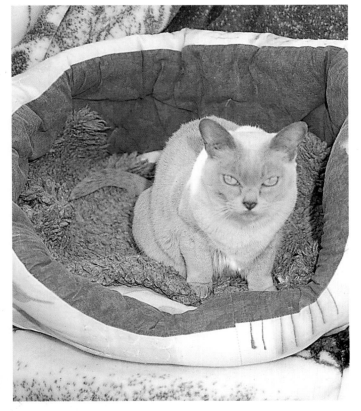

INTRODUCE IT TO ITS BED TO MAKE IT FEEL AT HOME.

STROKING THE NEW ARRIVAL WILL REASSURE IT, BUT WAIT FOR YOUR NEW-FOUND FRIEND TO APPROACH YOU FIRST.

On coming face to face with your kitten or cat for the first time on your mutual big day, don't abruptly bundle it into its carrier: spare a few minutes to give it some attention so that it knows that your intentions are friendly, and also be patient as its previous owner bids it farewell. Remember to ask for any tips, for example, regarding the diet or type of cat litter that it's been used to, and only then lift your cat gently into its carrying basket. As you wend your way home together, make soothing noises in response to any terrified yowls that your cat may make to express its fear at being torn away from the safety of its home by a stranger – it will inevitably be terrified, particularly if it's enduring a close encounter with a car for the first time.

Do not, however, under any circumstance, be tempted to remove it from its carrier to stroke or cuddle it: the best-case scenario is that chaos will ensue.

Once you have arrived home, set the cat's carrier in the room that you've temporarily allotted your cat and don't let it out until you have taken off your coat, have shut the door and are ready to give it your undivided attention as it takes its first tentative steps out of its basket and into its new home. Give it some words of gentle encouragement, but don't make a lunge for it to give it a reassuring cuddle, which would only scare it. Instead, sit back and let it explore its new surroundings. If, as is likely, it either slinks or bolts to a spot that offers it cover and a sense of security, such as behind the sofa, don't attempt to haul it out, just wait until its curiosity prevails and it's plucked up the courage to venture out again. Watch patiently as it explores the room and, when it feels confident enough to approach you, offer it a caressing stroke, but don't make any sudden movements. If it hasn't already discovered them, and when you have built up sufficient trust between you to enable you to pick it up (see page 80 for how to handle it), take it to its litter tray and water bowl – it may be very relieved to make their acquaintance – followed by its bed.

AFTER A DAY OF UPSET AND UPHEAVAL, YOUR CAT MAY BE IN NEED OF SOME REST AND RECUPERATON.

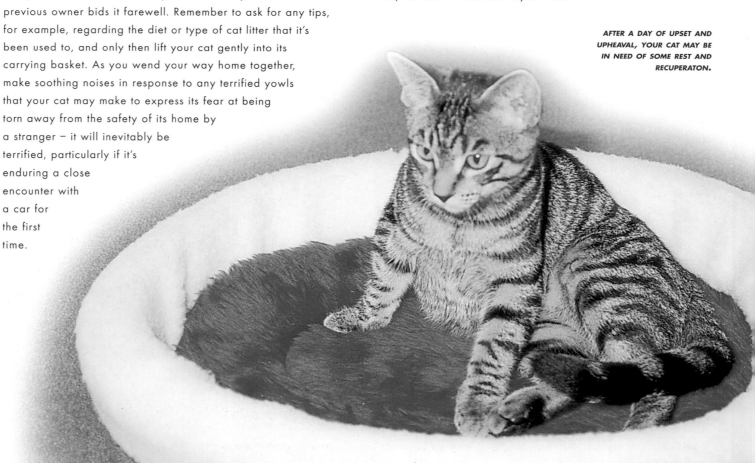

Don't feed your cat until you are certain that it is starting to feel at home (a good sign is when it starts washing itself, which indicates that it's feeling relatively relaxed). Thereafter, if both of you are still up to it, you could introduce it to the rest of the house – but not to the garden – taking your time to allow it to investigate each room in turn, a process that, depending on the size of your home, it may be sensible to stretch out over some days. Don't leave it to its own devices, but shadow it to ensure that it doesn't bolt – or creep inside a fridge-freezer! Finally, exploration complete, return to the room from which you started out together, which it should by now regard as the core of its new home.

At a kitten's bedtime, tucking a hot-water bottle or heated pad (see page 72) under one side of its bedding for the first few nights of its residency will provide some reassuring, sleep-inducing warmth (older cats may appreciate this, too). Some people also advocate placing a clockwork alarm clock near it – but make sure that the alarm's switched off – to simulate the familiar rhythm of its mother's heartbeat.

Whatever your new cat's age, it's best not to give it access to the great outdoors for at least a week (and in the case of nervous felines, three) to give it the opportunity to become thoroughly familiar with its home, to which it should then always return, if only at feeding time!

YOU'LL TERRIFY YOUR ALREADY TRAUMATISED CAT IF YOU MAKE A LUNGE FOR IT.

WHEN YOUR CAT STARTS TO FEEL AT HOME, ITS CURIOSITY WILL PREVAIL.

HANDLING YOUR CAT

Cats admittedly have loose skins, but unless your feline is a kitten whose mother has, until very recently, picked it up by the scruff of its neck – and even she will have found it increasingly difficult as it gained weight – don't attempt this. Although grasping the scruff of the neck can, in emergencies (see page 154), trigger a reflex reaction that causes the cat to freeze, a kitten or cat should never be lifted in this way because its skin will simply not be able to bear the cat's weight.

Before picking up your cat, try to ensure that it is relaxed – ideally, approach it slowly, all the while talking to it quietly – and never make a grab for it. The correct way in which to pick up an acquiescent cat who is standing on the ground is to slip one hand under its chest, just behind its front legs, and then, using a scooping motion, gently to push its back legs forward with the other hand, before lifting the cat until it is level with your waist. In this way, between them your hands will both be supporting your feline's entire weight and making it feel as secure and comfortable as possible. An alternative method that is often used by judges at cat shows is to hold the cat's front legs with one hand and to place the other under its abdomen

A KITTEN'S BONES ARE FRAGILE, SO NEVER SQUEEZE IT TIGHTLY LEST YOU BREAK THEM.

before carefully lifting the feline for inspection.

Never cradle a cat across your chest with its abdomen and face pointing upwards, as you would a baby, because this position will make it feel vulnerable and will also cause its back to slump awkwardly. Instead, slightly modify your lifting technique so that the cat is upright, with its face and body pointing outwards, in the same direction as yours, with its weight supported by one hand cupped under its hindquarters (you may find it easier to settle it in the crook of your arm) and the other lightly, but firmly, encircling its chest, again under the forelegs. Because some cats do not take kindly to being restrained in this way, however lovingly, the outward-pointing position has the advantage of ensuring that your face is not the first target of an irritable cat's claws.

Talking to it soothingly as you are holding your feline will reassure it of your friendly intentions, helping to settle it.

THE CORRECT WAY TO HOLD A CAT, WITH BOTH HANDS SUPPORTING ITS ENTIRE WEIGHT.

YOUR CAT AND CHILDREN

Teaching a child how to handle a cat correctly will ensure the safety of both, but may be difficult to drum into young children, who will probably be beside themselves with excitement at the arrival of a feline playmate. (And it's kinder to the new cat to arrange for them to be out of the house when you first introduce it to your home.) In fact, it's best to discourage children under the age of six from picking up your cat at all: kittens' bones are still relatively soft and fragile, and an overly enthusiastic hug

CHILDREN AND KITTENS ARE UNITED IN THEIR LOVE OF PLAYTIME, BUT ALWAYS ENSURE A KITTEN'S SAFETY.

from a child could easily cause a fracture, while a small child will certainly not be able to bear the weight of an older cat, and in any case could end up being badly scratched as the infuriated cat tries to escape its well-meaning tormentor. Be warned that if a cat suffers consistent mishandling by children, it could develop either exaggeratedly aggressive or timid self-defensive behavioural patterns.

TEACH YOUR CHILD TO RESPECT THE FAMILY CAT.

Kittens, who will not be able to resist the lure of a game for long, will usually get on better with a child than an older, more self-contained cat, who will be set in its ways. Even so, try as best you can to explain to your youngster that a kitten can easily be injured, that it needs to be left in peace to sleep when it is tired and that its tail is not a plaything. Although the feline nature is markedly different to ours, it may be expedient to humanise your cat when laying down feline-friendly laws to a young child: for example, 'You know how cross you feel when you're tired? Well the kitten feels just the same, so let's leave it alone for a while to have a sleep and you can play with it later'. In the case of older children, involving them in aspects of your cat's care will give them a sense of proud responsibility, but be vigilant about your feline's welfare and never delegate its overall care to them – assume a supervisory, if hands-off, role instead.

Finally, there are certain rules that you must abide by if cats and children share the same house.
• Never leave a sleeping baby where a cat could sit on it: the cat will be attracted by the baby's warmth and could inadvertently smother it.

• In the interests of maintaining both your child and your cat's health, discourage your child from human–feline face-rubbing, allow neither access to the other's food and, most importantly, ensure that your child stays away from the cat's litter tray to avoid the risk of toxoplasmosis infection (see page 103).

A HARMONIOUS FELINE–HUMAN FAMILY.

YOUR CAT AND OTHER HOUSEHOLD PETS

Felines and many other species of household pet will mix well, but only in certain circumstances. A cat will instinctively regard anything smaller than itself as potential prey, a viewpoint that will not change with familiarisation, so make sure that the aquaria of fish and the cages of mice, hamsters and birds, for instance, are cat-proof or you may end up with a massacre on your hands. A kitten will generally fit in well with a household's existing cats and dogs, in whom it may arouse protective instincts. In the case of an existing cat, a kitten will either be tolerated or ignored, while a dog will usually eventually

develop an affectionate modus vivendi with it, even if, as usually occurs, the kitten ends up ruling the roost. Difficulties may, however, arise if an older cat is introduced to a household that already includes an adult feline or canine, which will typically regard the new arrival as a threat to the established order. Being inevitably wary, the new cat will probably avoid contact with it, and if it has had bad experiences with dogs in particular, a bond will never be formed. And the smaller the dog, the harder co-existence will be, since the natural status quo determined by size will be blurred.

*CATS WILL OFTEN RUB ALONG
QUITE WELL TOGETHER.*

DOGS AND CATS USUALLY LEARN TO LIVE TOGETHER.

EATING TOGETHER SIGNIFIES MUTUAL ACCEPTANCE.

The introduction of a feline 'intruder' into a household that includes other pets will initially be fraught, involving much growling, hissing, spitting and posturing, but with time, patience and the use of certain strategies, your pets should eventually come to tolerate, if not enjoy, each other's presence in your – their – home.

- Keep existing pets away from the new arrival by shutting them in another room until you have had the time to acquaint it properly with both yourself and your home.

- Because a shared, 'family' smell is of crucial importance to both cats and dogs' sense of security, during the separation period place a blanket or cushion that one has been sitting on in the other's domain to familiarise each with the other's personal odour. This should firstly mean that when they finally come face to face the other won't seem so alien and, secondly, that the other's signature scent will come to be identified over time as a vital element of their home's overall smell.

- Supervise your respective pets' introduction to each other (keep a dog on a lead) and do not leave them alone together (again, segregate them in separate rooms) for at least a few weeks, until you are sure that they have grudgingly accepted each other and are unlikely to fight.

- Feed them in different parts of your home. It may take two or more weeks until they are relaxed enough with each other to eat together, and even thereafter don't force them to share the same food bowl.

- Divide your attention between each of them equally: although the feline newcomer needs to feel reassured, you may fuel your existing pet's resentment if it is made to feel that its position in your affections has been usurped by the recent arrival.

chapter 3

CAT-CARE FUNDAMENTALS

Cats that enjoy being bundled into their carriers and whisked to a strange-smelling examining room to suffer the indignity of being inspected from head to tail are few and far between, but a regular trip to the vet's is nevertheless a necessary evil if your cat is to remain healthy.

REGISTERING WITH A VET

If you didn't have it examined before adopting it, it's crucial that you make an appointment with your vet within a few days of having taken charge of your new kitten or cat. It's only a vet's experienced eye that will detect the first signs of either a life-threatening illness or a troublesome ailment, both of which must be treated as soon as possible. If you leave it too long, by the time that some innocuous signs have become full-blown symptoms, it may be too late to save the life of a feline who is rapidly becoming a fast friend.

A thorough check-up is not the only reason why a cat should be registered with a veterinary surgery as soon as you can arrange it: a kitten must have its first vaccinations against certain life-threatening, feline-specific diseases (see pages 86 to 90), while an older cat must have annual booster injections to maintain the immunity that previous vaccinations have given it. The correct timing of these vaccinations is of the essence, otherwise there will be a window of opportunity for these serious viruses to take hold when the feline's immune system is powerless to fight them off. Vaccination time is furthermore a good opportunity for the vet to check your cat's overall health and to give it a precautionary worming pill. Regular feline and veterinary get-togethers will also give you the chance to ask your vet's advice about any niggling concerns that you may have about your cat's health, dietary regime or behavioural quirks.

Although there is no state-supported health-care system for cats, financial concerns should never prevent your cat from receiving the veterinary attention that it needs, so consider spreading the cost of any future treatment by taking out an insurance policy (your vet will provide you with the details of health-insurance companies for pets, but note that these do not cover routine care). Remember, too, that certain animal-welfare organisations will treat a sick cat for either no charge or a minimal cost.

KITTENS AND CATS MUST BE REGULARLY VACCINATED AGAINST CAT-KILLING DISEASES.

ONLY A VET'S EXPERIENCED EYE CAN IDENTIFY SOME SIGNS THAT ALL IS NOT WELL.

VITAL VACCINATIONS

There are three viral diseases against which you must immunise your kitten or cat: feline panleucopenia, feline infectious respiratory disease and feline leukaemia, all of which are easily spread and potentially fatal to a cat who hasn't been vaccinated against them.

Indeed, the key to whether or not your cat's immune system will be able to battle these highly infectious viruses successfully, should it come into contact with them at any time from birth to old age, is found in the form of a hypodermic needle and a phial of the appropriate vaccine.

YOUR CAT WON'T THANK YOU FOR THE EXPERIENCE, BUT REGULAR EXAMINATIONS MUST BE ENDURED.

If your kitten's mother was immunised, she will have passed on some of her immunity to her foetuses through the placenta while pregnant and, after they were delivered, to her new-borns via the colostrum (the liquid that a nursing mother produces before and after her milk). The concentration of anti-viral antibodies (or maternally-derived antibody, MDA) in colostrum is at its highest for the first day or so after birth, a time when the kitten's bloodstream is also best able to absorb them from its gut. It is therefore important that an entire female's vaccination programme is vigilantly maintained (otherwise a queen may have no immunity to share with her litter) and that a kitten suckles as much as possible during the first days of its life. If you've adopted a feline, and especially a mature female who is either pregnant or has not been spayed, but have no record of any vaccinations that it may have had, take it to the vet's immediately for expert advice.

Because the level of MDA in colostrum is eroded over time, and a kitten's body cannot generate the necessary protective antibodies itself, a kitten should have its first vaccination (nowadays a single injection provides immunity against all three diseases) at the age of around nine weeks. This injection prepares your kitten's immune system to accept a stronger dose,

A MOTHER'S MILK PROVIDES SOME IMMUNITY.

but will not give it adequate protection against the trio of viral cat-killers, which is why your vet will ask you to return it two or three weeks later for a booster. (In the meantime, it is safer not to allow it to go outside in case it comes into contact with any of these serious viruses; because it may also temporarily act as carrier, your vet may advise you to quarantine it from other felines for a week.) The second dose of vaccine will stimulate your kitten's body to start producing protective antibodies, and thereafter all that your cat will require is an annual booster injection to nudge its body into carrying on the good work.

TEMPERATURE-TAKING: A FURTHER (VITAL) INDIGNITY.

The first time that your kitten is vaccinated, your vet will give you a record of vaccination, detailing when the first vaccination was given and its brand. Remember to take this record with you when you return your cat for its boosters so that it can be updated (reputable catteries, breeders of pedigree cats and the organisers of cat shows won't accept your feline without it). Try to ensure that you take your cat for its booster at the same time each year – many veterinary surgeries will automatically send you a reminder – because the feline body's maintenance of effective levels of immunity depends on the vaccine being administered just as they are starting to decline. If too long a time has elapsed since your cat's last booster, your vet may advise giving it two boosters two to four weeks apart to kick-start the regeneration of antibodies. If your feline is an indoor cat, don't let yourself be lulled into a false sense of security and be tempted to skip the immunisation programme by believing that, because it doesn't come into contact with other cats, it won't fall prey to a deadly feline viral disease because you yourself may inadvertently infect it by introducing a virus into your home on your clothes or shoes.

FELINE PANLEUCOPENIA

Also known as feline infectious enteritis (FIE) or feline parvovirus, the symptoms of feline panleucopenia are:

- unco-ordination in kittens
- loss of appetite
- chronic thirst, but often an inability to drink
- chronic fatigue and depression
- sitting in a hunched-up position
- pain in the abdomen
- a high temperature
- vomiting frothy matter
- watery and bloody diarrhoea

CAUSE OF INFECTION

Not only can the extremely contagious and long-living feline panleucopenia virus be spread by feline-to-feline contact, but because it is capable of airborne transmission, a cat may be exposed to it if it is brought into the home on your skin, shoes or clothes, via fleas or by sharing an infected cat's bedding, food bowl and litter tray.

PROGNOSIS

Feline panleucopenia is the among the deadliest of all of the incurable viral infections that target cats, and a kitten will be lucky to survive the severe dehydration that it causes.

Although an older cat, particularly if it has been immunised, stands a better chance of coming through feline panleucopenia, infection with this virus will involve a life-or-death struggle and the sick cat will require prolonged nursing (see pages 140 to 141).

When inspecting your prospective kitten or cat, as well as during the first month or so of its residency in your home while its full immunity has yet to develop, monitor it vigilantly for any symptoms that may indicate that a viral disease has invaded its body. And if you fear the worst, immediately quarantine the feline to reduce the danger of other cats becoming infected and then call your veterinary surgery for instructions. You'll probably be asked to bring your cat in at once for a blood test, but special arrangements will have to be made either to ensure that any other felines in the surgery are segregated from your potentially infected cat or for the vet to visit the patient in your home. The symptoms of feline panleucopenia, feline infectious respiratory disease and feline leukaemia that you should be looking out for (singly, as well as en masse), together with their causes and prognoses, are given below.

FELINE LEUKAEMIA

Also known as FeLV (or, erroneously, 'feline AIDS'), the symptoms of feline leukaemia are:

- anaemia (pale gums)
- loss of appetite and weight
- breathing difficulties
- chronic lethargy
- vomiting
- diarrhoea
- skin and mouth infections
- Tumours in any part of the body

CAUSE OF INFECTION

Feline leukaemia is most commonly passed from a mother to her kittens, as well as when young cats come into intimate contact (for instance, when bodily fluids are exchanged through fighting, grooming or sexual activity) with infected felines.

PROGNOSIS

Although it is often dubbed 'feline AIDS', feline leukaemia is actually cancer of the blood (which cannot be transmitted to humans). That having been said, however, its effect on the feline immune system is comparable with human AIDS in that a cat may become so weakened that it is incapable of fighting off even a mild infection, not least a serious virus like those detailed previously, making accurate diagnosis difficult. A kitten who contracts the virus will often succumb to it relatively quickly, but if an older cat is infected with feline leukaemia, it may take some time – even years – before the symptoms manifest themselves. Nevertheless, studies have shown that a cat who becomes infected with feline leukaemia is unlikely to survive beyond three years of its initial infection.

FELINE INFECTIOUS RESPIRATORY DISEASE

Also known as cat flu, the symptoms of feline infectious respiratory disease are:

- sneezing
- coughing
- catarrh
- laboured or rapid breathing
- pneumonia
- a runny nose
- drooling
- ulcers on the tongue and gums
- weeping eyes, conjunctivitis or the haw pulled over the eye
- loss of appetite
- chronic fatigue
- a high temperature
- vomiting

CAUSE OF INFECTION

The name commonly used to describe feline infectious respiratory disease, cat flu, is somewhat misleading because although the disease's symptoms are similar to those of human influenza, the viral culprits are different, which means that flu-ridden humans can't pass their virus on to cats and vice versa. When a cat contracts feline infectious respiratory disease, it will have been infected by either feline viral rhinotracheitis (FVR) or feline calicivirus, or sometimes both. Infection is caused by close feline-to-feline contact or the inhalation of viral agents when a cat that is already suffering from cat flu sneezes.

PROGNOSIS

Although your cat may have to endure a rough couple of days, and may need a course of antibiotics and devoted nursing to help it pull through, if it survives the onset of cat flu it is likely to live. The virus may, however, remain present in its body, which means that when it is run-down or stressed, mild symptoms of the disease, such as sneezing and a runny nose, may return. In addition, it may become a carrier of cat flu and may therefore infect other cats whose immune systems are not strong enough to resist the disease (so if you have a multi-feline household, ensure that all of your cats are immunised).

The prognosis is more serious for kittens and older cats, however, whose immune systems will be either under-developed on the one hand, or compromised on the other, and who will therefore be unable to put up an effective fight against feline infectious respiratory disease. In such cases, death is a sad probability.

WORMS AND WORMING

When you take your cat to the vet's for its annual vaccination, it will usually be given a worming pill to prevent its body from becoming host to such common parasites as tapeworms and roundworms or, albeit unusually in Britain, flukes and lung-, heart-, hook-, whip- and threadworms. Although a worm infestation is not life-threatening, if left untreated, it could, over time, sap your feline's vitality and weaken its immune system so that it becomes less resistant to any infections that may threaten its health. Lax hygiene may also result in worms being transferred from a wormy cat to its human carers, which is why you should always wash your hands after handling a cat or cleaning its litter tray (see page 103). An adult cat should be given worming pills specifically targeting round- and tapeworms every four to six months, as your vet advises.

Apart from crossing from feline to feline, cats can pick up roundworm eggs through eating infested prey. Adult roundworms (Toxocara and Toxascaris) live in the cat's stomach and small intestine, where they feed off the food that the cat has ingested and breed prolifically, the eggs being passed through the large intestine to emerge in the cat's faeces, traces of which may remain around the anus and be ingested by another cat during a mutual grooming session. Roundworm larvae inhabit cysts within the feline muscular tissue and, more seriously for kittens, sometimes also within the lungs, heart and liver.

CATS SHOULD BE GIVEN WORMING PILLS AS ADVISED BY YOUR VET.

Fleas, which are mainly responsible for a tapeworm infestation, swallow tapeworm eggs and then become hosts to their larvae. When a larva-carrying flea in turn sets up home in a cat's fur, the cat may swallow it while grooming, enabling the larva to pass through its digestive system and attach itself to the intestine by means of its hooked scolex, where it will grow into a mature tapeworm, an extremely long, thin parasite, whose body consists of many articulated segments, that lives off the food that the cat is digesting. The individual segments that pass out of the cat's body via the faeces contain the eggs that a flea may ingest, thus perpetuating the pernicious cycle.

When inspecting your kitten or cat for the first time, you should have been looking out for symptoms of worm infestation, which, although they are described on page 59, are worth reiterating in more detail. If a pregnant feline has roundworms (and she should be wormed both before the birth of her kittens and while

WASH YOUR HANDS AFTER CLEANING A LITTER TRAY.

she is nursing them), her unborn kittens may become infested with their larvae via the placenta, and, following their birth, via her milk, causing both their pre- and post-natal development to be retarded. Along with any unspecific warning signs that a kitten is not in the best of health, look out for a pronounced pot belly and flaky skin, and be especially wary if the kitten is coughing, seems to have been vomiting or has diarrhoea. Further points to note are that if your feline has been sick and you are very keen-eyed, you may be able to discern a mass of wriggling roundworms (which resemble thin threads of fibre) within the vomit. Tapeworm segments, on the other hand, look like grains of rice or melon seeds and may be seen in the fur around a cat's bottom (which may become chronically itchy) or within its faeces.

After you have adopted it, if you think that your kitten or cat may have a worm infestation, note down any relevant symptoms, scoop up a sample of its faeces from the litter tray, place it in a clean, sealable container (remember to wash your hands afterwards) and take it to your veterinary surgery for analysis. If this then shows that your feline does indeed have worms, your vet will prescribe the appropriate course of treatment for your cat.

*CATS MAY INGEST TAPEWORM
LARVAE WHILE GROOMING.*

FLEAS AND DE-FLEAING

Once, on taking our cats to the vet's for their inoculations, we found ourselves sharing the waiting room with a carrier containing a handsome tabby cat, which, the appalled veterinary nurse informed us, had been brought in by its owner with the request that it be put down. The reason given? Flea infestation. Thankfully, there was no question of the vet agreeing to this demand: because the cat was healthy and fleas are banishable, it would instead be rehomed. Its owner's outright rejection of the cat does, however, illustrate the extreme way in which a minority of people react when their cat harbours fleas.

Most cats endure a flea infestation at some point in their lives – it's simply part and parcel of being feline – during a stay in a cattery, even our, predominantly indoor, cats weren't immune from the magnetic attraction that the prospect of a meal of warm feline blood exerts on fleas. Yet with patience, time and the help of dedicated anti-flea measures, a cat that does become a host to fleas can be rid of them. Indeed, with the relatively recent development of effective preventative drops and injections administered by your vet, it need never be troubled by them at all.

Although cat fleas (Ctenocephalides felis) are spread by feline-to-feline contact, this needn't be direct because, despite their lack of wings, fleas are famously capable of jumping impressive distances relative to their diminutive size, and their four-stage life cycle enables them to survive for some time without a feline host. Having hopped onto a cat, settled into its fur and started to feed on its blood, after two or three days an adult flea will start laying eggs (two hundred within a flea's lifetime) wherever a cat may be lying – on its bedding or the carpet, for instance – the eggs hatching into larvae a few days later. The developing larvae, which sustain themselves on organic debris, such as flakes of dead skin, evolve into pupae within about two weeks, encasing themselves in cocoons in which they can survive for up to a year before becoming adult. Only then will these parasites need to find a source of fresh blood in order to thrive and perpetuate the flea population's existence.

LOOKING FOR FLEAS

A FLEA COMB REMOVES SOME, BUT NOT ALL, FLEAS.

YOU CAN BUY A VARIETY OF ANTI-FLEA PRODUCTS.

Try to pre-empt your cat falling victim to a horde of ravenous fleas by consulting your vet, who will usually recommend a repellent product (which will not harm your feline) that will prevent an infestation should a flea land on it. These are usually regularly administered by means of either an injection or drops that are absorbed through the skin. An alternative is an elasticated collar that has been impregnated with flea-killing chemicals, but the disadvantage of this is both its comparative ineffectiveness, especially in the case of longhairs, and the danger that it may induce an allergy in your cat, resulting in skin irritation and hair loss.

Whether or not you have taken preventative precautions, it's important that you check your cat's fur regularly for signs of an infestation of these pesky parasites, especially during the flea-friendly summer months (although central heating has made them year-round perils). If your cat scratches itself repeatedly and, on investigation, you can see reddish-black specks in its fur, these are likely to be flea droppings, and you will probably also be able to spot the dark-brown fleas responsible scuttling around in its fur. Having confirmed a flea infestation, you will first need to de-flea your cat using a proprietary flea powder or spray. Do this by standing your cat on a sheet of newspaper

and then applying a generous quantity of the product to the back of its head, making sure that it does not enter its eyes or ears, after which you should gently, but firmly, massage the product into its skin, working from its head to its tail through its flanks, abdomen and chest to its legs and paws. Follow the manufacturer's instructions – you may have to leave the product on the cat for ten minutes or so before brushing it out of the cat's fur and then burning the paper on which the dying fleas have dropped. Thereafter, to prevent reinfestation, you'll have to turn your attention to your home by washing your cat's bedding, vacuuming each room thoroughly and applying a proprietary environmental anti-flea product to the flooring and furniture. Again, follow the manufacturer's instructions, as it may be that you'll have to repeat the treatment over the next few weeks.

Never ignore fleas: not only could your cat develop flea-allergy dermatitis, hair loss or localised infections, but cat fleas have been known temporarily to transfer their attention to humans in desperate circumstances – that is, in the absence of a feline host – and, of course, they can act as intermediate hosts to tapeworm larvae (see page 92).

APPLY FLEA POWDER GENEROUSLY, AND MASSAGE INTO THE SKIN.

CAT IDENTIFICATION

If you give your cat the freedom to roam, there are any number of scenarios that may prevent it from returning home: it may become trapped in a neighbouring garden or shed or fall victim to a road traffic accident, for example, rendering it powerless to find its way back to you. Local newspapers regularly carry reports of cats that have gone missing, or of unidentified house cats that have been found, so if you don't want to suffer the anxiety and heartbreak of your feline friend becoming one of their number and perhaps never being reunited with you, identifying it is a must.

There are two ways of making your cat's identity known: an identity tag attached to its collar or microchipping it. If you decide to opt for the former, make sure that you fit your cat with a collar – perhaps a flea collar – that is designed specially for felines (available from pet shops) and that incorporates an elasticated section so that if your cat catches it on an immovable object there is enough slack to enable it to extract itself without choking. The tag itself (again stocked by pet shops) could either take the form of a hollow, unscrewable metal 'barrel' that contains a strip of paper on which to write your phone number and address or an identity disc on which

THE MICROCHIPPING PROCEDURE IS QUICK AND PAINLESS.

your details can be engraved. (A word of warning if magpies haunt your neighbourhood: Melchior was once gazing out of the window when a magpie, attracted by his glinting identity disc, swooped down out of nowhere and tried to pluck it off through the glass; the traumatised Melchior wouldn't go near that window for weeks!) A tip that may ensure your cat's safe return is simply to specify your phone number and the word 'reward' – greed may tempt even the most feline-indifferent person to contact you. Do not, however, include your cat's name because hearing it uttered could cause it to trust a potential cat-napper.

Many vets now recommend microchipping over a collar and tag. As its name suggests, a microchip is a microscopic chip so small that it can be injected under the loose skin at the back of a cat's neck, where it will remain without causing any discomfort. The microchip contains a code unique to your cat that is registered with a central computer database. Should your cat stray and be brought to a cat-rescue sanctuary, it will be scanned with a dedicated scanner, which will immediately identify the code borne by the microchip and hence, through the database, both your cat and your details, thereby facilitating your feline's return.

IT'S ADVISABLE TO INCLUDE YOUR PHONE NUMBER AND THE WORD 'REWARD' ON A CAT'S IDENTITY TAG.

NEUTERING YOUR CAT

When you were weighing up whether to adopt a male or female cat (see page 52), you no doubt decided whether you would have your cat neutered or whether you would be prepared to find homes for any kittens that your female might have or could tolerate a male's roaming and spraying. If you came to the conclusion that you would prefer your kitten or cat not to breed, consult your vet about having your feline neutered when you take it to be immunised. The vet will explain what the operation involves and should also advise you on its optimum timing (if you leave it too long, your kitten may astonish you with the living proof of its sexual maturity).

Vets usually recommend castrating a male cat when it is between four and nine months of age, when it has reached maturity, but any tom-cat habits have not yet become firmly established. Although vets differ as to how soon a female cat should be spayed, the general consensus is between four and six months. (Whatever your cat's sex, your vet will take its individual development into consideration when recommending at what age the operation would best be performed.) Both operations require general anaesthetic, which means that you should not feed or water your cat for at least twelve hours beforehand to prevent it from vomiting while unconscious. A male cat should remain at the surgery for a few hours

NEUTERING REDUCES A FELINE'S URGE TO STRAY.

YOUR PRE-OPERATIVE CAT WILL REQUIRE A GENERAL ANAESTHETIC, SO DON'T FEED IT BEFOREHAND.

afterwards – and a female may be kept in overnight – to ensure that it is fully recovered before being allowed to go home.

Castration is a simple procedure in which the testicles are excised (be prepared for your cat's vocal range to become a little higher), while spaying, in which the ovaries and uterus are removed, is a more invasive operation which subsequently requires stitches (and a further trip to the vet's may be required for their removal if they are indissoluble). When you bring your cat home after the operation, leave it to sleep in peace until it feels more itself, don't give it too much food, try to prevent a female from overexerting herself or worrying at her stitches and keep an eye open for infections. After a few days of rest and recuperation, however, all should be well.

HAVING KITTENS

If, whether by accident or design, you find that your cat is pregnant, her well-being before, during and after the birth of her kittens should become your priority, so as soon as you suspect that she is expecting (and the earliest sign are 'pinked-up', rosy nipples at around three weeks), you should start making preparations for the happy event.

The first thing that you should do is to take the expectant mother to the vet for a thorough check-up to ensure that she is healthy, free from parasites − if not, appropriate treatment will be prescribed − and that no complications are implicated. Following an examination of your cat, your vet will also advise you on the kittens' probable date of birth (around sixty-five days following conception), as well as how to feed and look after their mother in the meantime. Until she goes into labour, there is little active role that you can play in ensuring her welfare beyond adapting her diet to pregnancy so that both she and her unborn kittens remain well nourished. Your vet will probably recommend feeding her more often than usual − she could be eating for five or more − but only towards the end of her term, and ensuring that her diet contains calcium and vitamins A and D (a proprietary cat food formulated specifically for pregnant felines may meet these needs, but consult your vet before making the switch from her usual food).

PRIORITISE THE MOTHER-TO-BE'S WELL-BEING DURING THE SIXTY-FIVE DAYS OF HER PREGNANCY.

During the weeks leading up to the birth, your expectant feline will probably spend a considerable amount of time seeking out and investigating suitable spots in which to establish the maternal nest. Her exacting criteria include safety, seclusion, shelter, privacy, warmth and dim light, and if you want to discourage her from setting up camp in a place that would inconvenience the rest of the household, provide her with your preferred alternative.

A PREGNANT FELINE COULD BE EATING FOR SIX: HERSELF AND FIVE KITTENS.

You could, for example, cut away half of one side of a large cardboard box, line the box with layers of newspaper, place it somewhere dark, quiet and draught-free and perhaps half-drape it with an old towel for additional privacy. Encourage her to sit in it, and if she deigns to sleep in it and even starts shredding the newspaper, you'll know that she's accepted it. If she ignores it, however, and returns to her preferred site, either move the box there shortly before she gives birth or provide an emergency birthing bed, such as newspapers covered with a disposable fabric topped with a clean towel.

When her time approaches, your cat's nipples will start leaking milk and she may continually ask for your reassurance before washing herself intensively and increasingly scratching and squatting as birth becomes imminent. If all goes well, the kittens will emerge one by one, in rapid or slow succession (and it may take up to twelve hours or more before all of the litter have been born). Following each kitten's birth, their mother will remove its amniotic sac with her tongue, give her new-born a thorough wash, again with her tongue, to stimulate its breathing and encourage its fur to dry, and sever the umbilical cord (in Melchior's case, half of his tail, too) with her teeth. Finally, she will eat the placenta that followed the kitten – behaviour inherited from her wildcat ancestors that both gives the mother additional nutrition and deters predators from locating her and her kittens. It's best to supervise proceedings discreetly, but not

A CARDBOARD, NEWSPAPER-LINED BIRTHING BED.

to interfere actively unless it's an emergency (ask your vet what danger signs to look out for, and if labour seems to becoming difficult, call him or her out). With the kittens safely born, the new mother will curl her body around her offspring, both to give them easy access to her milk and to keep them warm. They will remain thus for a day or two, so apart from offering the recumbent mother some water or milk and food, placing a litter tray nearby and checking on the feline family occasionally, you can all take some time off to recover.

NEW FELINE MOTHERS SPEND A CONSIDERABLE AMOUNT OF TIME GROOMING THEIR KITTENS.

CARING FOR GROWING KITTENS

For the first few days of their lives, all that new-born kittens require are the warmth of their mother's body, the nourishment that her milk provides and sleep. Because they are utterly dependent on her, their mother will devote all of her attention to them for the first month or so of their lives, leaving their side only to eat, drink and use the litter tray. She may, however, decide to transfer her litter to a new nest site (thereby obeying an instinct to move them to a place where they will be safer from any danger of a predatory attack), doing this by carrying each kitten in turn by the scruff of its neck. As well as feeding them, she will spend a considerable amount of time keeping them clean, grooming them with her tongue and swallowing their bodily waste, which, for the first four weeks of their lives, they can only produce in response to the stimulus of her tongue licking their bottoms. Unless it is obvious that they are being neglected (unlikely, since most feline mothers lavish exemplary maternal care on their brood), when you may have to call in your vet for advice on remedial action, such as bottle-feeding, it's best to take a hands-off approach. Avoid any active interference, which may upset the mother and jeopardise the kittens' welfare. Do, however, ensure that you provide the mother and, by extension, her kittens, with water and plenty of nutritious food and that you change their bedding regularly. Their mother probably won't mind you handling her kittens gently once their eyes have opened, and, indeed, this is vital if they are to become socialised with humans.

MOST FELINE MOTHERS PROVIDE OUTSTANDING MATERNAL CARE.

FOR THE FIRST FEW WEEKS OF THEIR LIVES, KITTENS ARE TOTALLY DEPENDENT ON THEIR MOTHER.

Compared with human babies, kittens develop remarkably quickly. Born with their eyes and ears tightly shut and able only to squirm, they initially rely on their senses of smell and touch to locate their mother's teats and latch onto them to feed. Their mother's colostrum gives them some immunity from disease (see page 87), while her milk contains the building blocks of physical development and, if all goes well, they will grow with astonishing speed, doubling their birth weight within a week.

DON'T HANDLE BABIES IF THEIR MOTHER OBJECTS.

While their eyes usually open between four and ten days of age (although it will take a few more weeks before they are able to focus properly), their ears register their mother's communicative purrs, trills and chirrups, they in turn using a range of squeaks to attract her attention. They typically take their first staggering steps at around three weeks of age, after which their mobility improves by leaps and bounds, prompting their harassed mother constantly to call or haul them back to the nest. (When they seem confident that they can control their legs, and are taking responsibility for their own grooming, you could start introducing them to the litter tray.) At around four weeks, when they have mastered control of their limbs, kittens discover the joy of playing games. Playtime may be enormous fun, but it is also a crucial part of the feline learning process, when kittens begin to discover and practise such essential feline life skills as pouncing. Indeed, kittenhood is a voyage of discovery, supervised closely by their mother, who will try both to ensure their safety and to teach them all that they need to know in order to thrive and survive.

KITTENS SHOULD BE WEANED BY THREE MONTHS.

By around five weeks of age the litter should be displaying a full set of milk teeth, and the combination of teeth and mobility between three and five weeks, along with their mother's increasing disinclination to feed them at will, signals the time from which some solid food should be introduced to the kittens' diet. Although you should seek your vet's advice on how to supplement and vary their food, you should be safe giving them such highly nutritious dishes (in a shallow bowl) of increasing textural complexity as formula milk for kittens, human baby food, creamed rice, cottage cheese, scraped or minced cooked beef and flakes of steamed fish. They should have been completely weaned off their mother's milk between eight to twelve weeks, after which their diet should consist of a proprietary cat food (see pages 63 to 65) that has been specially formulated for kittens.

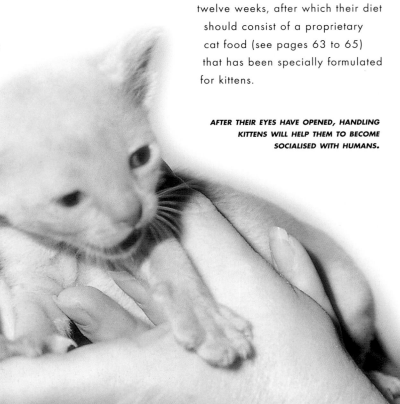

AFTER THEIR EYES HAVE OPENED, HANDLING KITTENS WILL HELP THEM TO BECOME SOCIALISED WITH HUMANS.

FEEDING DOS AND DON'TS

The section on what, and when, to feed your feline in Chapter 2 (see pages 63 to 65) stressed the importance of ensuring that your cat receives the correct balance of the nutrients that are vital to a feline's continued well-being. In practice, all that this usually means for an adult cat is giving it two meals a day of a tinned, foil-packed or dry proprietary food that has been specifically formulated for felines, as well as making sure that a bowl of fresh water is always available. This section delineates some further feeding dos and don'ts.

• Most cats will turn their noses up at food that isn't fresh. Although they usually make an exception for dry proprietary feline food, don't expect them to eat tinned food that has been left over from a previous meal.

• Try to accustom a cat, ideally from kittenhood, to a moderately varied diet, albeit based on its staple proprietary food. Give it a once or twice-weekly treat of cooked (to ward off toxoplasmosis, see page 103), good-quality fish, meat, liver or egg or raw cheese, but don't feed it too much of these foods and certainly not at the expense of its usual proprietary food. If you do, you may expose your feline to dietary deficiencies and may also find yourself pandering to the demands of an ultra-fussy eater.

WATER IS A VITAL ACCOMPANIMENT FOR DRY FOOD.

• Although liver contains vitamin A, an essential nutrient for felines, overconsumption may cause bone disease, specifically spinal arthritis, so feed it to your cat in moderation. Note that raw liver may result in diarrhoea.

• Your cat may be unable to tolerate milk or cream, either due to an allergy or because lactose (the sugar in cow's milk) does not form part of the natural feline diet. (It by-passes the stomach's digestive juices and is instead consumed by bacteria in the gut, resulting in diarrhoea). If your cat's digestive system reacts badly to it, don't give it milk.

GIVE YOUR CAT THE OCCASIONAL TREAT.

MANY CATS HAVE A LACTOSE INTOLERANCE.

- Don't give your cat raw fish because in its uncooked state the thiaminase enzymes within it break down thiamine, a B vitamin that is vital to feline health. Thiamine deficiency could lead to anaemia or Chastek's paralysis. Don't overcook fish or meat either, because heat also destroys thiamine. A diet that contains a high proportion of fish may lead to skin conditions like eczema or yellow fat disease, so limit your cat's piscine intake.

- Don't overfeed your cat or give it constant access to food: a fat feline is susceptible to heart disease and other potentially debilitating conditions.

- A large bone to gnaw on will benefit your cat's dental health, but because small or splintered bones could cause a cat to choke, and cooking makes the bones in meat, poultry and fish brittle, always remove such potentially dangerous bones from home-cooked food.

- Cats don't need, or generally greatly enjoy, vegetables, but if you want to interest your feline in some greens, note that cooking them makes them easier for the feline digestive system to process.

- If your cat has been ill or is old, it may have lost its appetite and its sense of smell may have been dulled. When trying to entice a convalescent or old cat to eat in order to build up its strength, tempt it with small amounts of strongly smelling food, such as tinned tuna, pilchards or sardines or choice morsels of fresh meat.

IF YOUR CAT ENJOYS A WELL-BALANCED DIET, IT WILL BE LESS LIKELY TO STEAL YOUR SUPPER.

- Although health problems may demand that you introduce them, your cat may refuse to countenance any changes to its customary diet. The best way to wean it onto a new food is to introduce it gradually by mixing it with your feline's current foodstuff in increasing proportions. If your cat refuses to eat the food, clear it away, but don't offer what it considers to be a more palatable substitute. When it is hungry enough, it will usually grudgingly consent to eat the novel food that it has previously spurned.

A SERVING OF TINNED FOOD SHOULD BE FRESH.

- When a cat reaches a venerable age, it's better to give it three or four small meals of its favourite foods a day instead of the two that it enjoyed in its prime. This strategy is more friendly to an ageing digestive system.

- Don't give a healthy cat vitamin or mineral supplements if you're feeding it a proprietary food. Kittens, mothers-to-be, convalescent or old cats may benefit from certain extra vitamins, but be guided by your vet.

- Serve your cat cooked food at its preferred temperature – that of warm blood – and not straight from the oven or fridge.

FELINE-RELATED HYGIENE MEASURES

FELINES ARE SCRUPULOUS SELF-GROOMERS.

Although ill or old cats, who may find self-grooming or reaching their litter tray difficult, may need a helping human hand, most adult cats are rigorous about maintaining high standards of feline hygiene, grooming themselves both thoroughly and regularly, as well as scrupulously covering their faeces with either earth or cat litter. (Melchior is untypically laissez-faire about the latter, instead leaving the tedious business of covering-up to the more fastidious Caspar.) There still remain certain risks of infection that are out of a feline's control, however, which it's important to take steps to address in the interests of maintaining both your cat and your family's health. The most basic are keeping your cat's bedding and bowls clean, as well as regularly checking its body carefully for signs of any physical problems. Others include the prevention and, if necessary, control of worms and fleas (see pages 91 to 941) and yet more the treatment of any infectious skin conditions – fungal dermatitis like ringworm, for example (see page 123) – that your cat may develop and then pass on to you or your family.

Counted among the few other conditions, known as zoonoses, that can be transmitted from felines to humans is cat-scratch fever (whose cause is exactly as its name suggests), which can result in a mild temperature and inflammation of the lymph nodes in humans, so always wash and disinfect any wound inflicted by a cross cat. A more serious zoonosis is toxoplasmosis, a flu-like disease caused by the protozoan parasite Toxoplasma gondii, which your cat may become host to through eating infected raw meat (because heat destroys the parasites, it's advisable to cook any meat that you give it), excreting the parasites in its faeces. If a pregnant woman

contracts toxoplasmosis, serious implications may ensue for her unborn child, ranging from malformation of the skull and blindness to liver infections and even stillbirth, so mothers-to-be should ensure that their skin never comes into contact with feline faeces. In fact, the following advice applies to all cat-owners.

- When cleaning a litter tray, always wear disposable plastic gloves, throw them away after use and wash your hands.

- Remove faeces from the litter tray as soon as possible, using a litter scoop, which you should store in a plastic bag.

- Thoroughly clean and disinfect the litter tray at least once a week, using hot water and disinfectant (but check the label to make sure that the disinfectant is cat-friendly because some can poison cats).

- At the same time, replace the cat litter (this should be done at least once a week, although a top-up will usually suffice after using the litter scoop).

- Wear gloves when gardening because it is a rare garden that does not harbour feline faeces.

Because children are especially vulnerable to attack by zoonoses, ensure that they never handle feline faeces (be wary about letting them play in sandpits which are left uncovered when not in use) and encourage them to wash their hands after handling or grooming a cat. Although this isn't always practical, hand-washing is a sensible precaution for adults, too, and a vital one before food is prepared. Similarly, discourage your cat from jumping onto kitchen surfaces, but, if it does so, disinfect them immediately.

COMBAT TOXOPLASMOSIS WITH RUBBER GLOVES.

GROOMING YOUR CAT

Your cat will spend a considerable amount of time grooming its fur, and will make an admirable job of it, too. A longhaired cat, however, will usually not be able to keep on top of the task unaided, and a shorthair will also need a helping hand to keep its coat in peak condition. (If you are planning to show your cat, immaculate grooming is essential, but because pre-show grooming is an art form and this section deals with grooming basics, consult a specialist authority or publication for further guidance.) An indoor cat's claws will furthermore require regular clipping, and whether or not your cat is an indoor or outdoor feline, your vet may advise you to institute a tooth-cleaning regime. (See pages 69 to 71 for details on grooming equipment.)

IF YOU DO LITTLE ELSE IN THE WAY OF GROOMING, AT LEAST COMB YOUR CAT USING A COMB APPROPRIATE FOR ITS COAT. A SHORTHAIRED FELINE SHOULD BE COMBED ONCE A WEEK, WHILE A LONGHAIRED CAT MAY NEED DAILY GROOMING. STARTING FROM ITS HEAD, WORK ALONG ITS BACK TO ITS TAIL BEFORE TURNING YOUR ATTENTION TO ITS UNDERSIDE.

All of these tasks are easily mastered, but if you are unsure how best to perform them, seek your vet's advice. And in the unlikely event that you really aren't equal to grooming your cat, a regular trip to a local feline beauty salon is an alternative option. Never, however, succumb to the temptation to have your cat declawed: not only does minimal attention render such drastic action unnecessary, but the removal of an essential part of a cat's self-defensive and climbing equipment is unkind, to put it mildly.

Because most domestic cats moult all year round, dead hairs accumulate on their coat which they will ingest while grooming, the resultant build-up being vomited up as sausage-shaped furballs. Not only will regular combing (once a week for shorthairs and daily for longhairs) minimise this uncomfortable problem, but it also provides an opportunity for you to keep an

GROOMING TIME GIVES YOU THE CHANCE TO CHECK YOUR CAT'S COAT FOR FLEAS AND SKIN PROBLEMS.

eye open for any skin problems or parasites, as well as increasing the bond between you and your feline. Their sheer abundance of fur makes it especially difficult for longhairs to prevent the build-up of tangles which, if not dealt with immediately, could result in such severe matting that the only solution is either to cut out the clump with a pair of round-tipped scissors or, in extreme instances, for the vet to shave your sedated cat. The sooner you accustomise your cat to being groomed, the easier the process will subsequently become.

MOST SHORTHAIRED CATS MAKE AN ADMIRABLE JOB OF KEEPING THEIR COATS SPICK-AND-SPAN.

Your cat's acquiescence can also be encouraged by holding the back of its neck firmly as you comb from its head along its back and tail before turning it over to address its underside. I comb our cats, using the appropriate steel comb for their different coat types, immediately before feeding them, a cunning endure-and-reward strategy that I've found very effective. Although it isn't always essential after a thorough combing, many feline coats benefit from having any loose hairs removed through being brushed with a natural- or nylon-bristled brush for the body, a toothbrush for the facial fur and finally perhaps a slicker brush to impart some sheen.

SQUEEZE THE BASE OF EACH CLAW IN TURN.

TRIM ONLY THE CLAWS' TRANSLUCENT TIPS.

IF YOU WANT TO AVOID BEING BITTEN . . .

An indoor cat may object to having its claws clipped, in which case prevent any outraged struggling by swaddling it in a blanket or towel so that only its head and front paws are protruding from the bundle. Squeeze the base of each claw in turn with one hand to extend it and then trim it with clippers wielded by your other hand. Because it contains blood vessels, it's important not to cut into the living quick (you'll see it as a pale-pink triangle), so only trim the translucent tips. You'll probably need to do this every two to four weeks, and the occasion will also provide a convenient chance to check that the paw pads haven't sustained any wounds or thorns.

If it's considered necessary, your vet will advise you how often to clean your cat's teeth, a technique that is easily learned (ask for a demonstration), although you must never apply too much pressure. At the same time, check that your cat's gums are rosy pink – an indication of good health – and that there isn't a

. . . USE A BRUSH TO CLEAN A CAT'S TEETH.

CLEAN A CAT'S EARS WITH DAMP COTTON WOOL.

BE VERY GENTLE WHEN WIPING A CAT'S EYES.

build-up of tartar on the teeth themselves, which would require scaling by your vet.

Finally, grooming time presents an opportunity to check the condition of your cat's eyes and ears; if they look a little gungy, clean them gently with some cotton wool moistened with tepid water. If any changes in its ears, eyes, teeth, claws or skin give you cause for concern, take your cat to the vet because they may indicate a potentially serious health problem.

CLAW-CLIPPING IS A MUST FOR INDOOR CATS.

FOSTERING FELINE FITNESS

Fat feral felines are almost unheard of, for not only is food harder to come by for ferals than for house cats, but they have to expend considerable time and energy in procuring it, and their predatory exercise regime keeps them fit and lean. Domestic cats, by contrast, often need only to miaow persistently for a meal to materialise, the only parts of their bodies that they exert in their quest for food being their vocal

FEEL YOUR CAT'S BODY TO CHECK FOR WEIGHT GAIN.

MOST CATS PREFER TO WALK ALONE.

cords. And if a domestic cat is also an indoor cat, which has limited opportunities for regular physical activity, it will be in greater danger of putting on weight and losing muscle tone.

YOUR VET MAY ADVISE WEIGHING
YOUR CAT REGULARLY.

Although cats are rarely inclined to eat for greed's sake, for a bored indoor feline, the highlight of the day is the materialisation of a full feeding bowl rather than the thrill of the chase, and it may thus pile on the pounds. Excessive weight gain, which puts extra strain on every organ, especially the heart, is just as much a danger to feline as to human health, so it is vital not to collude in creating a fat cat. When grooming your cat, take the time to feel its ribs, and if they are difficult to distinguish because they are padded with fat, consult your vet about instituting a weight-loss programme (and many proprietary cat-food ranges now include slimming diets).

Because weight gain creeps upwards when more calories are ingested than expended, the best way in which to prevent your cat from becoming fat is to ensure that it has ample opportunity for exercise. Access to the great outdoors is usually enough, but if your cat is confined to a small garden, consider building an outdoor run or activity centre, for example, including branches arranged at different heights for your cat to scale. If your cat is an indoor cat and your home is limited in size, two solutions to the exercise conundrum are to construct an indoor climbing frame or to devote at least half an hour a day to playing with your feline. Not only will a vigorous game enable your cat to exercise its muscles, it will also provide mental stimulation and strengthen the bond between the human and feline playmates. Be they indoor or outdoor felines, kittens or adults, all cats hanker after playtime, so even if you aren't around to participate, provide your cat with lots of toys with which to entertain itself.

PLAYTIME GIVES THE FELINE BODY A WORK-OUT.

GARDEN PATROLS WILL KEEP AN OUTDOOR CAT TRIM.

Opinion is divided about walking cats as we do dogs. Those that are against the practice point out that a cat's heart and lungs cannot comfortably sustain prolonged periods of exercise (see page 23) and that going on long, companionable rambles is furthermore alien to the feline nature – a cat is not, after all, a pack animal, but an individualistic creature focused on its core territory – and what happens when the pair of you encounter a dog? Advocates of cat-walking, by contrast, counter that many cats (especially Oriental breeds like Siamese) enjoy walking with their owners

and assert that the exercise is good for them. If you decide to try walking your cat, make sure that you fit it with an elasticated harness designed specifically for cats, never attach a lead to its collar or drag it after you and only stroll à deux for short distances. You never know, after a few weeks of accustomisation to this alien practice, your cat may take to being promenaded (unlike ours, who sat down mutinously and refused to budge, all the while wailing piteously). Ultimately, however, the decision as to whether or not it's amenable to 'walkies' will be made by your cat, not you.

KITTENS ARE FAMOUSLY FOCUSED ON PLAY, AN ACTIVITY THAT NOT ONLY HELPS THEM TO LEARN AND HONE THEIR HUNTING SKILLS, BUT ALSO STRENGTHENS THEIR MUSCLES AND SHARPENS THEIR REFLEXES. THE BODIES OF OLDER CATS, TOO, WILL BENEFIT FROM THE EXERCISE THAT PLAYTIME INVOLVES, ESPECIALLY IF THEY ARE INDOOR FELINES.

TRAINING YOUR CAT

Unlike dogs, cats are notoriously resistant to being trained – if anything, it's they who train their human housemates. Nevertheless, if you take the word 'train' to mean accustomising a cat to certain behavioural patterns rather than teaching it tricks, then it is possible to train it. In many instances, your cat won't need much training anyway: once an indoor cat has

MAKE CLEAR THAT HUMAN FOOD IS NOT FOR CATS.

IS IT TIME TO BUY YOUR CAT A SCRATCHING POST?

made its litter tray's acquaintance, for example, it will typically become instantly house-trained (see page 66). Because feline laws and imperatives differ from those of humans, however, your cat may not, for instance, understand why scratching at

furniture is forbidden when it's praised for stropping vigorously at its scratching post or why it's shouted at for jumping onto a kitchen surface to grab a tasty morsel when you otherwise willingly provide it with food. If your reaction is ambiguous or inconsistent, it will thus become confused about what is acceptable behaviour and what isn't. Remember, too, that there may be a reason for your cat's 'bad' behaviour: felines need to keep their claws in trim, for example, so if it is scratching the furniture, is this because it can't do so on a tree and you haven't provided a scratching post?

BAN YOUR CAT FROM KITCHEN SURFACES.

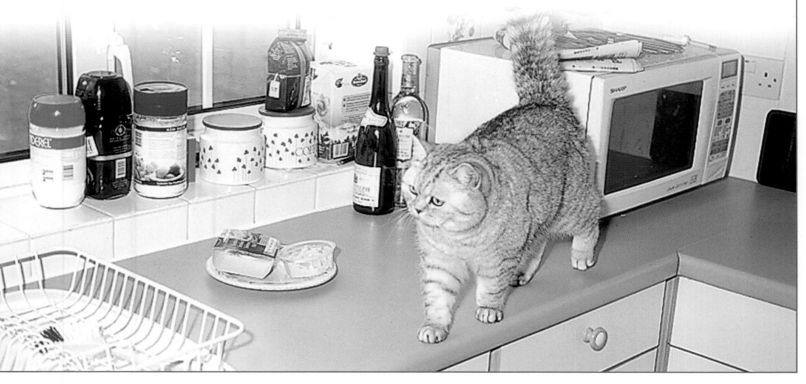

There are certain house rules that you'll have to drum into your cat if you are to live together healthily and harmoniously, and this is most successfully done by using the twin approaches of clarity and consistency. Before welcoming a feline into your home, decide what sort of habits you will tolerate and what is absolutely forbidden. Even if a cat continues to think in its heart of hearts that your rules are illogical, if you stick firmly to them and it knows that you will be displeased with it every time that it breaks them, it will reluctantly learn to comply.

TRAIN YOUR CAT TO STEER CLEAR OF DANGER AREAS.

When training a cat, there are two strategies that you could follow: aversion therapy and rewarding correct behaviour. Aversion therapy is best employed in emergency situations

A FELINE WILL SOON LEARN TO USE ITS CAT FLAP.

when a cat threatens to do something that could endanger its safety, for example, leaping onto a hot cooking hob, the response to which should be active discouragement. Conveying your disapproval with a loud and stern 'No!' will usually suffice if repeated each time that your cat misbehaves. Another way of training a cat to desist from doing something that irks you is to squirt a pump-action plant spray filled with water in its direction; although the mist of water droplets will not harm the cat, it can have spectacularly successful results if used in judicious moderation. And if a particular spot repeatedly receives a cat's unwanted attentions, try dabbing some vinegar or lemon juice onto it, the smell of which is so repellent to a feline that it will keep its distance. Never, however, hit a cat because this will simply cause it to distrust and fear you, often resulting in even more unco-operative behaviour because it has linked the punishment with you rather than the feline a ction that preceded it.

TAKE A CONSISTANT LINE ON WINDOWSILLS.

Discouraging bad behaviour is one thing, but training your cat to do something that wouldn't naturally occur to it, or that it would definitely prefer not to do – like returning

GIVE YOUR CAT THE OCCASIONAL TREAT.

home at night when it would rather be   out hunting – is quite another. I suspect that the question that a cat asks itself when a human makes an incomprehensible demand of it is 'Why? What's in it for me?' to which the best answer is 'food' (think about how rapidly your cat responds to the sound of its meals being prepared and how affectionately it treats you immediately before you place its food bowl in front of its nose). It may take repeated attempts, but if you reward your feline with its favourite titbit each time that it complies with your wishes, it will soon learn the lesson of human-prompted cause and feline-satisfying effect.

TRAINING CAN PLAY A CRUCIAL ROLE IN SAFEGUARDING YOUR CAT'S PHYSICAL WELFARE.

TRYING TO TRAIN YOUR CAT USING TERROR TACTICS CAN BE COUNTERPRODUCTIVE.

WHEN THE HUMAN'S AWAY . . .

When planning a stay away from home, making provision for your cat should be high on your list of things to do. If it's only for a night, put out enough food and water to cover evening and morning meals, make sure that the litter tray is fit for feline use and, if you have an outdoor cat, confine it to your home until your return. Longer human absences require more careful planning, however, because you cannot leave your cat – who, after all, depends on you for food, water, shelter and company – to fend for itself alone.

The kindest solution, the feline identity being focused on its home territory, is to stock up with sufficient food and cat litter to cover your period of absence and to arrange for a neighbour or cat-sitter to come into your home twice a day (or even better, to move in) to provide your cat with food, water and a bit of affection, to clean its litter tray and to make sure that it remains in good health (remember to leave your vet's details and to show its temporary carer where its carrier is kept in case of emergencies). If you have a cat flap, an outdoor cat could still enjoy trips outside, but for security's sake you may prefer it to become an indoor cat while you're away (don't forget to shut all

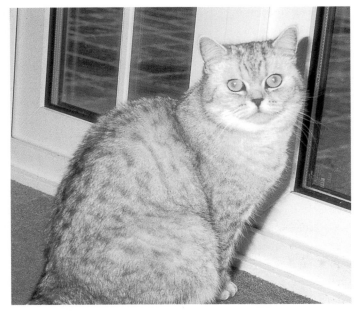

ENSURE THAT YOUR CAT WILL BE WELL CARED FOR IF YOU HAVE TO LEAVE IT HOME ALONE.

of the windows). Alternatively, you could take your feline, along with its cat-care accoutrements, to stay with a friend or relative.

A GOOD CATTERY SHOULD PROVIDE YOUR CAT WITH ITS OWN RUN SO THAT IT CAN TAKE SOME EXERCISE.

The only other option – and an expensive one – is to board your cat at a cattery, where it will be provided with food (although you may be asked to provide its usual fare if it is a fussy eater or has special dietary requirements) and shelter.

Before booking your cat into a cattery (ask your vet to recommend one), try to inspect it to check that the premises appear clean and well-run and that your cat will have its own, relatively spacious, run, where it will be warm and dry and will have no contact with other feline boarders to by-pass the twin dangers of fights and infection.

Along with your cat, remember to take its vaccination record and perhaps a favourite object or piece of bedding to act as a comfort-blanket.

USE A CARRY CAGE TO INTRODUCE YOUR CAT TO IT'S TEMPORARY HOME IN THE CATTERY.

FELINES ON THE MOVE

Whether you are taking your cat to the vet's, to stay at a cattery or to your new house, you will need to confine it to a cat-carrier (see page 60) for the duration of the trip. Before doing so, you will, of course, have to catch your cat, which can be quite a palaver if, like our two, it tends to flee as soon as it catches sight of its carrier. We have learned that the most effective way of transferring our cats to their carriers is first to shut any doors leading outside before extracting the carriers from their storage place. Then we calmly herd our reluctant felines into one room, closing the door before ushering each cat into its respective carrier. Their response to being 'caged' is a steady stream of anxious howls, which they keep up for a while in the car, although on longer trips they eventually settle down and snooze fitfully. If your cat faces a really long trip, it may be advisable not to give it food or water for a few hours beforehand if you can't ensure that it will be able to use a litter tray (within a stationary vehicle with the doors and windows closed) en route. If you're taking your cat abroad, remember that it will need to be microchipped (see page 95) and to travel with its own pet passport (provided by your vet), and if it will be a flying feline, check ahead with both the airline and country of destination to see what arrangements you'll need to make.

MANY CATS ACTIVELY RESIST BEING BUNDLED INTO THEIR CARRIERS, AND YOU MAY HAVE TO RESTRAIN YOURS FIRST.

SWADDLING A CAT IN A TOWEL WILL NEUTRALISE ITS CLAWS, MAKING IT EASIER TO PLACE IT IN THE CARRIER.

When moving house, you'll have to take steps to ensure that your cat doesn't become unsettled by the drastic changes occurring within its home environment and doesn't go missing as a result. Before the upheavals start on moving day, confine your cat to one room, along with its water bowl and litter tray, and warn any removal personnel not to enter that room; if this isn't possible, a less comfortable alternative is to confine it to its carrier. When it's time to leave your old home, never load your cat onto a removal van, but instead let it travel with you in its carrier so that it can derive some reassurance from your presence. Make sure that your feline's food, bowls, litter tray and litter are easily accessible – ideally stow them in the boot of your car – and haven't been packed away in an unmarked box. Once you've arrived at your new abode, again either keep your cat confined to its carrier or release it into a room where it'll be undisturbed and shut the door. After your possessions have been unloaded and relative peace prevails, introduce your feline to its new home by taking the same measures that you used when you welcomed it into your previous house (see pages 78 to 79) and don't allow it to go outside for a week or so until you are sure that it views its new abode as home.

CONFINING A CAT TO ITS CARRIER FOR THE DURATION OF MOVING DAY WILL ENSURE ITS SAFETY.

DON'T LET YOUR CAT INSPECT ITS NEW HOME UNTIL THE WORST OF THE UPHEAVALS ARE OVER.

CARING FOR AN OLDER CAT

Although our cats are now twelve years old, they haven't fundamentally changed since they officially became adult felines at nine months. That having been said, they have become rather more blasé about the joys of active playtime and, being semi-indoor cats, have a tendency to put on weight, which is why their vet has advised feeding them a proprietary cat food formulated for senior felines who need to slim.

How can you tell that your cat is entering old age? Working out the human equivalent of a feline's age is an imprecise science, and there is some argument about the traditional assertion that multiplying the years that your cat has lived by seven is a good general rule of thumb. Most authorities, however, agree that after notching up twelve years a cat is in its mid-sixties, after fifteen years its mid-seventies, while after twenty years it's approaching its centenary. Just as in humans, a feline's ageing process varies according to the individual, so it's best to monitor your cat for signs that its age may be catching up with it. These include loss of appetite, weight and condition (possibly indicating degeneration of the liver or kidney disease), increased thirst, constipation or incontinence, stiffness, skin tumours and dental problems (see Chapter 4 for further details). If you have any cause for concern, take your cat to the vet, who will advise the appropriate remedial treatment, which will often involve a dietary adjustment.

AS A CAT AGES, IT STARTS TO SLOW DOWN AND SPENDS MORE TIME SLEEPING.

Because older cats have an increased requirement for vitamins and minerals, your vet may advise switching it to a diet specifically formulated to meet this need at a relatively early age (ours were eight, or approaching fifty human years). When it has become clear that your cat has graduated to the ranks of the really senior citizens of the feline world, your vet may advocate feeding it four small meals a day, as well as a diet that contains dietary fibre to counter constipation and is rich in protein and fat to provide its body with extra energy and insulation. An older cat will spend most of its time sleeping, but when it awakes its first thought will typically be 'I'm awake: I must be hungry!' and because food may be one of its few remaining pleasures, oblige it with a small, but highly palatable, meal. Make sure that it has a cosy bed in a warm spot in which to sleep and that its food and water bowls, as well as its litter tray, are close by. It will also increasingly appreciate your company and affection, so take the time to stroke and talk to it and keep up a gentle grooming regime (an older cat's increasing lack of mobility makes self-grooming difficult). If your cat begins to suffer from failing eyesight and hearing, make sure that you don't disorientate it by moving familiar objects around and note that these senses won't warn it of the approach of potential dangers.

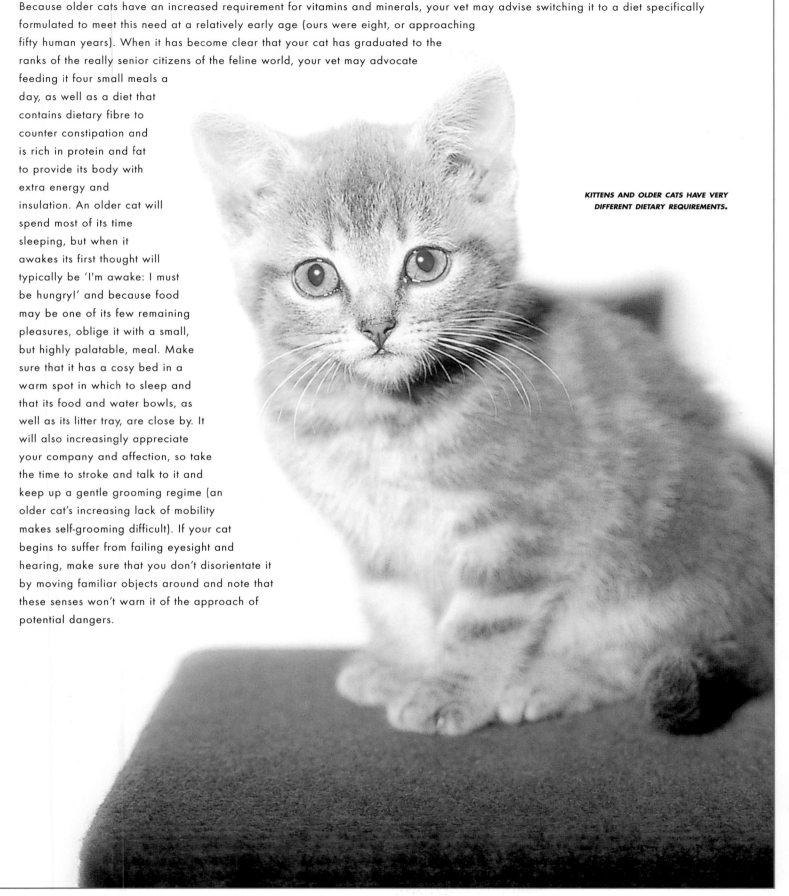

KITTENS AND OLDER CATS HAVE VERY DIFFERENT DIETARY REQUIREMENTS.

A FELINE SENIOR CITIZEN'S WORLD REVOLVES AROUND THE TWIN PLEASURES OF SLEEP AND FOOD.

When caring for an older cat, the golden rule is to be guided by your vet, who should see it every three months or so, or as recommended, to monitor its health. Your vet will be able to ascertain with clinical accuracy when your cat is reaching the end of its natural days or when the pain caused by a chronic condition can no longer be alleviated and your cat's quality of life has plummeted irrevocably. If euthanasia is recommended, accept that your experienced vet, who has its best interests at heart, is certain that there is no hope that your cat will recover and recognises that prolonging its life will condemn it to further suffering. Remember, too, that the euphemism that is frequently used for euthanasia, 'putting to sleep', accurately describes the administering of a painless injection that is the last act of kindness that you can authorise for your old friend.

OLD CATS TEND TO SUFFER FROM WEIGHT LOSS, AND YOUR VET MAY ADVISE REGULAR WEIGHING SESSIONS.

chapter 4

FELINE AFFLICTIONS AND THEIR TREATMENT

In this chapter, we'll take a voyage around the feline body to home in on the afflictions to which a cat's skin and coat, ears, eyes, nose and mouth may fall prey. Certain ailments are minor, while others may be symptomatic of more serious threats to a cat's health, some of which are detailed in Chapter 5. No matter how trivial they may seem, as soon as you notice that your feline is suffering from any of these symptoms, it's important to take the appropriate measures to restore it to full physical fitness, the first usually being taking it to be examined by your vet, who will instruct you how best to care for it. Because you may be advised to monitor its vital signs, to administer pills and other forms of medication or to nurse your under-par cat, basic guidance on how to perform these procedures is also given in this chapter. As ever, however, when identifying and treating feline ailments, be guided by your vet.

AFFLICTIONS OF THE SKIN AND COAT

Two of the most common afflictions of the skin and coat that affect cats – flea infestation (see pages 93 to 94) and matted fur due to inefficient grooming (see pages 104 to 105), as well as the necessary remedial actions – were detailed in Chapter 3. In addition, keep a hawk-like eye open for all of the following afflictions of the skin and coat during your regular grooming sessions. Although you can easily treat some yourself, others will require the specialist advice of your vet, as well as prescription medication.

YOUR CAT MAY FALL VICTIM TO ANY NUMBER OF FELINE AFFLICTIONS.

Symptoms
- Round patches of bald skin, maybe crusty around the edges: see ringworm
- Red or purple bean-like protrusions: see ticks.
- Grey insects and tiny white eggs: see lice.
- Flaky and bald patches, inflammation and chronic itchiness: see mange mites.
- Minute yellow spots: see harvest mites.
- Tiny yellow larvae within an open wound: see maggots.
- Thinning hair on the abdomen and lower back: see alopecia.
- Chronic itchiness, scabs, weeping lesions or localised loss of hair, particularly on the legs and back: see dermatitis and eczema.
- Greasy fur, crusty skin and hair loss around the tail: see stud tail.
- Greasy fur and spots on the chin or lips: see feline acne.

RINGWORM

Despite its misleading name, ringworm is not a type of worm, but a form of fungal dermatitis (Microsporum canis) that is transmitted by direct contact with infected animals or even inanimate objects and that manifests itself as round patches of bald skin, sometimes crusty around the periphery, usually on the head, ears and forepaws. Among the most infectious of all of the zoonoses, ringworm is easily transmitted to humans, especially children and women, and speed is of the essence in banishing it. If you suspect that your cat has ringworm, whisk it to the vet, who will inspect the lesions under ultra-violet light. If they appear fluorescent, and ringworm is therefore confirmed, you will be given a course of anti-fungal tablets and ointment or shampoo with which to treat your cat. Remember to wash your hands after administering any medication, to burn infected bedding and thereafter to keep your cat's immediate environment scrupulously clean. You may also be advised to quarantine your cat until it is ringworm-free, which may take many weeks.

TICKS

Ticks are small, eight-legged parasites that lurk in grassy and woodland habitats waiting for a warm-blooded host onto which to latch with their mouthparts. Your cat may pick up sheep or deer ticks (Ixodes ricinus) or hedgehog ticks (Ixodes hexagonus) either while out on patrol or by coming into contact with an infested animal, and you will see them as red or purple bean-like protrusions on the skin. Because there is a danger that a tick bite may impart a number of potentially debilitating diseases, notably Lyme disease – to you, as well as your cat – and cause localised infections, you must rid it of these parasites immediately. They cannot simply be pulled off, however, for once they have sunk their mouthparts into their host's skin, ticks excrete a substance that cements them firmly into place, so that although you may have removed their bodies, their mouthparts will remain embedded within the skin, redoubling the risk of infection. To force a tick to relinquish its grip, you therefore have to kill the tick while it is still attached to your cat, which can be done by applying a suffocating layer of petroleum jelly, nail-varnish remover, surgical spirit or alcohol with a cotton bud and leaving it to do its work before removing the dead tick with a pair of tweezers. Alternatively, you could treat a tick-infested cat with a proprietary spray (stocked by most veterinary surgeries).

ONLY A DEAD TICK WILL RELINQUISH ITS GRIP.

LICE

Tiny grey parasites, lice (Felicola) are spread through contact with infested felines or objects, but are usually only suffered by cats in poor general condition. One type of cat louse sucks a cat's blood, while its biting fellow feeds on dead skin and fur. The first sign of an infestation is when a cat starts scratching itself repeatedly, whereupon you may be able to discern the culprit insects or their minute white eggs (nits) on its skin. If left to thrive, lice can cause a cat to become dangerously anaemic and sickly, so bathe an infested cat with an insecticidal shampoo, apply a follow-up preparation and use a fine-toothed comb to rid its coat of both the lice and their nits, a process that will probably have to be repeated.

REMOVE LICE AND NITS WITH A FINE-TOOTHED COMB.

MANGE MITES

The mange mite that occasionally targets cats is Notoedres cati, which, because it embeds itself deep within the feline skin, causes the surrounding area to become severely irritated and inflamed and may also result in hair loss. Evidence of excruciatingly itchy mange-mite infestation is typically seen on the ears and head, in the form of patches of flaky and bald skin. Spread by feline-to-feline contact, mange is uncommon in house cats that are well cared for, but, if it occurs, your vet will advocate treatment with antibiotics and insecticides.

HARVEST MITES

As their name suggests, the heyday of harvest mites, or chiggers (Trombicula autumnale), is during the late summer, when these parasites may make the leap from grass to cat.

The signs of a harvest-mite infestation are the tiny yellow spots that pinpoint where the parasites have burrowed under the feline skin, causing the cat to scratch the irritated areas. The infestation is relatively short-lived, however, particularly if treated with a preparation recommended by your vet.

MAGGOTS

It is usually only neglected felines and cats in extremely poor condition that succumb to maggots, the larvae that hatch from the eggs of flies that have alighted upon matted fur, an open wound or chronically inflamed skin, often around the rectum if a cat is suffering from persistent diarrhoea, and especially during the summer. Notwithstanding the cat's pre-existing poor health, which will have prevented it from swatting away the culprit flies in the first place, an infestation of maggots is deadly serious because these parasites will literally eat away and poison its flesh. It is vital that the cat sees the vet as soon as possible, but initial first-aid can be administered by cutting away clumps of dirty fur, removing any visible yellow maggots with tweezers and wiping the affected areas with a feline-friendly antiseptic solution.

ALOPECIA

Neutered cats are prone to the form of hair loss called alopecia, which is caused by hormonal imbalances and causes the fur on the abdomen and lower back to thin significantly, albeit without causing any irritation. Because there is no danger of infection, and the cat is suffering no discomfort, there is nothing that you need do, although your vet may recommend a dietary adjustment or hormone-therapy treatment (HRT).

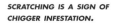
SCRATCHING IS A SIGN OF CHIGGER INFESTATION.

DERMATITUS AND ECZEMA

You will first be alerted to the presence of the allergic conditions dermatitis and eczema in your cat if it constantly scratches and licks itself – particularly its limbs and back – because these skin conditions cause chronic itching. Although not in themselves serious, the cat may lick the affected areas so frantically in its attempt to alleviate the maddening itchiness that either scaliness, scabs or weeping lesions, and hence infections, may develop, along with hair loss. Having first checked that no parasites, especially fleas, are responsible (and if they are, take the appropriate countermeasures), present your cat to the vet. It may be that it has a dietary or environmental allergy or else a hormonal imbalance, which the vet will help you to identify and treat. Whatever the cause, cleaning and drying the skin prior to the regular application of a soothing preparation will probably be prescribed, sometimes along with the wearing of an Elizabethan collar (see page 139) to prevent your cat from further aggravating its skin condition.

STUD TAIL

Despite its macho name, stud tail can sometimes occur in entire females and neutered males, as well as in strutting toms. Tom cats are, however, more prone to this testosterone-influenced skin condition, in which the oil-producing glands at the base of the tail become blocked and the fur becomes covered in grease, sometimes causing hair loss and encrustation of the skin. Although the only danger to health inherent in stud tail is if the skin becomes inflamed (when antibiotics will be required), you may wish to clean the area with a mild shampoo.

FELINE ACNE

Teenagers may be comforted to know that cats can get blackheads and spots, too, and for the same reasons as humans: the clogging-up of the skin's sebaceous glands, to which a build-up of grease from food residues may contribute. Feline acne typically erupts on the lips and chin, areas which a cat finds difficult to reach while grooming.

Although this skin condition usually clears up on its own, you should monitor any outbreaks of feline acne for the development of abscesses (see page 148), which could have serious consequences.

If a spot looks particularly angry, you could encourage it to burst by dabbing it with cotton wool soaked in warm water and then apply a feline-friendly antiseptic. If your cat suffers from chronic acne, however, consult your vet, who may prescribe a course of antibiotics.

SKIN ALLERGIES PROVOKE CHRONIC ITCHING.

AFFLICTIONS OF THE EARS

You will usually be alerted to any trouble brewing within your cat's ears if you see it scratching them repeatedly or shaking its head – signs of chronic irritation – whereupon you should immediately take a closer look. As well as enabling you to identify the source of the problem better, wiping the inside of your cat's ear flaps with a wad of cotton wool soaked in warm water often proves a helpful initial hygiene measure. Never, however, insert a finger, cotton bud, tweezers or any other object into your cat's ear canal as the consequences in terms of infection or damage to the ear's delicate internal structure could be serious. Similarly, if ear drops are prescribed, do not introduce the dropper as far as the ear canal, but instead massage the ear gently to encourage the liquid medication to disperse inwards. And if you suspect that a foreign object, perhaps a grass seed, has become lodged in your feline's ear, its extraction should be left to your vet. Because the symptoms of many ear afflictions are so similar, an accurate home diagnosis can be difficult to make, so take your cat to the vet's if you suspect that it is suffering from any of the following.

Symptoms
- Ear-scratching, head-shaking and brown discharge within the ear: see ear mites and outer-ear infection.
- Blood blister on an ear flap: see aural haematoma.
- Flaky, red skin or sores around the edges of the ear flap: see sunburn.
- Tilting of the head and a wobbly gait: see middle- and inner ear infections.
- Lack of response to sounds: see deafness.

EAR MITES

Sometimes also called ear canker or otodectic mange, an infestation of ear mites (Otodectes cynotis) occurs within the feline ear canal and is spread by contact with an infested animal, not always another feline. Kittens are particularly prone to the unwelcome attentions of these tiny white mites, and the danger signs include repeated ear-scratching, in extreme cases sometimes causing hair loss and bleeding, and head-shaking as the cat tries to rid itself of the excruciating irritation that is caused by the mites' aggravating presence. On closer

examination, you will usually see – and, perhaps, smell – a reddish-brown, waxy discharge and possibly encrustation, the ear's defensive response to chronic irritation and the signal that you should take your cat to the vet's. If the diagnosis is confirmed by a sighting of the mites under a magnifying torch, the vet will usually first clean the cat's ears thoroughly and then give you some ear drops with which to eradicate them over a period of a few weeks. Although they aren't blood-suckers, instead deriving nourishment from feline earwax, don't ignore an infestation of ear mites because not only would you be prolonging your cat's distress if you did so, but a bacterial infection could subsequently set in.

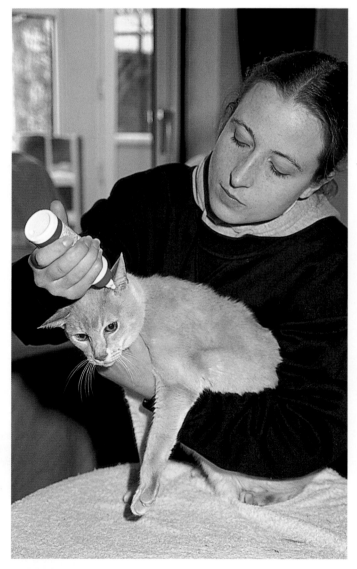

APPLYING EAR DROPS REQUIRES CAUTION.

AURAL HAEMATOMA

Typically seen on the outside of a cat's ear flap, a blood blister, or haematoma, results from either a cat fight or from the feline repeatedly, and forcibly, scratching at an irritated area, causing the blood vessels on the surface of the skin to burst and the released blood to be trapped between the ear's cartilage and epidermis. There are two reasons why you should seek the vet's attention: firstly, because it is more than likely that the underlying cause of the cat's scratching is chronic and needs to be addressed and, secondly, because as the blood within the blister slowly disperses, it may cause a distortion evocatively named 'flop ear' (or sometimes the 'cauliflower ear' notorious to boxers), which is why the vet may take the precaution of draining away the blood and may also prescribe antibiotics to ward off infection.

SUNBURN

As unlikely as it may seem, white or light-coloured cats are susceptible to sunburn. Because their skins are scarcely pigmented, and because the tips and edges of their ears aren't protected by a dense layer of fur, these areas, along with the

EAR DROPS ALLEVIATE MANY AURAL AFFLICTIONS.

YOUR VET MAY PRESCRIBE A SOOTHING PREPARATION.

nose and eyelids, are the most typically damaged by the sun's powerful, ultraviolet rays. If you notice that one, or both, of your cat's ear flaps are rimmed with red, flaky skin, and especially if you know that it enjoys sun-bathing, consult your vet for confirmation that it is suffering from sunburn. Although the damage progresses slowly, the flaking skin may be replaced by sores, scabs, ulcers and ultimately full-blown squamous-cell carcinoma, a destructive form of cancer that may require the ear to be amputated if allowed to spread. If you are vigilant, however, it shouldn't reach this stage, and you should prevent it from doing so either by keeping your cat out of the sun or by applying sunblock formulated for children to the most vulnerable parts of its body.

OUTER-EAR INFECTION

If, during a grooming session, you notice a pungent-smelling, brown, waxy discharge within your cat's ear, it is likely that it has either been infested with ear mites (see above) or, more seriously, and particularly if the discharge contains pus, that a bacterial or fungal infection (sometimes called by the Latin designation otitis externa) has taken hold. In order to prevent the condition worsening and causing irreparable damage, as well as to put a stop to any discomfort or pain that your feline may be enduring, it's important to take your cat to the vet's as soon as you can. If an outer-ear infection is diagnosed, you'll be given the appropriate anti-bacterial or -fungal medication to administer at home.

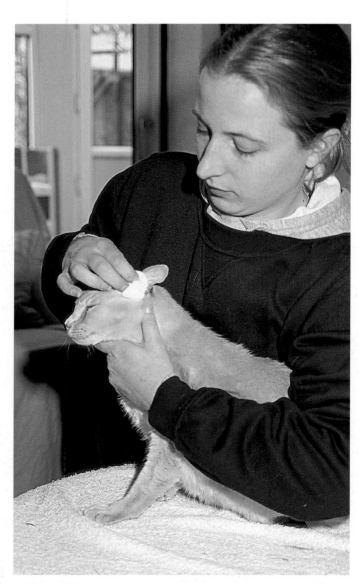

CLEAN A CAT'S EAR WITH MOISTENED COTTON WOOL.

MIDDLE- AND INNER-EAR INFECTIONS

If neglected, an infection of the outer ear, whatever the cause, may spread inwards, into the middle ear, dangerously close to the vestibular organ that controls the feline sense of balance (see page 26) in the inner ear. Although you may not detect a middle- or inner-ear infection from the presence of discharge, if your normally agile cat becomes wobbly on its feet, staggers around in a circle (the direction identifying the infected ear) or its sense of balance otherwise appears to have been compromised, warning bells should start ringing. Further symptoms of a middle- or inner-ear infection include intermittent deafness and the cat – which will be starting to suffer considerable pain and distress – constantly tilting its head to one side. Take your profoundly disoriented cat to the veterinary surgery without delay, where any deep-seated discharge may be drained away and a course of powerful medication prescribed. Time is of the essence if nerve damage and permanent deafness are to be avoided.

DEAFNESS

Although it may sometimes be caused by a middle- or inner-ear infection, white cats with blue eyes, in which deafness is a genetic defect, and older cats are at risk of losing their sense of hearing. Just as in humans, deafness in felines manifests itself as a lack of response to sounds, which is unusual in creatures whose sense of hearing is exceptionally acute. Since hearing aids are not available for cats, there is nothing that can be done except to make sure that your cat's deafness does not expose it to danger. Confinement to the home or a securely fenced garden may therefore be advisable to ensure that your cat, who may not hear a car approaching, does not fall victim to a road traffic accident.

AFFLICTIONS OF THE EYES

Many feline eye problems, which often stem from scratches inflicted during cat fights, are both relatively insignificant and easily cleared up with the correct treatment, but, as with any physical malfunction, mustn't be neglected in case an infection blows up and the eyesight is threatened. Other eye afflictions, however, are potentially very serious, and because the similarity of the symptoms that indicate that all is not well with a feline eye can make it difficult for you to identify a condition correctly, it's essential that the diagnosis is made by a vet, who will also advise you on the appropriate remedial action.

It almost goes without saying that a feline's eyes are extremely sensitive, so always treat them with the utmost delicacy and never poke anything into them, even a gentle finger. As part of its treatment, your vet may, however, advise you to bathe your cat's eyes with either warm water or a feline-specific ocular preparation – don't use eye drops formulated for human use – in which case do so by gently pressing a pad of cotton wool generously soaked in the liquid against the afflicted (closed) eye. Although an eye bath will temporarily soothe the irritation and may expedite the removal of a foreign body, your cat probably won't appreciate this procedure, so be warned that you may have to pre-empt it struggling by swaddling its body in a towel so that only its head protrudes. The same advice applies if you've been instructed to apply a feline eye ointment, which you should squeeze along the lower eyelid before closing both lids and gently massaging the eye.

A CAT'S BRIGHT EYES MAY SUCCUMB TO CERTAIN OCULAR AFFLICTIONS.

Symptoms
- Clear tears running from the eye: see blocked tear ducts.
- Pawing at the eye: see foreign bodies.
- Repeated blinking or a half- or fully closed eye: see scratched cornea and conjunctivitis.
- The third-eyelid pulled over the eye: see haw problems.
- Turned-in eyelids: see entropion.
- Cloudy discharge from the eye: see conjunctivitis.
- A swollen, unblinking eye: see glaucoma.
- An opaque eye: see glaucoma and cataract.
- Bumping into obstacles and a lack of response to movement: see blindness.

CAUTION! A CAT'S EYES ARE EXTREMELY SENSITIVE.

BLOCKED TEAR DUCTS

Being unsentimental creatures, felines don't cry, so if your cat appears to be weeping, the discharge is clear and it seems otherwise fit and well, its tear ducts are probably blocked. Although you could give its eye, along with the affected fur beneath, a preliminary bathing with warm water (see above), you should still seek your vet's expert opinion as soon as you are able in case further treatment is needed.

CHECK EYES FOR SIGNS OF FOREIGN BODIES

FOREIGN BODIES

You'll usually be alerted to the presence of a foreign body in a cat's eye if it is obviously, and repeatedly, pawing at the affected eye, an action that felines otherwise never demonstrate, even when grooming their faces. Immediate inspection of the problem eye is required, and if the object is on the surface of the eyeball, you may be able to dislodge it by bathing the eye (see above). Do not attempt this if the foreign body has penetrated the surface of the eye, however, in case you cause serious damage, and instead whisk your cat to the vet's for immediate attention.

SCRATCHED CORNEA

If your cat is either blinking constantly (which cats rarely do) or keeping one of its eyelids closed or half-closed, it is probably doing so because its eyeball is sore, usually due to either a scratched cornea or an infection. By lowering its eyelid, the cat is attempting to protect its painful eye from the drying effect of the air and to soothe the irritation with a film of moisture. The first step is to bathe the eye, as detailed above, and then to consult the vet to prevent an infection, and ultimately possibly ulceration, from taking hold.

HAW PROBLEMS

When a cat is sleeping, it sometimes does so with its eyes open, but with the haws – commonly known as the third eyelids, but more properly as the nictitating membranes – pulled across them to provide protection. This is quite normal, but if a haw, which is usually retracted and tucked into the inner corner of the wakeful eye, is visible when the cat is going about its everyday business, it may indicate damage, either to the haw or to the eye beneath, or more general illness.

If only one haw is visible, the problem will typically be confined to that eye; if both are pulled across each eye, however, the cat may be sickening for something serious, such as feline viral rhinotracheitis, one of the viruses implicated in feline infectious respiratory disease (see page 90). If the condition persists for longer than a day, consult your vet for a diagnosis and the appropriate treatment.

CATARACT

In common with their human counterparts, feline senior citizens, and also diabetic cats, may develop cataracts within the lenses of their eyes, which can be identified by the presence of a white film or white pupil. Although there is no danger of infection, a cataract can cause progressive loss of sight and an increased danger of glaucoma, so seek your vet's advice about having it removed, which may be advocated if cataracts are affecting both of the cat's eyes and hence significantly impairing its vision.

CONJUNCTIVITIS

The symptoms described above for a scratched cornea, accompanied by visible inflammation of the eye and, more tellingly, by cloudy discharge, often signal conjunctivitis induced by a chronic allergy or a bacterial or viral infection, such as feline infectious respiratory disease, and specifically feline viral rhinotracheitis (see page 90). Any eye infection must be treated as soon as possible lest it develops into an irreversible, sight-threatening condition, so waste no time in presenting your cat to the vet.

GLAUCOMA

If one of your cat's eyes appears to be swollen – perhaps so much so that it cannot close its eyelids – and the eye itself looks cloudy or glassy, the situation is serious. It may be that your cat has suffered a blow to the head, causing internal bleeding, or that it has a grave infection or a tumour, all of which can cause glaucoma, a condition in which the aqueous humour within the eye is unable to circulate freely, resulting in a dangerous build-up of pressure. Often also associated with old age, glaucoma can ultimately result in some extreme scenarios, including blindness, and, if at all, can only be treated by the vet, who may deem it necessary to remove the afflicted eye.

BLINDNESS

If your normally sure-footed feline starts to bump into obstacles or doesn't respond to rapid movements, it may be that it can no longer see them. One way of checking is to sit your cat on a table and then gently to cover each eye in turn with one hand while moving an outstretched finger of the other towards its open eye. If it blinks, it has registered the movement, but if it remains unmoved, loss of sight is indicated. On closer examination, your vet should be able to determine the cause, which, depending on the diagnosis, may mean that its blindness is only temporary and that its eyesight can be restored, as is sometimes the case if the cause is neurological or a cataract, for example. If, however, its loss of sight is permanent, you'll have to keep your vision-impaired cat inside for the rest of its life and ensure that the position of its bed, litter tray, food and water bowls – and preferably the furniture, too – is never changed so that it does not suffer the anxiety of not being able to locate these familiar components of its everyday life.

ENTROPION

Entropion, or rolled-in eyelids, may either be a congenital condition (common to Persians) or the result of a chronic eye inflammation. Because it causes constant discomfort and irritation, your vet may advise surgical correction, which is often the only cure.

APPLYING CREAM TO A CAT'S EYE

AFFLICTIONS OF THE NOSE

Caspar once alarmed us – and himself – by suddenly developing a runny nose a few weeks after his booster immunisation and shortly after a further routine trip to the vet's. Because this is a potentially serious sign, we rushed him back to see the vet, whose diagnosis was that, in the absence of any other symptoms and, as sometimes happens when felines are under stress, the second, anxiety-inducing visit had caused the active agents within the vaccine temporarily to surface. After a week of precautionary antibiotics, all was well. Caspar, however, who was obviously unable to clutch a handkerchief, had a most unpleasant time mopping up the stream from his nose with his tongue, despite being aided every so often by a human wiping his nose with cotton wool dampened with warm water. (Although it wasn't necessary for us to do this, note that you can temporarily ease any soreness caused by chronic mucus production by smearing a light layer of petroleum jelly over a cat's nose.)

Because we'd been vigilant about maintaining Caspar's immunisation programme, we knew that it was unlikely that he was suffering from a full-blown case of feline viral rhinotracheitis, one of the viruses that goes under the umbrella name of feline infectious respiratory disease (see page 90), but if your cat has a runny nose and its immunity to this serious illness is questionable, cat flu may be a chilling possibility. Another cause may be a localised infection. In both instances, urgent veterinary treatment will be required, to take your cat to the vet's as soon as you can.

Other internal nasal problems include irritation caused by an allergy or a blockage within the nose, when, as in all instances of nasal problems, you should consult your vet immediately. Inhalation treatment may be advocated, in which case follow the vet's instructions. Never squirt a nasal decongestant formulated for humans up a cat's nose, however, and never try to remove a foreign object from a feline's nose yourself.

External nasal problems include sunburn (see page 127) and scratches inflicted during fights, both of which should be carefully monitored to ensure that they do not develop into chronic conditions, at the same time as keeping the cat's nose clean by regularly wiping it with water-soaked cotton wool.

A CAT'S NOSE INDICATES ITS GENERAL HEALTH.

AFFLICTIONS OF THE MOUTH

Whereas Caspar's episode of nasal distress was immediately apparent to us, I'm ashamed to say that we had no idea that Melchior was suffering from the onset of localised dental disease until the vet discovered two affected teeth during a routine check-up. Although the condition was not advanced, it could only worsen, eventually leading to the collapse of the teeth concerned and possible infection, so Melchior was anaesthetised, the decaying teeth were extracted and his remaining teeth were scaled (Caspar didn't escape the anaesthetisation-and-scaling procedure either). That was many years ago, and since then our felines have had to put up with having their teeth brushed weekly (see page 71 for equipment and page 106 for guidelines), partly as result of which they can now boast excellent dental health.

Whether or not you brush your cat's teeth, it's important to look inside your cat's mouth as a matter of routine to check for any problems that may be brewing within its gums, mouth lining and tongue. Signs that a condition has become chronic include bad breath, drooling and obvious pain when eating – or even a disinclination to eat – but it's clearly better to pre-empt the development of these secondary symptoms by monitoring your cat's dental health. Many ailments of the mouth, teeth and gums are both minor and curable, but others may indicate a significant threat to your feline's health, so consult your vet if any of the symptoms listed below are giving you cause for concern.

Symptoms
- Bad breath and a layer of yellow or grey material on the top of the teeth: see tartar.
- Red, inflamed gums: see gingivitis.
- Pale gums: see anaemia.
- A swollen cheek and inflamed gum: see abscess.
- A sore on the inside of the upper lip: see rodent ulcer.
- Sores on the tongue or gums: see mouth ulcers.
- A swelling under the tongue: see ranula.

SCALING REQUIRES A CAT TO BE ANAESTHETISED.

TARTAR

Although tooth-eroding sugar isn't to blame for feline dental decay, unlike among humans, the high calcium content of most cats' diets can result in this nutrient being deposited on their teeth. Furthermore, because many house cats subsist on soft, tinned food, there the deposits may remain to calcify, in contrast to their feral fellows, which scrape the deposits away while devouring the tough bodies of their prey. (Note that dried food may therefore be better than tinned for your feline's dental health; alternatively, give it a chewy or tooth-friendly treat every so often.) It's best to brush your cat's teeth at least once a week to prevent the build-up of tartar (dental calculus), an accumulation of which will require your cat to be anaesthetised to enable the vet to remove it by scaling. If your cat's breath smells bad, examine its teeth to see if they are covered with a layer of tartar, which, if left untreated, could result in gingevitis, progressing to periodontal disease.

GINGIVITIS

If your cat's gums look red and sore, it is probably suffering from gingivitis, an inflammation of the gums caused by a build-up at the neck of the teeth of tartar and plaque, bacteria-harbouring food deposits. Chronic gingivitis is indicated when the gums are severely swollen and prone to bleeding. Unless the condition is addressed, it may advance to become periodontal disease, whereby infection sets in and attacks the tissues and bone surrounding the teeth, ultimately causing their destabilisation, death of the dental nerves and hence also of the teeth, which will then need to be extracted. It's therefore vital that you act as soon as you see the danger signs, preferably in the earliest stages of the condition, when only a thin red line along the part of the gum immediately adjoining the teeth will be visible.

ANAEMIA

Feline gums should be rosy pink in colour, but if they appear unusually pale, and the cat hasn't suffered a shock, anaemia is indicated, especially if the feline seems listless. This debilitating condition is caused by a reduction in either the red blood cells or a dilution of haemoglobin within the blood, and may be a symptom of feline leukaemia (see page 89). Take your cat to the vet's for diagnosis and treatment as soon as possible.

ABSCESS

An abscess may be caused when an infection has taken hold in the root of a damaged tooth, resulting in widespread swelling and inflammation and causing the cat exquisite pain when pressure is applied – for example, while eating – when its distress will be obvious. The usual remedy is for the vet to extract the problem tooth and to prescribe a course of antibiotics with which to clear up the underlying infection and hence abscess.

RODENT ULCER

By pawing at its mouth, your cat may be unwittingly alerting you to an irritating mouth condition, and if it seems to be targeting its upper lip, gently roll the lip back to investigate further. If you can see a sore, it may be a rodent ulcer

(eosinophilic granuloma), which, although not in itself especially serious, is likely to persist, to your cat's distress, if not subjected to veterinary treatment.

MOUTH ULCERS

Sores on the tongue or gums may be symptomatic either of local irritation or else of the more threatening feline infectious respiratory disease (see page 90) or kidney disease (caused by increased levels of ammonia within the saliva), both of which require the urgent attention of your vet.

MOUTH PROBLEMS

RANULA

You should always investigate the inside of your cat's mouth if it seems to be suffering discomfort when eating, and if you then see a translucent swelling under its tongue, it's likely to be a ranula, a fluid-filled cyst that is formed when the saliva ducts become blocked or damaged. Ranulas generally respond well to veterinary treatment.

MONITORING A CAT'S VITAL SIGNS

Whether or not your cat has developed any worrying symptoms, if it doesn't seem itself and you are concerned about its health, monitoring its vital signs may help you to decide whether you should take it to the vet's. Although the vet's first step would be to take its temperature, you would be emphatically advised against doing so yourself unless you are experienced in the procedure and also possess the correct type of thermometer. To explain further, the temperature-sensitive strips that you can place across a child's forehead are useless when it comes to felines, as is putting a digital or glass thermometer in its mouth and telling it to keep still for a minute or two. The only accurate way of gauging a cat's temperature is to insert a thermometer designed especially for animals into its rectum (the cat may struggle against this indignity, causing a human-specific thermometer to break and internal damage to be wreaked). Although taking a cat's temperature should therefore be left to the vet, for the record, a cat's normal temperature is between 38 and 38.6°C (100.4 and 101.5°F), a higher reading therefore indicating infection or illness, although if a cat is feeling stressed, a slightly higher reading may also result (as always happens when Caspar, who has no particular reason that we can discern for his anxiety, finds himself in the veterinary surgery, another obvious manifestation of his uneasiness being 'stress-moulting', the rapid shedding of hairs).

YOU CAN FEEL A CAT'S PULSE BEAT AT A CERTAIN POINT WHERE THE BACK LEG MEETS THE TORSO.

What you can safely do, however, is check your cat's pulse by holding your finger against the inside of its 'thigh', the spot where the back leg adjoins the torso, where the femoral artery runs close to the skin's surface, for thirty seconds (it may help to ask someone else to act as a time-keeper so that you can concentrate on taking the pulse).

GENTLY PLACING TWO FINGERS OVER A CAT'S HEART ENABLES YOU TO JUDGE THE STRENGTH OF ITS HEARTBEAT.

Count the pulse beats as you feel them and then, when the thirty seconds are up, double the total so that you obtain a per-minute figure. The normal pulse rate for an unstressed cat ranges between 110 and 140 beats a minute. If the cat seemed agitated as a result of having been restrained, you can probably discount a slightly higher rate, but if it appeared calm or apathetic, a significantly higher, weak or erratic pulse should be taken as a signal to take it to the vet's as soon possible – your cat could be really ill – for further investigation and remedial treatment.

GIVING MEDICATION

If the vet has prescribed medication for your cat, you will have to perfect the art of administering it, both to ensure that it has the desired effect and to avoid distressing your feline patient through your clumsiness. While the recommended procedures for administering eye preparations and ear drops (see pages 126 and 129) have already been covered, and applying ointment to the skin is a straightforward process (always wash your hands afterwards), those for giving internal medication –

powders, pills and their liquid counterparts – will be made easier with the help of a little insider know-how.

Introducing powdered medication into the feline body is relatively easy: if it is mixed into a ball with a little of your cat's favourite fresh food, such as tuna, it will usually be readily swallowed without your cat realising the deception.

Although it becomes automatic with practice, the first few times that you give a cat a pill, you'll probably find the process tricky, not least because you may have to restrain your protesting cat with one hand and administer the pill with the other. You may therefore find it easier either to lift the cat onto a table and ask someone gently to hold its front legs and restrain its rear end or to wrap it in a towel so that only its head protrudes. See the following pages for further instructions on administering pills and liquid medication.

If any medication that isn't intended to make the cat vomit has this effect, discontinue the treatment and consult your vet, as it may be that your cat is allergic to it. And if you have difficulty giving your cat medication, ask your vet for a demonstration.

TAKING A CAT'S TEMPERATURE IS A JOB THAT IS BEST LEFT TO THE PROFESSIONALS.

1 With your feline immobilised, encircle its jaw with one hand, so that your thumb and forefinger are on either side of its mouth, and tilt its head backwards.

2 Now apply a little pressure with your thumb and forefinger (alternatively, gently push down on the lower jaw using the index finger of your other hand) until its mouth opens and then, using your free hand, quickly pop the pill as far to the back of its mouth as you can. (You could use a pill dispenser, or 'popper', rather than your fingers, but don't push the tube too far into the cat's mouth in case you damage its delicate interior).

3 Finally, close the cat's mouth and hold it shut with one hand while stroking its throat with the other to encourage it to swallow its medication. Only then release your hold, but watch your feline to ensure that it has actually swallowed the pill and doesn't instead spit it out (lip-licking is a sure sign that the pill has gone done).

4 If you're administering liquid medication, use a dropper (preferably a plastic one, not glass, in case the cat bites and shatters it) or a syringe and either introduce the liquid in the same way as you would a pill or hold the cat's mouth shut with one hand and inject the liquid into the space behind a canine tooth. The medication should be administered a drop at a time to prevent your cat from choking on a flood of liquid. In both instances, when you're done, again keep the cat's mouth closed and stroke its throat until it swallows its medicine.

CARING FOR AN INJURED OR SICK CAT

There may be occasions when you have to provide more dedicated nursing care than simply administering medication: for example, if your cat's skin has suffered significant damage as a result of infestation, infection or injury, in which case your vet may advocate a bandage or an Elizabethan collar. A feline who has succumbed to a serious illness, however, may require more devoted nursing to encourage it to recover its health and strength.

Although the following general tips may prove helpful, you must obey your vet's instructions to the letter to ensure that your cat receives the care that it badly needs following a severe physical trauma.

A SICK FELINE REQUIRES PLENTY OF REST.

BANDAGES AND ELIZABETHAN COLLARS

Because a feline's flesh repairs itself remarkably quickly following an injury, it is not usually necessary to bandage any scratches or superficial wounds that your cat may sustain. The exceptions are, however, if it persistently licks or scratches at a skin injury, thereby both retarding the healing process and introducing the risk of infection, or if the wound is so large or deep that it could be infected as it heals. If your vet has instructed you to apply an ointment, your cat may furthermore lick it off, in which case you may need to enlist the help of a bandage (and the gauze, crêpe and cotton bandages sold for human use are also fine for use on felines).

A tail can be bandaged in the same way as a paw or leg, but a wound to the abdomen will require a body bandage. Your vet will advise you how to make, or obtain, one of these and also, if it is advocated, how to bandage a cat's eye or ear.

If your cat is suffering from a chronically itchy or inflamed patch of skin, particularly anywhere on its head, your vet may recommend that it wears an Elizabethan collar – a forward-pointing, funnel-shaped contraption resembling an Elizabethan ruff that is secured around the neck – to prevent it from licking, pawing or scratching at its skin before it's healed. Keep your cat inside for the duration because your feline's temporarily limited field of vision may endanger its safety. The collar may

be removed occasionally to enable the cat to eat, drink, groom itself and use the litter try without hindrance, but as soon as it shows any signs of turning its attention to the affected area, it's time to replace its collar.

Before bandaging your cat, gently wash the affected skin with cotton wool soaked in dilute saline (salt) solution and then, if the vet's advised you to do so, apply ointment before reaching for a clean piece of gauze.

When bandaging a paw or leg, first apply the gauze, then wrap the paw in cotton wool and finally commence bandaging, working from the foot up the leg and overlapping each turn that you make. The cat won't welcome being swaddled in a bandage, which it will regard as an alien irritant and will often try to remove, so it's important that the bandage is neither loose enough to unravel easily, nor so tight that it impairs the circulation. Never secure the end of a bandage with a safety pin, which could spring open and prick the cat, or tie it off in case the cat worries at the knot with its teeth, thereby causing the bandage to unravel. Instead use a strong sticking plaster, one end of which should be applied to the fur above to keep the bandage in place (when it's time to remove it, don't pull it off, but cut it away with a pair of scissors).

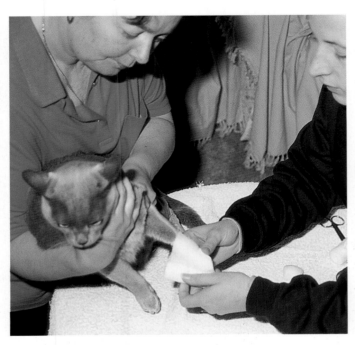

FIRST APPLY GAUZE TO THE INJURED AREA.

WRAP THE PAW IN COTTON WOOL, THEN BEGIN TO BANDAGE.

NURSING A SICK FELINE

During, and following, an episode of serious injury or illness, your vet may advise you to supplement any prescription medication with round-the-clock nursing to aid your cat's recovery. This involves confining the patient to bed (which, because your cat will be probably be feeling abnormally weak, shouldn't present a problem) in a dim, warm and quiet spot. Make sure that the bed is as comfortable as possible, but use only disposable or washable bedding, which, for the sake of cleanliness, should be changed regularly, especially if the invalid is incontinent. If the patient is unable to stand up, reposition its body every few hours to prevent pressure sores from developing.

Place the litter tray nearby, but note that if your cat is simply too weak to reach it, you may have to lift it into the tray two or three times a day. Leave a bowl of fresh water next to the patient's bed, too, and give it small portions of its favourite food as often as it will accept them (see page 102 for advice on how to tempt a sick or old cat to eat). If the cat can't, or won't, eat, your vet will usually deem it necessary for you to give it liquidised food (ask for advice on what best to feed it)

YOUR CAT WILL NEED PLENTY OF ATTENTION IF IT IS SICK OR INJURED.

through a syringe, in which case you should follow the same procedure as described for administering liquid medication (see page 137).

YOUR CAT MAY NEED SOME HELP WITH GETTING AROUND, AS WELL AS LOTS OF TENDER LOVING CARE.

It's important to maintain an ill cat's morale, and little makes a fastidious feline feel more depressed than being dirty. So if these parts of your cat's body need cleaning, bathe its nose, lips or eyes in a very dilute mixture of salt and water, dry them off gently and finally, if they are sore or cracked, smear a little petroleum jelly — but use a prescription ointment for the eyes — over them. An inflamed rear end or soiled fur should first be cleansed with mild shampoo diluted in warm water and then dried and dressed with a little petroleum jelly. Finally, lightly and carefully comb or brush the invalid's coat. (Remember always to wash your hands after cleaning or handling a feline patient.)

A sick cat will be reassured by your attention and affection — tending to a feline's psychological state can be as important as ministering to its physical well-being — so spend some time talking to it soothingly, but don't make too much of a fuss of it because rest is vital to its recovery. And if all goes well, the care that you and your vet have given it will enable your invalid slowly to recover, and one of the first signs that it is on the mend will be when it starts trying to wash its face.

WITH CARE AND LOVE, YOUR CAT SHOULD SOON BE AS HIGH - SPIRITED AS EVER!

chapter 5

SYMPTOM DIAGNOSIS AND EMERGENCY ACTION

If your cat has developed a physical problem, it will usually alert you to both its presence and cause by a change in its behaviour: if a feline repeatedly scratches its skin, for instance, a number of underlying irritants may be implicated, as outlined in Chapter 4. This chapter highlights the symptoms that may warn of a potentially serious threat to a feline's health, as well as outlining the emergency action to take should your cat suffer one of a number of accidents that could endanger its life.

Although the following pages will help you to identify the problem and, in the case of an accident, advise you on initial first-aid treatment, always rush an ailing or injured cat to the vet's as soon as possible. In many cases, it is only prompt veterinary expertise and attention that can save a feline's life.

SYMPTOM DIAGNOSIS

The following sections delineate some of the symptoms that may point towards a possibly grave condition that will require veterinary treatment; others, however, may be minor or temporary symptoms and problems. Some of these conditions have already been covered where indicated, and where an asterisk appears, refer to the emergency-action section for guidance on initial treatment.

Although they have been presented separately, some symptoms may occur in combination – vomiting and diarrhoea, for instance – so don't consider them in isolation, especially if your cat seems listless, has lost its appetite or otherwise doesn't seem its usual self. Writing down a list of your cat's symptoms before taking it to the veterinary surgery will both help you to remember them and give the vet valuable information on which to act.

If your feline doesn't appear unduly bothered by a symptom, wait for twenty-four hours to see if it clears up (vomiting for example, may simply be caused by having swallowed a number of hairs, by having eaten too much or too quickly or by having

A CAT WILL USUALLY ALERT YOU TO A PROBLEM.

ingested something that disagrees with the cat's digestion), but if it persists thereafter, take it to the vet's.

Finally, while you should never ignore a chronic symptom, don't be too alarmed by the doom-and-gloom pictures that the following lists may paint and remember that if they are addressed in time, many of these symptoms can be halted in their tracks: Caspar, for example, has suffered bouts of both colitis and cystitis in the past, but, following the appropriate veterinary treatment, has made a full recovery and is today free of both conditions.

CHECKING FOR SYMPTOMS

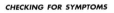

LUMPS AND BUMPS

Hard, throbbing, pus-filled lump: abscess*.

Soft, fluid-filled swelling: cyst.

Soft, blood-filled swelling: haematoma; see also aural haematoma (page 127).

A number of hard nodules: fungal infection, feline leprosy.

Tumour: benign or malignant growth; see also feline leukaemia (page 89).

MOBILITY PROBLEMS

Lack of co-ordination: poisoning*, feline infectious peritonitis, eclampsia (in mother cats), stroke; see also feline panleucopenia (page 88).

Trembling: shock, poisoning*, hypothermia, neurological disorder.

Twitching and spasms: poisoning*, eclampsia (in mother cats), tetanus.

Staggering: poisoning*, injury, concussion, eclampsia (in mother cats), encephalitis; see also middle- and inner-ear infections (page 128).

Fits* or convulsions: poisoning*, calcium or thiamine (vitamin B1) deficiency, infection, head injury, epilepsy, meningitis, feline infectious peritonitis, brain tumour, hepatitis, nephritis (kidney disease), hypoglycaemia (diabetes), eclampsia (in mother cats).

Limping or stiffness: injury (sprain, fracture), foreign body in the paw, bone infection, rickets, vitamin A poisoning, tumour, nephritis, cystitis, tetanus, arthritis, rheumatism, inflamed or dislocated joint, spinal damage.

Stiff neck: vitamin A poisoning.

Swollen leg or paw: injury (sprain, fracture), infection, abscess*, tumour, arthritis, oedema (dropsy), inflamed or dislocated joint.

Paralysis: injury, concussion, poisoning*, iliac thrombosis, stroke, encephalitis, brain tumour, spinal damage, tetanus.

RESPIRATORY PROBLEMS

Chronic sneezing: allergic reaction to airborne pollutants, asthma; see also feline infectious respiratory disease (page 90).

Wheezing: bronchial asthma, heart disease, lungworms.

Coughing: foreign body stuck in the throat, allergic reaction to airborne pollutants, growths in the mouth or throat; bronchitis, heart disease, lungworms, heartworms; see also worms (pages 91 to 92), feline infectious respiratory disease (page 90).

Catarrh: fungal infection; see also feline infectious respiratory disease (page 90).

Abnormal breathing patterns: heatstroke, hypothermia, shock, poisoning*, foreign body stuck in the nose, asthma, injury of the lung or chest, fungal infection, bronchitis, pneumonia, pleurisy, heart disease, anaemia, post-partum haemorrhage or eclampsia (in mother cats); see also feline infectious respiratory disease and feline leukaemia (pages 89 and 90).

URINARY PROBLEMS

Chronic thirst: poisoning*, gastritis, enteritis, diabetes, nephritis, hepatitis, pyometra or puerperal metritis (in mother cats); see also feline panleucopenia (page 88).

Increased urination or urinary incontinence: psychological unsettlement, nephritis, old age, diabetes, urethral infection or damage, hormonal imbalance (in females), neurological or spinal damage.

Bleeding from the penis: bladder infection.

Blood-tinged urine: injury, urinary-tract blockage or infection, nephritis, cystitis.

Straining when urinating: urinary-tract blockage or infection, cystitis, calculi (or urolithias, urinary-tract stones).

GASTRIC AND BOWEL PROBLEMS

Abnormal eating patterns: increased need for nourishment, diabetes; see also worms (pages 91 to 92) and feline leukaemia (page 89).

Drooling: foreign body stuck in the throat, mouth affliction, heatstroke, poisoning*, ulcerative glossitis, fits* or convulsions; see also feline infectious respiratory disease (page 90).

Vomiting: furballs, indigestion, gastritis, enteritis, poisoning*, feline infectious peritonitis, feline dysautonomia (Key-Gaskell syndrome), hepatitis, pancreatitis, nephritis, diabetes, puerperal metritis, pyometra or eclampsia (in mother cats), intestinal blockage, constipation; see also worms (pages 91 to 92), feline panleucopenia, feline infectious respiratory disease and feline leukaemia (pages 88 to 90).

Abdominal pain: constipation, poisoning*, feline infectious peritonitis, enteritis, hepatitis, nephritis, calculi (or urolithias, urinary-tract stones), pancreatitis, puerperal metritis (in mother cats), intestinal blockage; see also feline panleucopenia (page 88).

Diarrhoea: food intolerance, stress, gastritis, enteritis, feline infectious peritonitis, hepatitis, spinal damage; see also worms (pages 91 to 92), feline panleucopenia and feline leukaemia (pages 88 and 90).

Blood or mucus in the faeces: constipation, colitis, enteritis; see also feline panleucopenia (page 88).

Constipation: lack of water and a dry diet, furballs, intestinal blockage, rectal prolapse, liver disease, feline dysautonomia (Key-Gaskell syndrome), loss of muscular tone in older cats, lack of exercise, spinal damage; see also worms (pages 91 to 92).

Anal irritation: blocked anal glands; see also worms (page 91 to 92), maggots and eczema and dermatitis (pages 124 and 125).

EMERGENCY ACTION

If, despite all of your safety precautions, the worst comes to the worst and your cat has an accident or another type of life-threatening encounter, the following reference section may prove helpful in giving it emergency treatment. Once you have stabilised its condition, however, you should immediately phone the vet for further advice and instructions. Thereafter, you'll probably be asked to take it to the vet's at once for expert remedial – even life-saving – treatment.

Although a traumatised feline will probably not in any case be interested in eating or drinking, do not offer it any food or water in case a pre-operative general anaesthetic is required. Remember, too, that a cat that has met with any kind of mishap will be terrified by what has befallen it, so try to stay calm in case you drive it into an even greater state of panic, talk to it soothingly and reassuringly and handle it with the utmost gentleness.

DISINFECT A SKIN WOUND WITH COTTON WOOL DIPPED IN SALINE SOLUTION.

A final word of caution: never give your cat an aspirin: despite its status as a human panacea, aspirin has a toxic effect on the feline body and may cause irreversible liver damage.

SCRATCHES, MINOR CUTS AND PUNCTURE WOUNDS

If a cat has suffered at the teeth or claws of another feline, it's important to disinfect the wound because the injured cat will inevitably lick it, thereby introducing infection-inducing bacteria and increasing the danger of an abscess developing. The same applies to minor cuts inflicted, perhaps, by a splinter of glass or a thorn (if it is still embedded in the skin, remove it with a pair of tweezers). Puncture wounds caused by claws or teeth, and even deep scratches, rarely bleed for long, and once the bleeding has stopped, if necessary clip away the surrounding hair and then clean and disinfect the wounded area with cotton wool dipped in saline solution (a small amount of salt dissolved in warm water). If such a wound appears to have become infected or otherwise gives you cause for concern, seek veterinary advice.

ABSCESSES

If an abscess does develop from a wound that has become infected, you will feel it as a throbbing swelling. Because the pus within it needs to be drawn out before the healing process can begin, you can help the process along by pressing a pad of cotton wool soaked in hot (but not boiling) saline solution against the abscess and holding it there for a minute or so before gently drying the abscess, repeating the process four hours later if necessary. When the abscess bursts, wipe away the pus and again disinfect the area with warm saline solution (to which some feline authorities recommend adding a few drops of hydrogen peroxide). If the abscess proves stubbornly resistant to home treatment, take the cat to the vet's – in any case a sensible precaution because antibiotics may be required to prevent reinfection – for the abscess to be lanced. Once clear of pus, the site of the abscess should be kept open for a day or so (and cleaned every few hours) to avoid a new abscess forming.

INSECT STINGS AND SNAKE BITES

The instinctive response of many cats to flying insects is to try to catch them, which may have painful consequences if the insect in question is a bee or wasp. Unless your cat has been stung in the mouth or on the periphery of the eye, when you should immediately apply an ice cube and then whisk it to the vet's to prevent the ballooning swelling from seriously impeding its breathing or vision, you can treat insect stings yourself. To do this, if it is visible and appears easily removable, pull out the sting with a pair of tweezers and then clean the area with saline solution. The pain of a wasp sting may be alleviated by wiping it with vinegar, and that of a bee sting with a mixture of water and a few drops of hydrogen peroxide. If the sting has broken off, however, which will make its removal difficult, it may be wiser to seek the help of your vet, who may also prescribe an antihistamine ointment.

If you are certain that your cat has been bitten by a snake, but are not sure whether it was of the venomous variety, take it to the vet's at once so that a general anti-venom can be administered before it is too late.

GIVE A TRAUMATISED CAT SOME GENTLE REASSURANCE.

NEEDLES AND THREAD

Lengths of thread exert a magnetic attraction on many felines, which can be particularly dangerous if the thread is attached to a needle. If you think that your cat has swallowed a needle and thread, first open its mouth in the same way as you would to give it a pill (see pages 136 to 137) and check inside to see if the needle has become stuck in its mouth. If you can see the needle, it's best to arrange for the vet to remove it as soon as possible rather than risk damaging the cat (which will no doubt struggle wildly) by trying to extract it yourself. And if you can't see the needle, but still suspect that your cat has ingested it, again take it to the vet's for an X-ray. If your suspicion is confirmed, an operation may be required to extract the needle, which could otherwise cause a serious injury on its passage through the feline digestive system.

If you see a length of thread or string hanging from your cat's rectum, do not attempt to pull it out lest you damage its bowel. If a significant amount of thread is dangling free, cut it to a length of about 5 centimetres (2 inches) so that your cat cannot see it, or get a good hold on it, thereby similarly injuring itself. In most instances, the thread will eventually be excreted through the natural movement of the bowel, but if it is still visible after a few days, consult your vet for further advice.

BURNS

Different types of burn require different emergency treatment, but all will necessitate a follow-up visit to the vet's because the depth – and therefore seriousness – of a burn may not be evident to the inexperienced eye. Scalds or heat burns should first be cooled either under cold running water or with an ice cube (although some authorities advocate smothering the burn with petroleum jelly, others believe that this simply serves to seal in the heat) and then loosely covered with a piece of cloth, but not bandaged.

Chemical, caustic or acid burns, which may be more widespread, require instant action to remove the corrosive substance from the cat's fur and skin. To do this, fill a bucket, sink or bath with tepid water, add a handful of either sodium bicarbonate (for acid burns) or boracic acid (for caustic burns), don a pair of rubber gloves to protect your own skin and then lift the cat into the water. Be warned, however, that your cat – which will be both frightened and in pain – will struggle, so be firm, but not brutal. Finally, when you think that you have removed all traces of the culprit substance, wrap the cat in a blanket and take it to the veterinary surgery.

IF YOUR CAT HAS A CLOSE ENCOUNTER WITH FIRE, COOL THE BURN WITH COLD WATER OR ICE.

POISONING

Rat and mouse poisons contain substances (such as warfarin, arsenic, phosphorus and thallium) that are just as toxic to felines as to rodents, as are many insecticides and other garden pest-control products. Among the more innocuous-seeming household products that may poison your cat can be counted disinfectants (especially those containing phenol), household paint (if it contains lead), creosote, wood preservatives, tar and turpentine. If you intend to use any of these products around your home or garden, it's therefore crucial to keep your cat away from their immediate vicinity. Unfortunately, however, you may not be able to prevent a wandering feline from coming into contact with them in a neighbouring garden.

Although you probably won't have seen your cat ingest a toxin, if it has been poisoned, you'll be alerted to the seriousness of the situation by the dramatic symptoms listed above (see pages 144 to 146), indicating that it requires urgent veterinary treatment if it is to survive, so before you do anything else, phone the vet for advice. If you believe that the cat has been poisoned by licking a toxic substance off its fur, you may be advised to wash it off (see page 151) as soon as you can. And

ADMINISTER SALT AND WATER SOLUTION THROUGH A SYRINGE

although an emetic – usually in the form of a generous quantity of salt mixed with warm water administered through a plastic syringe (see page 137) – will encourage the cat to vomit up its toxic stomach contents, do not apply this remedy unless your vet has advocated it because regurgitating a corrosive substance could have disastrous consequences for your cat.

PESTICIDES, CERTAIN PAINTS AND A HOST OF OTHER HOUSEHOLD PRODUCTS COULD POISON YOUR CAT.

REMOVING TOXIC SUBSTANCES FROM A CAT'S FUR

If your cat has clearly had a brush with a freshly creosoted fence or painted wall, do not ignore the evidence in the belief that the feline will simply lick it away itself: not only may this be an insurmountable task, but many such substances will poison your cat if it ingests them through self-grooming. You will therefore have to wash the substances off the feline's fur using a mild shampoo (remember to wear rubber gloves so that your skin remains untainted), followed by a thorough rinsing and drying. Cutting off the affected area of fur may still be necessary. Thereafter, your priority should be a trip to the vet.

ELECTRIC SHOCK

The most common scenario in which felines receive electric shocks is when they chew through an electrical cable. Should this happen to your cat, turn off the power supply before ministering to your stricken feline, whose mouth may still be connected to the cable, but if this is inaccessible, pull on a pair of rubber gloves (in any case a sensible precaution, especially if the shock has caused your cat to release a quantity of electricity-conducting urine) and pull your cat free. The unfortunate cat may have suffered heart failure, so if it appears to be comatose, check its pulse and, if this is weak, try to resuscitate it (see page 153) before ferrying it to the vet's.

CHOKING AND FITS

If your cat starts choking (as opposed to preparing to vomit or to expel a furball), and provided that it will allow you to get close enough to examine it, immobilise it by wrapping it in a towel and then open its mouth to see whether its windpipe has been blocked by a foreign object. You may need to depress its tongue with a pencil to get a clear view; shining a torch into its mouth may also help. If there is indeed something in its mouth, reach inside and pull it out with a blunt pair of pliers or tweezers (if you use your fingers, you may be bitten), but if you have no success, you may have to resort to using the emergency procedure recommended for drowning (see page 152). The next step is to take your cat to the vet's immediately.

The sight of a cat having convulsions can be just as frightening for the human spectator as the experience is for the feline suffering the fit, who may be frothing at the mouth and losing control of its bladder and bowels as its body goes into uncontrollable spasms. It's important to keep calm and phone the vet at once for instructions, which you should follow to the letter. You will probably be advised not to approach the cat, but to cover it with a blanket until the fit subsides, whereupon you should wipe away any froth from its mouth and nose to ease its breathing and clean up any accidents. Thereafter, transfer the cat to a dark, quiet and warm place and cover it with a clean blanket until it can receive veterinary attention to ascertain the cause – and poisoning (see page 150) is a distinct possibility – that will dictate the treatment.

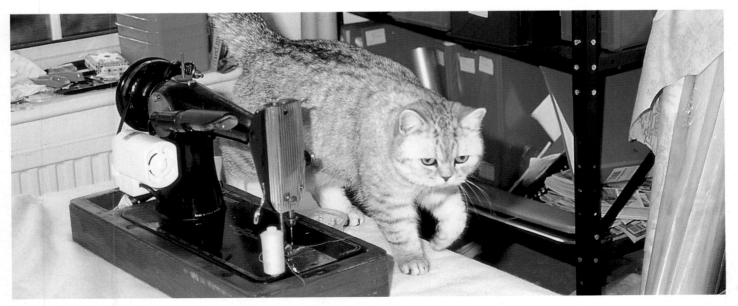

FORESTALL YOUR CAT RECEIVING AN ELECTRIC SHOCK BY TUCKING ELECTRICAL CABLES OUT OF ITS WAY.

DROWNING

Should you find your cat lying prone in a puddle or pond, its life is at threat from drowning and you will therefore need to expel the water from its lungs before it succumbs. To do this, first grasp both of its back legs (not its tail) firmly in one hand, raise them so that the cat is upside down and give its back a sharp slap, which should force the water out of its lungs. If that doesn't work, however, the next step is to hold its back legs with one hand and the scruff of its neck with the other and then to swing it firmly downwards. If the situation looks really desperate, and only then, again grasp the cat's back legs and swing it vigorously around in a circle, which should create sufficient centrifugal force for the fluid to be ejected from the lungs through the mouth. Thereafter, you may need to resuscitate the cat by breathing into its nostrils (see page 153).

BROKEN BONES

Even if you don't think that your cat has been involved in a fall or accident, if it is limping badly and the suspect area is swollen, it may have broken a bone. You can test for this by gently lifting the cat onto a table to ascertain whether the suspect leg looks different from its partner or your cat avoids putting any weight onto it. If you think that your cat has sustained a fracture, wrap it gently in a blanket, taking care not to jolt or put pressure on the limb, place it in a large cardboard box and take it to the vet's for an X-ray and whatever further treatment, perhaps a splint, plaster cast or internal pinning, is deemed necessary. Fractures in other parts of the body require urgent veterinary attention

STEMMING BLEEDING

If your cat is bleeding, but not haemorrhaging, from a wound, you may be able to stem the blood flow by applying a wad of clean fabric (perhaps a handkerchief) or cotton wool to the wound, pressing it down firmly and then bandaging it (see pages 138 to 139).

In cases of profuse bleeding, before applying a pressure bandage, it is usually advisable to try to stem the flow of blood by pressing a wad of cotton wool firmly against the appropriate artery: on the hollow between the neck and shoulder for head and neck wounds; on the bone above the inner elbow (the raised artery should be visible) for the front legs; for the back legs, the corresponding point on the inner thigh; and underneath the base of the tail for tail wounds. Although applying a tourniquet may be effective in halting a haemorrhage, don't attempt this unless you know exactly what you are doing. Thereafter, wash the area with saline solution and apply a pressure bandage. If blood seeps through the bandage, put another over the top, but don't remove the first in case you retard the clotting process. In both instances, it's important to rush your cat to the vet's as soon as possible because the wound may need stitches and antibiotics.

STEM THE FLOW OF BLOOD, THEN BANDAGE

RESUSCITATING AN UNCONSCIOUS CAT

Having monitored the unconscious cat's pulse (pages 135 to 136) to ascertain the strength of its vital signs and hence the gravity of its condition, if the situation looks grim, prompt action may save its life. This is especially vital if the feline's eyes are bulging and its gums are turning blue, both of which indicate oxygen deprivation. There are three ways of resuscitating an unconscious cat whose heart may have stopped beating and who has stopped breathing: firstly, by giving it a heart massage to stimulate its heart to resume beating, secondly, by kick-starting the breathing process either by applying pressure to the lungs or, thirdly, by administering mouth-to-nose resuscitation. In all cases, if the cat is wearing one, the first step is to remove its collar to prevent its airways from being restricted, the second being to shift the cat onto its side.

A heart massage can be given by rubbing the flats of both of your hands over the cat's chest, in the process making sure that you apply as little pressure as possible in case you exacerbate any existing damage. With luck, the heart will start to pump blood again, but artificial respiration may nevertheless still be required. Using the flat of one hand, jab it sharply against the cat's chest behind the elbow to encourage air to leave the lungs, then remove your hand for five seconds to enable the lungs to take in air before reapplying the pressure. If this fails to kick-start the breathing process, the next step is to administer mouth-to-nose resuscitation. To do this, first open the cat's mouth and pull out its tongue so that it does not obstruct its windpipe and wipe away any blood, vomit or foreign objects within using a clean cloth. Close the cat's mouth again, tilt back its head slightly, and then, using your lips, blow air into the cat's nostrils for a count of three, take a two-second breather and then repeat the manoeuvre until, it is hoped, your cat shows signs of life.

Whether or not your cat responds positively to these procedures, it will require urgent veterinary treatment (see page 154 for how to transport it as safely as possible to the vet's).

IF YOUR CAT IS UNCONSCIOUS, JUDGE THE GRAVITY OF THE SITUATION BY FIRST TAKING ITS PULSE.

THE NEXT STEP IS TO ASCERTAIN WHETHER THE CAT'S HEART IS STILL BEATING.

RESTRAINING AND HANDLING AN INJURED CAT

If your cat has had a traumatic or injurious experience, it may have been rendered frantic with shock and pain, in which case you will have to restrain it, both so that you can examine it and to prepare it for transportation to the veterinary surgery. One way of doing this is to encircle the upright cat's chest with one hand and, with the other, to grip the scruff of its neck firmly, which should trigger a kittenhood reflex that makes it freeze, enabling you to pick it up (not by its scruff, but by supporting its chest and nether regions) and wrap it in a blanket before transferring it to a cat-carrier or cardboard box. In more extreme circumstances, you may have to chase the panic-stricken cat into a room, shut the door and throw a towel or blanket over it so that you can pick it up without sustaining painful lacerations from its teeth and claws (putting on a pair of thick gardening gloves may literally save your skin). Try to calm the feline down during the immobilisation process by talking to it quietly and comfortingly.

If the injured cat is already immobile – perhaps following a fall or traffic accident – it's generally not advisable to alter the position in which it is lying lest you inflict additional damage on the cat's body. That having been said, however, the best way to prepare it for transportation, and lessen the risk of injuring it further, is gently to shift it onto its side. As delicately as you can, and with your palms facing upward, place one hand under its chest, where the front legs meet the torso, and the other under its pelvis, where the back legs adjoin its body. (Never, however, lift up its head in case you cause it to choke on blood or vomit, although if you can arrange its head so that it is a little lower than its body while still being supported, this will ward off brain damage.) Thereafter, first lift it onto a blanket or towel and, preferably with you holding one end of the blanket or towel and someone else the other to minimise any jolting, transfer the makeshift stretcher into a large cardboard box (or a cat-carrier, although a box may be more secure). Cover the cat with another blanket to keep it warm – and, if possible, place a warm hot-water bottle near it – to prevent it from going into deeper shock, before taking it to the veterinary surgery, doing your best to make the transportation process as smooth as possible to avoid aggravating the cat's injuries.

IMMOBILISE A PANIC-STRICKEN CAT BY WRAPPING IT IN A TOWEL.

chapter 6

CAT BREEDS

LONG-HAIRED BREEDS

IN THE WILD A LION MAY GROW A LONGER 'RUFF' OR MANE AROUND THE NECK.

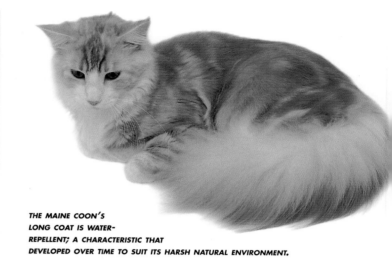

THE MAINE COON'S LONG COAT IS WATER-REPELLENT; A CHARACTERISTIC THAT DEVELOPED OVER TIME TO SUIT ITS HARSH NATURAL ENVIRONMENT.

Fabri de Peiresc, brought a long-haired cat to France from Turkey, and the first clearly described long-haired cats in Europe were given the name Angora cats, called after the capital city of Turkey – now Ankara – where these cats appear to have been known for centuries.

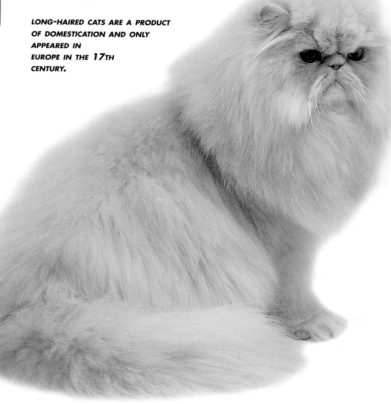

LONG-HAIRED CATS ARE A PRODUCT OF DOMESTICATION AND ONLY APPEARED IN EUROPE IN THE 17TH CENTURY.

In the wild, there are no long-haired cats, although some, like lions, do grow ruffs or manes of longer fur. Even the Amur Tiger and the Snow Leopard, which both endure particularly harsh winters near the snow line, only grow hairs about 12.5 cm (5 in) long, which size for size, are quite short compared to domesticated long-haired cats. Long hair on a wild cat would be impractical: it would get tangled and matted, pick up burrs and thorns, as well as parasites and be impossible to groom properly.

Long-haired cats are only mentioned in historical records long after the cat had become domesticated, and were only mentioned in Europe in the 17th century when it was claimed that a long-haired cat was imported into Italy from Persia in 1620 by Pietro de Valle. At the end of the century, French scientist and traveller, Nicholas

TURKISH ANGORA

After the Crystal Palace Cat Show in 1871, in London, standards for Persians and Angoras were written by Harrison Weir. Subsequent breeding within the guidelines has meant that stocky build remains an essential characteristic of Longhairs, but their faces are much shorter and their coats much longer.

There are, however, some long-haired cats which are not Persian and hail from climates where a longer, thicker coat is an asset. The Norwegian Forest Cat and the Maine Coon have a different body type to Longhair/Persian cats, with slimmer legs and trunks and narrower faces with longer noses. Despite their long hair, these cats don't require as much grooming as their 'exotic' cousins whose fur sheds copiously at each stroke of their silky coats!

By the time of the cat shows of the 19th century, both Persian cats, said to have come from the Persian province of Chorazan, and the Angora were known in Europe, and considered as 'status symbol' pets. But the Persian type became the most fancied and the Angora was soon to disappear from show benches and homes. Recently, the original Turkish Angora Cat became established as a new breed in the United States from imported cats bred deliberately at Ankara Zoo to protect the species from extinction.

For most people, the name 'Persian' thus became synonymous with long-haired cats, and although the British Cat Fancy (CFA) now officially uses the designation Long-haired for self-coloured cats, with other colours classified as separate breeds. In the United States, these cats are still called Persians, and the different colours are listed as varieties.

NORWEGIAN FOREST CAT

BIRMAN

DATE OF ORIGIN: unknown

PLACE OF ORIGIN: Burma (now Myanmar) or France

ANCESTRY: disputed

OTHER NAMES: Sacred Cat of Burma

COLOURS:

SELF (SOLID) AND TORTIE POINTS: seal, chocolate, red, blue, lilac, cream, seal tortie, blue tortie, lilac tortie and chocolate tortie

TABBY POINTS: colours as for self and tortie points

COAT LENGTH: long, with full ruff around neck and slightly curled on stomach

TYPE OF FUR: fine and silky, snarl- and tangle- resistant

SIZE: 4.5—8 kg (10—18 lb)

A cat of mystery, the Birman is also known as the Sacred Cat of Burma, although it has no connection with the Burmese breed (see page 211). With its pale-coloured body, dark points (mask, ears, tails and legs) and long coat, the Birman does bear a resemblance to the Colourpoint Longhair (Himalayan Persian in US) (see page 168 except for one striking feature – the white gloves on the Birman's paws, which are possibly due to a recessive white-spotting gene, although the romantic tale of the Birman's origins is far more entertaining.

SEAL TABBY POINT BIRMAN

The legend goes that before the time of Buddha, the Khmer people of Southeast Asia built beautiful temples to honour their gods, in particular, the god Song-Hyo and the goddess Tsun-Kyan-Kse. A golden figure of the goddess, with sapphire eyes, was kept at the temple of Lao-Tsun, guarded by 100 pure-white cats. One of these cats was called Sinh, the companion of an old priest called Mun-Ha – whose silver-white beard was said to have been braided by the god Song-Hyo himself. One night, foreign raiders attacked the temple, killing Mun-Ha as he knelt in devotion before the statue of the goddess. Immediately, Sinh jumped on the body of his master and faced the goddess. The soul of the priest entered the cat and, as it did so, its eyes became sapphire-blue, like those of the goddess. The cat's face, ears and legs took on the colour of the fertile land – except for the paws, which remained pure white because, according to the legend, they had touched the priest's beard. (On the Birman's rear paws, the white 'boots' extend up the back of the hock to a point known in North America as the 'laces'.)

BLUE TABBY POINT BIRMAN

BLUE POINT BIRMAN

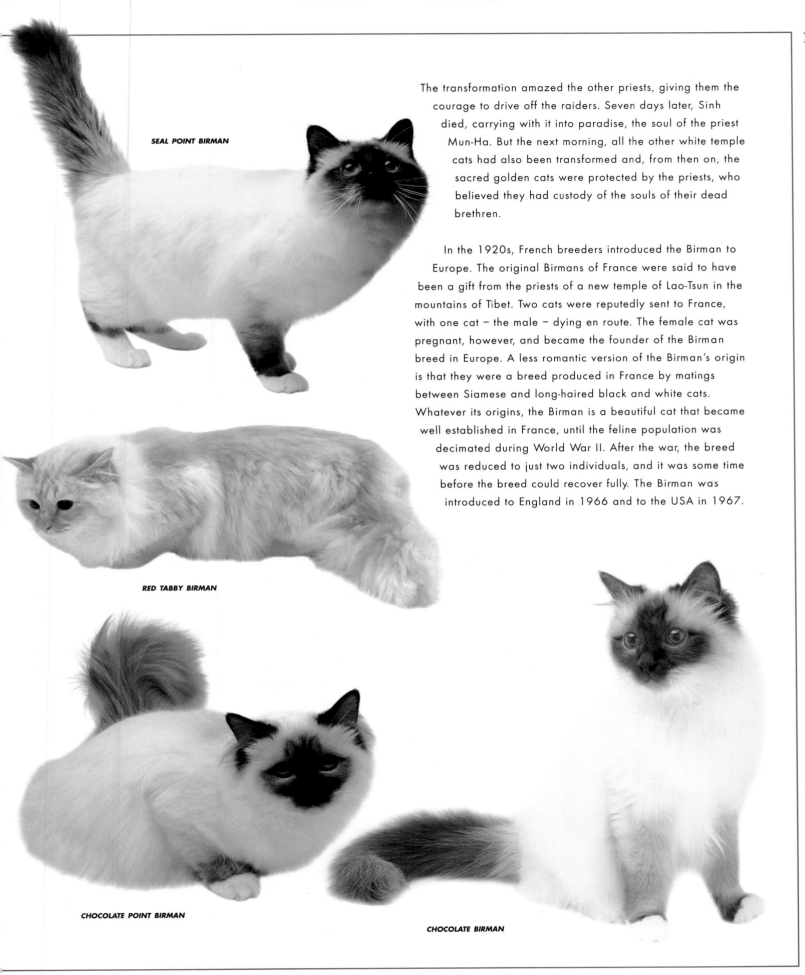

SEAL POINT BIRMAN

RED TABBY BIRMAN

CHOCOLATE POINT BIRMAN

CHOCOLATE BIRMAN

The transformation amazed the other priests, giving them the courage to drive off the raiders. Seven days later, Sinh died, carrying with it into paradise, the soul of the priest Mun-Ha. But the next morning, all the other white temple cats had also been transformed and, from then on, the sacred golden cats were protected by the priests, who believed they had custody of the souls of their dead brethren.

In the 1920s, French breeders introduced the Birman to Europe. The original Birmans of France were said to have been a gift from the priests of a new temple of Lao-Tsun in the mountains of Tibet. Two cats were reputedly sent to France, with one cat – the male – dying en route. The female cat was pregnant, however, and became the founder of the Birman breed in Europe. A less romantic version of the Birman's origin is that they were a breed produced in France by matings between Siamese and long-haired black and white cats. Whatever its origins, the Birman is a beautiful cat that became well established in France, until the feline population was decimated during World War II. After the war, the breed was reduced to just two individuals, and it was some time before the breed could recover fully. The Birman was introduced to England in 1966 and to the USA in 1967.

A strong cat, with a stocky body, thickset legs and large, round paws, the Birman is a very gentle and highly intelligent cat. Its coat is not as fluffy in texture as the Himalayan/Colourpoint Longhair, but more silky – like that of a Turkish Angora in length and texture. In winter months, a ruff around the neck is apparent. For many fanciers, the Birman's most striking features are the eyes that are almost round, slightly slanted and a beautiful, deep sapphire-blue.

BLUE POINT BIRMAN

The Seal Point and the Blue Point Birman were the original colours of the breed introduced by the French in the 1920s, and for some purists these remain the only true Birman colours, although breeders have introduced other point colourings including chocolate and lilac (where the points are a pinkish-grey, with the nose leather to match), red (flame), tortoiseshell and tabby points, which must show clear 'frown' marks between the eyes and lighter 'spectacles', as well as spotted cheek pads, striped legs and a ringed tail. Furthermore, in the US, some breeders have produced short-haired Birman-patterned cats known as Snowshoe Cats or Silver Laces (see page 204).

LILAC POINT BIRMAN

RED BIRMAN

SEAL TORTOISESHELL BIRMAN

ANGORA/ORIENTAL LONGHAIR

DATE OF ORIGIN: 1970s

PLACE OF ORIGIN: Britain

ANCESTRY: Siamese/Abyssinian crosses

OTHER NAMES: Javanese (Europe), Mandarin and previously known in the US as Oriental Longhair

COLOURS:

SELF (SOLID) COLOURS: black, chocolate, cinnamon, red, blue, lilac, fawn, cream, caramel, apricot and white (blue–, green– and odd–eyed)

TORTOISESHELL COLOURS: tortoiseshell, chocolate tortoiseshell, cinnamon, blue, lilac, fawn and caramel tortoiseshell

SMOKE, SHADED, SILVER SHADED AND TIPPED COLOURS: as for self and tortie except white

TABBIES (ALL PATTERNS): brown, chocolate, cinnamon, red, blue, lilac, fawn, cream, caramel, tortie, chocolate tortie, cinnamon tortie, blue tortie, lilac tortie, fawn tortie and caramel tortie

SILVER TABBY COLOURS (ALL PATTERNS): as for standard tabbies

COAT LENGTH: medium-long

TYPE OF FUR: very fine with tendency to curl, no thick undercoat

SIZE: 2.5—5.5 kg (5—11 lb)

The Angora breed suffers from a little confusion because it has a number of names: in continental Europe it is known as the Javanese – even though some North American cat associations use this name to refer to some colours of the Balinese! In North America, the British Angora was once called the Oriental Longhair, implying that it was a descendent of the Oriental Shorthair. There is now, however, a true breed called the Oriental Longhair (see page 182) with that descent.

The most important thing to note about the Angora, is that this cat is not related to either the Oriental Longhairs, or the Turkish Angora saved from extinction by the breeding programme at Ankara Zoo and now a protected breed. The modern Angora, would perhaps best be called the 'British Angora' since this breed was developed in the UK by Maureen Silson in the mid 1960s when a sorrel (red) Abyssinian was mated with a Seal Point Siamese in an effort to produce a Siamese with ticked points! The descendants inherited the cinnamon trait – producing cinnamon Oriental Shorthairs – and the gene for long hair, which led to the creation of the first Angora, who was called Cuckoo.

BLACK ANGORA

The elegant, lithe-bodied Angora, is one of the oldest breeds of cat. It may well have been the first long-haired cat to arrive in Europe, although it was never as popular as the more sturdily built Persian. The Angora has a similar temperament to the other Oriental breeds, being lively and inquisitive, but also capable of long periods of inactivity, which they love to spend sleeping in warm, comfortable places. Angoras have a very fine, silky coat and, having no woolly undercoat, they require less grooming than Persians/Longhairs and their coat lies flat on their bodies. Angora coats are slow to mature and young cats often have short coats for quite some time. Their bodies are carried on long, slim and well-muscled legs – the forelegs are shorter than the hind legs – and end in small, oval paws with tufts of fur at the toes. Their tails, which are carried up, are long and fluffy and taper to a fine end. Their ears are large and pricked atop a small (in proportion to the body) wedge-shaped head with large, almond shaped eyes. Angoras' eyes are green in all coat colours – except in white cats, when they are blue- or odd-eyed.

BLACK SILVER SHADED ANGORA/ ORIENTAL LONGHAIR

TURKISH ANGORA

DATE OF ORIGIN: 1400s

PLACE OF ORIGIN: Turkey

ANCESTRY: unknown, possibly household cats

OTHER NAMES: none

COLOURS:

SELF (SOLID) AND TORTIE COLOURS: white, black, red, blue, cream, tortie and blue–cream

SMOKE AND SHADED COLOURS: as for self and tortie except white

TABBY COLOURS (CLASSIC AND MACKEREL): brown, red, blue and cream

SILVER TABBY COLOURS (CLASSIC MACKEREL): silver

BICOLOURS: all self and tortie colours, with white

COAT LENGTH: medium–long

TYPE OF FUR: fine and silky with negligible undercoat

SIZE: 2.5—5 kg (6—11 lb)

It has been suggested that the Turkish Angora traces its descent from the manul, or Pallas' cat (Felis manul) found in the steppes, rocky terrain and wooded mountainsides of central Asia. This handsome wild cat is orangey-grey with black and white head markings, and the story goes that the Tartars domesticated it and took it to Turkey. It is more likely though, that the Turkish Angora is a distant relative of the Persian, with the two lines developing separately over the centuries and the Turkish Angora becoming established in the Turkish capital, Angora (now Ankara). It seems that the gene for long hair mutated in – or spread to – a group of cats with the lithe body build (known to breeders as 'foreign'), and because there were limited opportunities for breeding outside the group, the long-coated characteristic became fixed, so that a true-breeding, long-haired cat with a foreign body evolved.

In the 16th century, Turkish Angoras were sent as diplomatic gifts by the Sultan to Europe and were the first long-haired cats to be seen there. At first they were very popular, but later they lost ground to the Persians and newer Longhair breeds. While they continued to thrive in their homeland, by the end of World War II, the Turkish Angora was extinct in the Western world. In the 1950s and 1960s however, breeding pairs of Turkish Angoras were said to have been brought from Ankara Zoo and taken to the USA where a breeding programme was established, while other Turkish Angoras were taken to Sweden and Britain. These cats formed the foundation stock for the pedigree Turkish Angoras of North America and continental Europe, and the Turkish cats of Britain.

WHITE TURKISH ANGORA

In many respects, the Turkish Angora is similar in appearance to the Angora (see page 161) as both share the elegant, lithe body shape with long, slim legs. Furthermore, both have small paws with tufts of fur on the toes and small wedge-shaped heads. The ears are large and pricked and, like the Angora, the Turkish has a long, fluffy tail, carried elegantly up.

The medium-long coat is very fine and silky, and shimmers when the cat moves. It is shed in the summer months, when the Turkish Angora appears more of a short-hair cat – with the exception of its luxurious tail.

The medium-long coat is very fine and silky, and shimmers when the cat moves. It is shed in the summer months, when the Turkish Angora appears more of a short-hair cat – with the exception of its luxurious tail.

In Turkey, Angoras were to be seen in many colours, each with their own descriptive names such as sarman (red tabby) and teku (silver tabby). Today, Turkish Angoras are recognised in a variety of colours, shades and patterns, such as tortie-and-white, black – which must be coal black and solid from the roots to the tip of each hair – and Smoke. Smoke Turkish Angoras appear to be full-coloured cats when they are in repose, but when the cat moves, the subtle colours of the undercoat become apparent. Combined with their inherent grace, the colourings of the winter coat do indeed look like swirls of smoke.

It is, however, the blue-eyed, white Turkish Angoras – which regrettably like other white cats of most other breeds are often deaf in either one or both ears – who are the great favourites. To many fanciers though, the Ankara kedi, as they are known still in Turkey, the 'odd–eyed white' – one blue and one orange – is the classic colour and eye combination of the historical, pure breed.

BALINESE

DATE OF ORIGIN: 1950s

PLACE OF ORIGIN: USA

ANCESTRY: Long-haired Siamese

OTHER NAMES: sometimes called Javanese in the US

COLOURS:

CFA RECOGNISED: lilac point, blue point, chocolate point and seal point

OTHER COLOURS/VARIANTS: Javanese point colours in CFA – seal point, seal tortie tabby point, chocolate tortie point, red tabby point, blue tabby point, seal tabby point and chocolate tabby point

COAT LENGTH: medium–long, with a tendency to curl, but generally shorter than other long–haired breeds

TYPE OF FUR: fine and silky with no undercoat

SIZE: 2.5—5 kg (6—11 lb)

CREAM POINT BALINESE

For many years, long-haired kittens had appeared from time to time in the litters of particular Siamese bloodlines. In 1928, a long-haired Siamese was registered in Britain with the CFA, but generally, such long-haired offspring were regarded by cat breeders and fanciers as 'faulty' since their long hair disqualified them from being shown as Siamese. In the main, these lovely cats were passed on to owners as house pets. In the 1940s, however, Marion Dorsey produced Balinese kittens and a number of breeders in the US began working towards gaining recognition for these cats as a separate breed. Since the gene for long hair (l) is inherited in a recessive manner, any long-haired Siamese must be homozygous (true breeding) for long hair. This means that it must carry two of the longhair genes, and that any offspring that result from mating two such cats will also be long haired.

In 1955, 'Longhaired Siamese' were exhibited, but breeders of Siamese cats protested at the name. The breed was renamed Balinese, a name suggested by these cats' svelte lines and graceful movements, emphasised by the flow of their long, silky coat. Indeed, the Balinese in motion is reminiscent of the dancers of the Indonesian island, even though they hail from North America!

The Balinese resembles the Siamese in most ways: it has a slender, fine-boned, sleek body with a long, wedge-shaped head and deep blue, almond-shaped eyes. From the front, a Balinese's head is wide between the ears (which may be tufted), narrowing to a fine muzzle in a straight line, while in profile the nose should be straight and the chin strong. From all aspects the Balinese is a splendidly elegant-looking cat. The coat is medium long, without the fluffy undercoat of other Longhair cats, and the hairs lie more or less flat against the body. This also makes these cats easier to groom and keep tangle-free than other long-haired cats.

From a distance it can be easy to mistake a Balinese for a Siamese – that is until you see the Balinese's tail. Long and plumed, and like the Siamese, no kink or squint is allowed. In colouring, as with other long-haired, pointed cats, there is less contrast between body and point colour than is normally seen in Siamese. The CFA in America recognises only four basic point colours: seal, blue, chocolate and lilac. Breeders in other associations in Britain and Australia have, in addition, produced red-, cream-, tortie- and tabby-point Balinese, which are recognised by the CFA under the breed name of Javanese (see note right). As with all pointed cats, the coats of the Balinese darken with age, making a show cat's career quite short.

As might be expected, Balinese share many characteristics as pets with Siamese. They are incredibly acrobatic – their tubular bodies allow them to perform the greatest feats in tight spaces (mainly kitchen drawers and cupboards!). They love climbing – especially up curtains – and playing in shopping bags and will often ride on the shoulders of their owners. Highly affectionate, they also demand attention in return, and yet they still manage to retain an elegant air of aloofness! Lively and spirited cats though they are the Balinese are almost, though not quite, as talkative as Siamese!

NOTE:

In North America, the name Javanese is used to describe the varieties of Balinese cats that do not correspond to the four traditional Siamese point colours. In New Zealand, the self and spotted varieties of Balinese are called Javanese, while in Britain, the Javanese is a separate breed – the result of attempts to recreate the Angora. The Javanese was granted Championship status in 1984, and has recently been introduced to the USA.

SEAL TORTOISESHELL BALINESE

TURKISH VAN

DATE OF ORIGIN: pre-18th century

PLACE OF ORIGIN: Lake Van region, Turkey

ANCESTRY: household cats

OTHER NAMES: The Swimming Cat

COLOURS: the coat is white with markings in the recognised colours on the face and tail

BICOLOURS: auburn, cream and white with amber, blue or odd eyes

OTHER COLOURS: black, blue, tortoiseshell, blue-cream, with white

COAT LENGTH: long (coat is longer in winter months than in summer)

TYPE OF FUR: fine and silky, no undercoat

SIZE: 3—8.5 kg (7—19 lb)

Unique among small cats, the Turkish Van loves water and is an enthusiastic swimmer! Of the big cats only tigers are strong swimmers, and most domestic cats will shy away from water of any kind – even though they will sit mesmerised for hours watching goldfish in a bowl!

This breed of cat has been domesticated for several hundred years around the area of Lake Van in Turkey. Like the Turkish Angora, the Turkish Van had limited opportunities to breed outside of its native region, allowing the long-haired characteristic to become fixed, so that they became a true long-haired breed with a foreign body. Legend has it that the (ideal) white blaze or patch in the centre of the Van's forehead is the thumbprint of Allah and it is also maintained that the cats living locally at the town of Van itself are all-white with odd eyes – one green, one blue. Whatever truth there is in these popular beliefs, the restricted colour of the Van's coat makes it so distinctive that the name is also given to the pattern when it occurs in other breeds.

The modern history of the Turkish Van began in 1955, when two cats were brought home as holiday souvenirs by two British tourists who then went on to establish the breed in the UK. Although the breed spread quickly across Europe, it was not accepted by the registries until 1969. By 1982, Turkish Vans had reached North America where they were accepted by the CFA and TICA.

WHITE-AUBURN TURKISH VAN

In the GCCF, however, only the auburn and cream colours are allowed, while the other registries permit black-based colours. While other breeds know the colour simply as red, Turkish Van breeders use a much more poetic designation, 'Auburn', where ideally, the coat should be chalk-white and the red marking confined to the top of the head (markings should not extend below the level of the eyes or beyond the base of the ears) and the full brush of the feathery tail – which is as long as the cat's body. The Auburn pattern, accompanied by large, oval, amber-coloured eyes with pink rims, was the original appearance of the Turkish Van when it arrived in the West in the 1950s.

Tortie-and-White Vans appeared when black was introduced into the breed, but this pattern is difficult to breed to the breed standards – often patches of colour appear on the Van's body – which means that 'perfect' show tortie Vans are scarce, although there are lots of tortie Vans as adored pets!

In their native Turkey, Vans developed an immensely thick winter coat to protect themselves from the freezing temperatures. In the summer, they moult copiously, shedding nearly all the winter coat. The soft coat is water resistant and tends to 'break' open over any curves, rearranging itself with the cat's every move. It is a strongly muscled cat, ideally proportioned for swimming: the body is long, the legs medium length and the paws are rounded and small, with furry toe tufts and pink pads. In temperament the Van retains its sense of independence, inherited from its ancestors – rural cats used to extremes of temperature and tough lives.

WHITE-AUBURN TURKISH VAN

COLOURPOINT LONGHAIR/HIMALAYAN

DATE OF ORIGIN: 1950s

PLACE OF ORIGIN: UK and USA

ANCESTRY: Longhair, Siamese

OTHER NAMES: Himalayan Persian (USA)

COLOURS: body is ivory/cream with all point colours available

COAT LENGTH: long (12 cm/5 in)

TYPE OF FUR: very thick and silky with no woolliness

SIZE: 3.5—7 kg (8—15 lb)

CHOCOLATE COLOURPOINT

The Colourpoint Longhair, known more poetically in the US as the Himalayan Persian, is a man-made breed synthesised initially during breeding experiments to solve genetically related diseases in cats. In the 1920s, Swedish geneticist Dr. Tjebbes crossed Siamese, Persian and Birman cats. Then, in the 1930s, two Harvard Medical School researchers in the US decided that further breeding – this time with cats of known pedigree – was necessary in order to establish the inheritance of certain characteristics. They mated Siamese with smoke, silver tabbies and black Longhair/Persians, but this time as a deliberate attempt to establish a Siamese-patterned cat with a Persian coat and body type.

The first Himalayan/Colourpoint Longhair kitten, called Debutante, was born in 1935. In the meantime, other cat breeders were also experimenting in the US and in Britain to develop this breed of beautiful cats. It was called Himalayan, not because of any geographical links to the mountain range, but because this name is used for the same colour patterns in other fancy-bred small livestock, such as rabbits. In Britain, the breed was accepted – but called Colourpoint Longhair – in 1955.

LILAC COLOURPOINT

TORTOISESHELL TABBY AND WHITE MAINE COON

The head is ideally slightly longer than it is wide, with high cheekbones and ears that are large, well tufted and wide at the base. The neck is medium long, while the body is long and the chest broad. Unlike a Persian/Longhair, a Maine Coon's legs and tail are long.

In spite of its long, thick coat, a Maine Coon is remarkably low maintenance and is water-repellent, so washing is rarely required!

Rugged in coat and build, they withstand the hardest of winters and are also one of the largest breeds physically – males commonly weigh up to 7 kg (15 lb); females up to 5 kg (11 lb) and there are stories of giants of 18 kg (40 lb)! While they enjoy the company of humans, Maine Coons are very independent cats – otherwise you'd need a very large lap for them to sit on!

Throughout the history of the Maine Coon there have never been any restrictions – official or otherwise – on the patterns and colours accepted in the breed (with the sole exceptions of lilac, chocolate and Siamese patterns). Consequently Maine Coons are bred in a delightful range of colours including self, bicolours, tortoiseshells, tabby-torties (known as torbies!), shaded and, of course, tabbies – the brown classic tabby is undoubtedly the best known. Originally, only brown tabbies were given the name Maine Coon (because of their close resemblance to racoons) and all other colours and patterns were given the appellation Maine Shags.

Eye colours range from green, through gold and copper to blue, with odd eyes in white cats also permitted. In shows, eye and coat colours and combination account for only 15% of the points awarded. Much more important to judges are the head, body and coat condition.

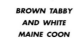

BROWN TABBY AND WHITE MAINE COON

RED SILVER AND WHITE MAINE COON

BLUE TABBY MAINE COON

WHITE GOLD EYE MAINE COON

BLUE/SILVER MAINE COON

NORWEGIAN FOREST CAT

DATE OF ORIGIN: 1930s

PLACE OF ORIGIN: Norway

ANCESTRY: farm cats

OTHER NAMES: Skogkatt or Skaukatt, Wegie

COLOURS: all coat colours and patterns acceptable, with or without white, except chocolate, lilac and Siamese patterns

COAT LENGTH: semi-long

TYPE OF FUR: Double. Thick undercoat covered by smooth, water-resistant outer hair

SIZE: 3—9 kg (7—20 lb)

Domestic cats first arrived in Scandinavia some time around AD 1000 via the Vikings' trade routes with the Byzantine Empire in the east, the capital of which was Constantinople (now Istanbul). There is evidence that cats were traded directly between the Vikings and Byzantium, since the cat population of Norway has coat colours in common with Turkish cats that are rare elsewhere in Europe. Long-haired cats are common throughout Scandinavia: while Norway has its 'Wegie', Denmark and Sweden have their own versions called the 'Racekatte' and 'Rugkatt' respectively.

BLACK TORTOISESHELL NORWEGIAN FOREST CAT

The Norwegian Forest Cat, or Norsk Skaukatt is a uniquely Scandinavian breed of cats, having evolved in the cold, northern climate of Norway. Its exact origins are unknown but, like the Maine Coon, it adapted to living in the cold and wet by growing a magnificent double coat made up of a soft woolly undercoat to keep the body warm and a long, glossy, hanging outer coat designed to shed the snow and rain. As with the Maine Coon, such a coat requires very little grooming, but in common with all other long-haired cats, the outer coat is shed once a year, leaving just the magnificent bushy tail to show that it is truly a long-haired cat. The heavily furred tail — which reaches to the shoulder blades — is long and carried high.

BLUE AND WHITE NORWEGIAN FOREST CAT

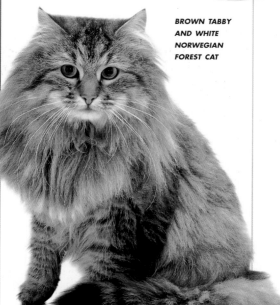

BROWN TABBY AND WHITE NORWEGIAN FOREST CAT

SILVER TABBY AND WHITE NORWEGIAN FOREST CAT

BLUE-EYED WHITE NORWEGIAN FOREST CAT

The Wegie's large size, strong legs – the hind legs are longer than the forelegs – large, heavy paws and strong, sharp claws make it a champion climber – perhaps these very agile cats are the descendants of the mythical giant cats that pulled the chariot of the Norse goddess, Freya! In Norse fairy tales collected and written down in the 19th century, a 'fairy-cat' with a long, bushy tail often appears.

From a race of hardy outdoor cats used for hunting vermin on farms, a group of breeders began to develop the pedigree breed in the 1930s. At least one Norwegian Forest Cat was shown in Oslo, Norway, before World War II, but planned breeding did not begin in earnest until the 1970s.

The breed arrived in the US in 1979, and in Britain in the 1980s. There are now some 400 registered Forest Cats in Norway, and many more abroad, especially in neighbouring Sweden. While large and strong, Norwegian Forest Cats should never appear stocky and the face should be angular, giving a fine impression of alertness and intelligence, rather than of 'sweetness'! All colours are permitted – no points are allocated to coat colour in the scoring system at shows – more important is the quality of the coat.

Tabbies and bicolours, however, predominate in the breed, reflecting the random bred cat population from which the Wegie is descended.

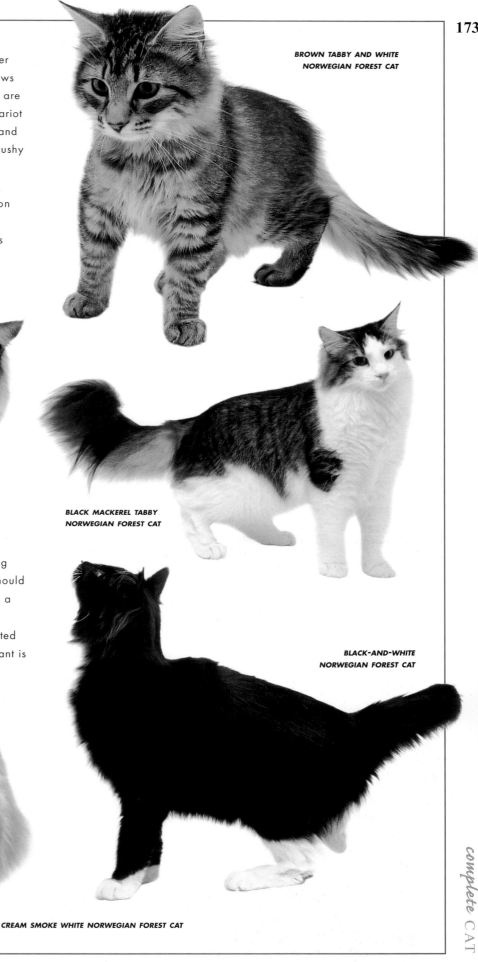

BROWN TABBY AND WHITE NORWEGIAN FOREST CAT

BLACK SMOKE AND WHITE NORWEGIAN FOREST CAT

BLACK MACKEREL TABBY NORWEGIAN FOREST CAT

BLACK-AND-WHITE NORWEGIAN FOREST CAT

CREAM SMOKE WHITE NORWEGIAN FOREST CAT

SIBERIAN FOREST CAT

DATE OF ORIGIN: 1980s

PLACE OF ORIGIN: Eastern Russia

ANCESTRY: household and farm cats

OTHER NAMES: none

COLOURS: in Russia, the Siberian is allowed in only black- and red-based colours. Elsewhere a wider range of colours is recognised:

SELF (SOLID) COLOURS AND TORTIE: black, red, blue, cream, tortoiseshell and blue tortie

SMOKED, SHADED AND TIPPED COLOURS: as for self and tortie

TABBIES, SILVER TABBIES (CLASSIC, MACKEREL, SPOTTED): brown, red, blue, cream, tortie and blue tortie.

BICOLOURS: all allowed self, tortie and tabby colours with white

COAT LENGTH: long

TYPE OF FUR: ldense, waterproof undercoat, with long, coarse guard hairs to shed rain and snow

SIZE: 4.5—9 kg (10—20 lb)

These cats are very similar in appearance to the Norwegian Forest Cat (see page 172) and, like them, have a wonderfully thick, dense and oily coat ideally suited for the extreme cold of a northern climate. It's likely that this breed has existed for thousands of years, independently of man. Russian cats were shown at early cat shows arranged by Harrison Weir – who, in fact, owned one himself – but the breed was largely forgotten during the 20th century when relationships between the Soviet Union and the rest of the world cooled. Recently, however, there has been an increasing interest in formalising the breed. Siberians were imported into the United States in 1990, thanks to the efforts of Elizabeth Terrell of the Starpoint Cattery – a name that can be found in the pedigrees of most of the top Siberians in America.

As interest in the Siberian grew, a greater variety of coat colours and patterns has been introduced, but some Russian clubs fear that cats exported for breeding in the West are not always the best. The face of the Siberian Forest Cat in Russia is different to that accepted in the West. In Russia a more 'wildcat' appearance is preferred, with a broad face and slightly tilted eyes giving it a more Asiatic cast. Outside Russia, the TICA standard for the Siberian head is less markedly wild – here the impression should be of 'roundness and circles' with a sweet expression and almost-round eyes. Furthermore, in its homeland, the Siberian is permitted in only black- and red-based colours to preserve its wild appearance. Consequently, the Siberian Forest Cat is developing two distinct looks internationally.

RED MACKEREL TABBY AND WHITE SIBERIAN

The Siberian Forest Cat is a strong cat with a long, well-muscled and powerful body and sturdy legs, ending in large, round and fur-tufted paws. In both sexes, the hind legs are slightly longer than the forelegs when straight, and the body is carried with a slightly arched spine.

Around the neck is a ruff, enhancing the short, sturdy proportions. The ears are medium in size, with rounded tips that are angled outwards, giving the cat an ever-alert appearance. Between the ears the head is broad and flat. The magnificent tail is thick, with a rounded tip while the hind quarters are shaggy. The topcoat is strong and slightly oily to shed rain and snow, while the dense woolly undercoat is thick enough to keep out the Arctic winds of Siberia. Every aspect of the Siberian Forest Cat demonstrates that it is designed to survive in the toughest conditions and climate on earth.

SILVER, TABBY AND WHITE SIBERIAN

RAGDOLL

DATE OF ORIGIN: 1960s

PLACE OF ORIGIN: USA

ANCESTRY: uncertain

OTHER NAMES: none

COLOURS:

POINTED, MITTED AND BICOLOUR: seal, chocolate, blue and lilac

COAT LENGTH: medium

TYPE OF FUR: very dense and silky

SIZE: 4.5—9 kg (10—20 lb)

The Ragdoll is a relatively new breed first developed in the 1960s in California, USA, by the breeder Ann Baker, and is sometimes mistaken for the Birman (see page 158). Both breeds have point colours – which can be seal, blue, chocolate or lilac – and may have white on the head, body and legs (when it is known as bicolour), white on the abdomen and feet (mitted), or no white at all (colourpoint). The body build of the Ragdoll is, however, heavier than that of the Birman.

Ragdolls are the result of an attempt to produce a cat with a gentle disposition and in this the breeders certainly succeeded, for the Ragdoll is famous for its habit of completely relaxing when they are touched or picked up. Ann Baker formed a breed association, but these Ragdolls were not accepted by other associations. Other breeders however, were to produce the breed of Ragdolls accepted today by the major registries. In addition, the Ragdoll was the first breed of cat in history to receive its own trademark!

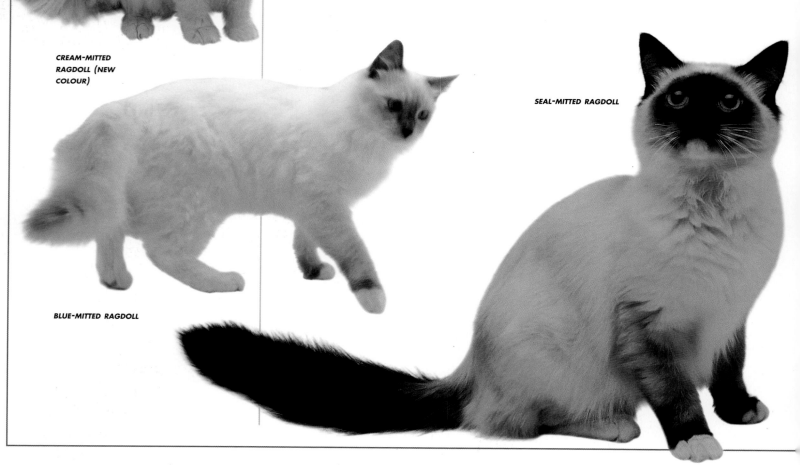

SEAL COLOURPOINT RAGDOLL

CREAM-MITTED RAGDOLL (NEW COLOUR)

BLUE-MITTED RAGDOLL

SEAL-MITTED RAGDOLL

The first Ragdolls were bred from a white, probably non-pedigree, long-haired queen called Josephine, and a Birman, or Birman-type tom called Daddy Warbucks. According to Ann Baker, Josephine had been severely injured – her pelvis was broken after she was hit by a car – and when she picked up the Ragdoll kittens they went limp in her hands. This led to the claim that Ragdolls were unable to feel pain or fear or to fight other animals, and that this trait was a direct result of Josephine's accident. That Ragdolls feel no pain is a myth – they have the same pain threshold as other cats – but they do indeed have a very docile nature, making them ideal and loving pets. They are also an easy breed to train because they respond extremely well to tasty treats as rewards! These characteristics are actually the result of genetic mutations in the selective breeding process among highly domesticated animals. Breeders also point out that all the varieties known as Ragdolls could be produced by a white queen if the mate carried the Siamese and long-hair genes, and if either also carried the white-spotting (piebald) gene (white spotting can be present undetected in a white Long-hair/Persian).

A large cat – some toms can weigh up to 9 kg (20 lb) – the Ragdoll's body is strong and muscular, with a short, heavy-set neck and a deep chest. The legs are medium length, with the front legs covered in a shorter fur than on the body. The paws are large, round and tufted with fur, and the pads are dark brown or black. The head is medium sized and tapering, with full cheeks and a rounded muzzle.

SEAL TORTOISESHELL POINT RAGDOLL

SEAL BI-COLOUR RAGDOLL

BLUE-MITTED RAGDOLL

The beautiful oval eyes are blue, while the ears are wide at the base, with rounded tips which tilt slightly forwards. As with all long-haired cats, the Ragdoll's coat is beautifully silky, but also very dense. The coat is longer around the neck, but short over the shoulders, and medium length on the sides, abdomen and hind legs.

BLUE COLOURPOINT RAGDOLL

Ragdolls are essentially pointed cats, born white and slowly developing their colours and patterns over the first two years. In the early years of the breed, the seal point and its dilute, blue, were the most common colours to be found in Ragdolls, but later breeders succeeded in producing chocolate and lilac colours. The breed standards recognise the usual markings for bicolours and colourpoints, but require good contrast, and the body colour on Ragdolls can be deeper than that accepted on other pointed breeds.

BI-COLOUR RAGDOLL

SOMALI

DATE OF ORIGIN: 1963

PLACE OF ORIGIN: Canada and the USA

ANCESTRY: Abyssinian

OTHER NAMES: Long-haired Abyssinian

COLOURS:

TABBIES (TICKED): usual (called ruddy in the US), chocolate, sorrel (red), blue, lilac, fawn and cream

TORTIES: usual tortie, chocolate, sorrel, blue, lilac and fawn tortie

SILVER TABBIES (TICKED): colours as for tabbies and torties, but must have white chests and underparts

COAT LENGTH: medium-long, with ruff and full breeches

TYPE OF FUR: Fine and silky, ticked (at least three and up to 12 bands of colour on each hair)

SIZE: 3.5—5.5 kg (8—12 lb)

With its beautiful shaggy coat, fluffy 'trousers' or breeches, exaggerated ear tufts and a fine, full tail like a fox's brush, the Somali is a wild-looking cat, vigorous and athletic. Yet, like their Abyssinian relations, Somalis are very gentle in nature, soft in voice and make for great companions.

This breed of cat was named after Somalia, a country next to Ethiopia (formerly known as Abyssinia), in order to emphasise the breed's similarity to the Abyssinian. In fact, the Somali is the long-haired variety of the short-haired Abyssinian.

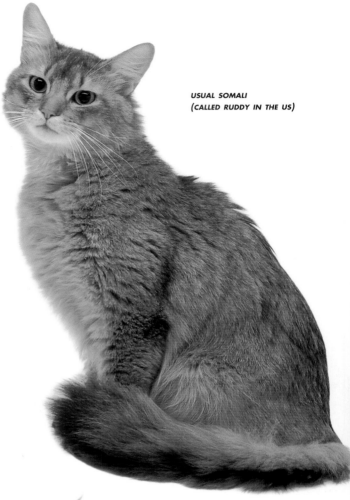

USUAL SOMALI (CALLED RUDDY IN THE US)

BLUE SOMALI

At first, the Somali was not recognised by the registries because it was believed that some out-crossing of Abyssinians to long-haired breeds must have taken place. In fact, certain breeding lines of Abyssinians are now known to have carried the recessive (l) long hair gene (see pages 49–53) for many generations – long-haired kittens had appeared occasionally in Abyssinian litters in the UK and, in the 1940s, breeder Janet Robertson exported 'Abys' to North America and Australia, where descendants of these Abys also produced long-haired kittens. In the 1960s, Canadian breeder Ken McGill produced the first official Somali and, from his stock, the breed was fully developed in the US in the 1970s. The breed appeared in Europe in the 1980s and by 1991 had received worldwide recognition.

Like its Abyssinian forebears, the Somali has the same ticked coat, although it is silkier, softer and very much longer. Instead of two or three bands of ticking on each hair, the Somali can have up to 12 bands. The colouring, which may be 'usual' – called 'ruddy' in the US – or sorrel (red), is deeper and much richer. The usual or ruddy colour was one of the first to be accepted for showing. Here, the base coat is a red-brown shade of apricot while the ticking is black. On all Somalis, the ticking is much darker on the ground coat and, in autumn and winter when the Somali is in glorious full coat, they produce a beautiful, vibrant shimmer. The coat is full, but not woolly, and a full ruff around the neck is typical of the breed. It takes a long time for the coat and colouring to develop fully: kittens are born very dark and only achieve a full ticked ruddy colouring at about 18 months.

Lithe and muscular in build, the Somali's legs are long, with oval-shaped, tufted paws. The head is a moderate wedge shape, and all Somalis have dark-rimmed eyes – as if they have been outlined in kohl or eyeliner – surrounded by 'spectacles' of lighter hair. On the cheeks and forehead there are clear tabby markings – it is said the prophet Mohammed once embraced a tabby cat and, in so doing, left his initial 'M' on its forehead!

Since the long hair gene (l) is recessive, Somalis always breed true for long hair. Crossed with an Abyssinian, however, a Somali will have short-haired kittens carrying the gene for long hair. These offspring will have a much plusher coat than most 'normal' Abyssinians. Mated together, they will result in both long-haired and short-haired offspring. Notwithstanding, all 'short-haired Somalis' must be registered in North America as Somalis, even though they are genetically identical to many Abyssinians that may also be carrying the long-hair gene!

CHOCOLATE SOMALI

BLUE/SILVER SOMALI

TIFFANNIE

DATE OF ORIGIN: 1980s

PLACE OF ORIGIN: Britain

ANCESTRY: Burmese-Chinchilla crosses

OTHER NAMES: none (not to be confused with the Tiffany, US appellation for the Chantilly)

COLOURS:

SELF (SOLID) AND SEPIA COLOURS: black, chocolate, red, blue, lilac, cream, caramel and apricot

TORTIES: black, chocolate, blue, lilac and caramel torties

SHADED COLOURS: as for self and sepia

TABBIES (SOLID, SEPIA, ALL PATTERNS): brown, chocolate, red, blue, lilac, cream, caramel, apricot, Black tortie, chocolate, blue, lilac and caramel tortie

COAT LENGTH: long, with ruff at neck

TYPE OF FUR: very fine

SIZE: 3.5—6.5 kg (8—14 lb)

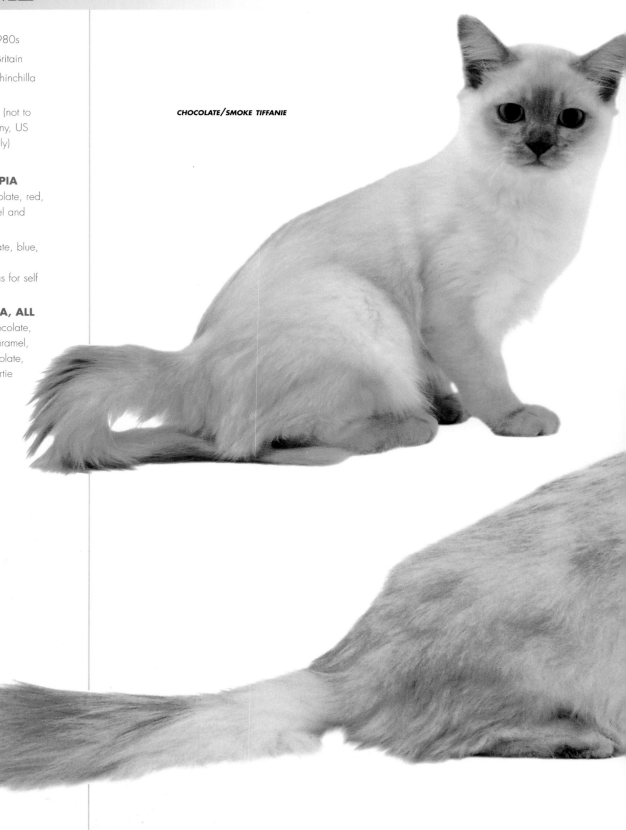

CHOCOLATE/SMOKE TIFFANIE

The attractive – and attractively named – Tiffannie are unusual for combining long, silky   hair with the shaded tones of the colours of the Burmese (see page 211). Although it is sometimes confused with its US namesake – the Tiffany (elsewhere called Chantilly) – the Tiffannie has nothing to do with the breed. Instead, the Tiffannie is essentially a long-haired Burmese and is the only Asian long-haired cat. Born a pale café au lait colour, the subtle sable colouring and long coat develop only gradually and the colour generally remains lighter than in a Burmese cat of the same age. Like all kittens, the Tiffannie is born with blue eyes, but these change to grey then to the adult golden colour.

The Tiffannie's origins can be traced back to an accidental mating in London, England, in 1981, between a Chinchilla Long-hair/Persian and a lilac Burmese which belonged to Baroness Miranda von Kirchberg. The first generation were short-haired, shaded Burmillas (see page 216) but

subsequent generations ultimately revealed the recessive long-hair and sepia-pointing genes. Although the breed was developed with the assistance of Burmese breeders, the two breeds remain distinct.

While their coat is semi-long, very fine and silky, as one would expect in the offspring of a Persian/Long-hair, the body retains the Burmese conformation: a medium-sized, muscular body with a round chest and straight back. The head is a short wedge, with a distinct nose break in profile, while the medium-sized ears continue the lines of the face. Eyes are neither almond-shaped, nor round and are set slightly obliquely. The legs are medium long and the paws rounded, while the tail is long and elegantly plumed. In temperament, the Tiffannie has combined the characteristics of its parent breeds once again to great effect – they are more lively than the average Long-hair/Persian, yet less boisterous than the average Burmese! The breed standard for the Tiffannie does, in fact, place emphasis on good temperament. This, combined with low maintenance in a long-haired cat, will undoubtedly ensure that the delightful and beguiling Tiffannie will become an even more popular breed worldwide.

BLUE SHADED SILVER TIFFANIE

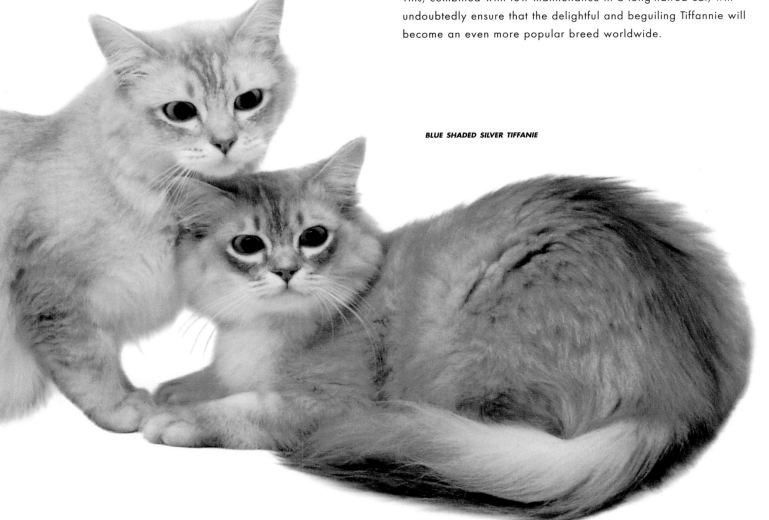

LONG-HAIR/PERSIAN

DATE OF ORIGIN: 1800s

PLACE OF ORIGIN: Britain

ANCESTRY: Middle-eastern longhairs

OTHER NAMES: called Persian in the USA

COLOURS: see main text

COAT LENGTH: up to 10 cm (4 in) long

TYPE OF FUR: soft and thick but not woolly

SIZE: 3.5—7 kg (8—15 lb)

Longhairs/Persians are both an important part of the pedigree cat world – having appeared regularly in shows for well over one hundred years – and greatly prized as pets by owners worldwide. The long coat is the result of the recessive gene (l) and the most likely place of origin was Asia Minor, where, according to legend, the Persian cat was created by a magician from a little flicker of fire, the spark of two distant stars and a swirl of grey smoke.

In 1876, long-haired cats were referred to as 'Asiatic cats', but they had been seen in Europe some 300 years before this.

Today, most cats of the long-hair type are known as Long-haired in Britain, where only selfs are called Longhairs (each colour is classified as a separate breed, of which there are nearly 50!) In the USA, these cats are known as Persians and the colours are listed as varieties which, for show purposes, are divided into five divisions: solid (self), shaded, smoke/tabby, part-coloured and point-restricted colours. Nevertheless, the ideal body type is pretty much the same – a big, cobby body, low on the legs, with a round, broad head, full cheeks, large, round eyes and small, rounded ears and, of course, the beautiful, long, silky and full coat. While the early Persians/Longhairs had short, compact faces, they were not the flat faces seen today. European breeders still prefer what they term a 'moderate' nose, while American breeders and many show judges look for the flatter, or 'ultra-type' face. This trend reached its most extreme in the 'Peke-faced' Persian/Long-hair where the narrow nostrils and restricted tear ducts caused by this face shape meant that these cats often suffered for their appearance. This look is no longer desired by many breeders today.

RED PERSIAN

BLUE CREAM PERSIAN

BROWN PATCHED TABBY PERSIAN

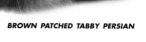

CREAM POINT PERSIAN

BLACK SMOKE PERSIAN

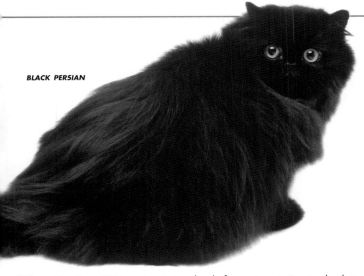

BLACK PERSIAN

CREAM PERSIAN

When Harrison Weir set out standards for cat varieties in the late 19th century, the colours he described in Persians/Longhairs were white, black, blue, grey, red and any other self colour, with brown, blue, silver, light grey and white for tabbies.

By 1901, the recognised colours in Britain were black, white, blue, orange, cream, sable, smoke, tabby, spotted, chinchilla, tortoiseshell, bicolour and tricolour. The orange Persians/Longhairs were the ancestors of the red self colours and red tabbies, and the tricolours were most likely tortie-and-white.

TORTOISESHELL PERSIAN

The self colour group of Persians/Longhairs today includes whites, blacks, blues, chocolates, lilacs, reds and creams. While black – listed as Breed Number 1 in the UK – is the oldest variety of all, in 1910 there were in fact only 10 registered individuals. It was not until the end of World War II, when

American breeders 'rescued' the breed, that black Persians/Longhairs became significant in numbers. The white selfs were among the very first long-haired cats in Europe, renowned then as now, for their blue eyes, but also for their deafness, which is associated with the dominant white gene W. Due to the way this gene acts, some white Persian/ Long-haired kittens show small clusters of coloured hairs on their heads, revealing the underlying colour genotype and giving an idea of what the kitten would have looked like without the action of the recessive white gene. Today, deafness is selectively bred against by careful cross-breeding using coloured Persians and by neutering deaf kittens.

Blue has always been one of the most popular varieties – a trend said to have been set by Queen Victoria, who was inseparable from her two Blues – and Blues now even have shows dedicated solely to them!

WHITE PERSIAN

BROWN TABBY PERSIAN

complete CAT

CHINCHILLA PERSIAN

TABBY COLOURPOINT PERSIAN

The rarest of all the self Persian/Longhairs is the red self, which was originally called orange. Such cats are difficult to breed to perfection – although show standards require red selfs to be free from tabby markings – and the long coat does help obscure some of the 'tabbiness'. A truly unmarked red Persian/Long-hair is probably an impossibility, due to the way the orange gene (O) works.

Tabbies have always been bred by cat lovers and, in 1871, they were included in the classification for the first famous cat show held by Weir in London. Today, both the mackerel (lined) and classic (blotched) tabby patterns are recognised in North America, while in the UK, only the classic type – termed simply 'tabby' – competes. These tabbies continue to be bred in the basic colours, such as brown (i.e. genetically black), which is both the original colour and essentially the natural tabby, along with silvers and reds while, more recently, newer colours and patterns have been introduced, such as 'shaded cameos' in red, cream, cream-shell (essentially a cream chinchilla) blue-cream and tortie.

SEAL TORTOISESHELL COLOURPOINT PERSIAN

The fall of the breed's long coat makes a great display for tortoiseshell colouring. The first torties classified were standard black and reds, but soon red Persians/Longhairs were mated with blues and the blue-creams, or blue torties appeared. Tortie-and-whites were once called 'chintz cats' – and are still known today as 'Calicoes' in the US because of their resemblance to the bright patterns on printed calico cotton – while the original bicoloured cats (black, blue, red and cream) were known as 'magpie cats'. The ideal pattern for the bicolour Persian/Long-hair, which is well known in fancy-bred mice and rabbits, is called the 'Dutch coat' pattern, where the white areas are confined to the underparts. In bicolour Persians/Longhairs, this perfect marking is very difficult to achieve and, consequently, some flexibility is allowed. A distinct variant in patterns – though genetically the same as the bicolour – is the Van Pattern: a white body and legs, with a coloured tail and face markings not extending below the level of the eyes or beyond the base of the ears.

BLUE TABBY PERSIAN

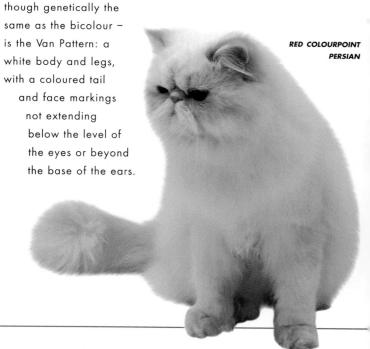

RED COLOURPOINT PERSIAN

RED TABBY PERSIAN

BLUE COLOURPOINT PERSIAN

Shaded and Tipped Persian/Long-hair varieties developed out of the early silver tabbies and the best-known member of this group is undoubtedly the Silver Chinchilla – most often called simply, Chinchilla. One of the earliest and most famous chinchillas was called Silver Lambkin and it seems that he gave rise to both silver and golden kittens. The silver variety was what breeders were aiming for, and the golden was ignored for some time because some breeders maintained they were the result of 'illegal' or accidental matings between self-coloured Persians/Longhairs and Chinchillas. Shaded Silvers (called 'pewter' in the UK) and shaded goldens are similar to the Chinchillas, except that the degree of tipping is greater, so the colours appear much darker. The Shaded Silver is recognised in the US as a black-tipped cat with green or blue-green eyes, and in red and tortoiseshell versions (called shaded cameo and shaded tortoiseshell) while in Britain, only the black versions are recognised (as pewters) with orange or copper eyes. The Golden Persian, which has deep tipping on an apricot base, looks like a golden version of the Shaded Silver (Pewter) and is one of the most recent, and most attractive, varieties of the Persian/Long-hair breeds, even though the genetics of this colour are still disputed. Whatever colour or pattern, the Persian/Long-hair are famous for their long, silky coats, which require daily grooming to keep them looking like a supreme champion which, to their owners, each cat is. The daily grooming routine is not only enjoyed by the cat, but helps to cement the very special bond between the cat and its

owner – a very strong relationship for which this breed and its owners are well known! Furthermore, if the owner takes a little time to groom, the Persian/Long-hair will not swallow so much of its own hair, thus avoiding fur balls, which can block the intestines. One of the quietest and least active of the breeds of cat, they are generally regarded as indoor cats. But this does not mean that Persians/Longhairs don't enjoy outdoor activity – they display the same feline characteristics when guarding their territory or hunting as any other breeds.

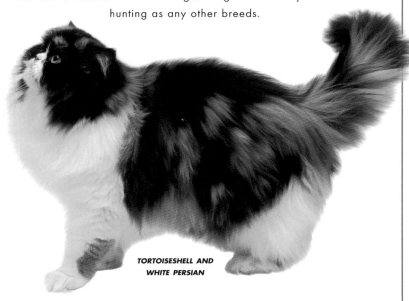

TORTOISESHELL AND WHITE PERSIAN

DILUTE CALICO, BLUE TORTOISESHELL AND WHITE TABBY PERSIAN

BLUE CREAM PERSIAN

SCOTTISH FOLD

DATE OF ORIGIN: 1961

PLACE OF ORIGIN: Scotland

ANCESTRY: farm cats, British and American Shorthairs

OTHER NAMES: Highland Fold

COLOURS: all colours and patterns including pointed, sepia and mink

COAT LENGTH: can be long-or short-coated

TYPE OF FUR: soft and dense, standing away from the body in the long-hair

SIZE: 2.5—6 kg (6—13 lb)

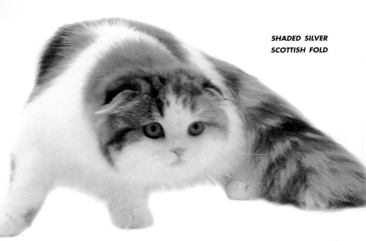

SHADED SILVER SCOTTISH FOLD

While folded ears are common among dog breeds, in cats they are rare. All Scottish Folds can be traced back to Susie, a white farm cat born in Tayside, Scotland. Two years later, Susie bore two more folded-ear kittens, one of which, a white female, was given to a local shepherd, William Ross, and his wife Mary and named Snooks. The uniqueness of the 'abnormality' was noticed and soon a breeding programme was established with the help of two geneticists, Pat Turner and Pete Dyte. It was discovered that Susie carried the dominant long-hair gene (l) which could also be carried in any short-haired offspring, only appearing in later generations. Long-haired Scottish Folds, however, are still rare.

The short-hair variety can trace its ancestry back to Snooks, who was mated with a British Shorthair (see page 192) and produced Snowball, a white male. In 1971, Mary Ross sent some of her Folds to geneticist Neil Todd in Newtonville, Massachusetts, where further breeding developments using British and American Shorthairs (see page 196) continued. The main centre for breeding is still in the US.

Scottish Folds must be mated to cats with normal ears otherwise any homozygous (Fold-to-Fold mated) offspring may suffer from deformities of the joints and cartilage that start to become evident when the kitten reaches four to six months old. The cause of these deformities is something of a mystery since they affect only a proportion of cats, including those Folds that are heterozygous (Fold-to-Other-Breed mated). In long-haired Folds especially, the deformities may go unnoticed under their beautiful coats, so checking long-haired kittens' tails for thickening joints is vital.

The folded ears are the result of a dominant gene that is responsible for varying degrees of fold. They are present from birth, but the extent of folding may not become fully apparent until the kitten matures. The original Scottish Fold, Susie, had what is now called a 'single fold', where the ears bend forwards. Today's show cats have 'triple folds' where the ears are folded tightly and flat against the head, set according to the breed standards 'in a cap-like fashion' to expose a rounded cranium'. The head is indeed well—rounded, and the shape is further enhanced by the prominent cheeks, whisker pads and large, rounded eyes.

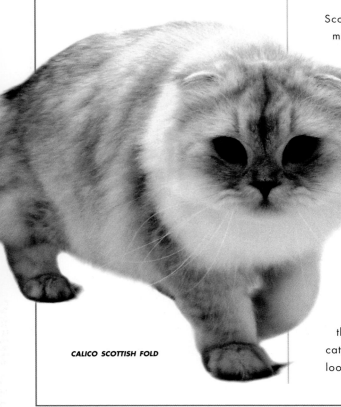

CALICO SCOTTISH FOLD

Like the Scots themselves, Scottish Folds are robust, strong and seemingly impervious to the cold! They are also highly resistant to many common feline diseases. Though placid cats, and perhaps a little 'reserved' or undemonstrative, they are good natured. Their 'sad' look is too often misinterpreted as an indicator of their inner feelings!

COUPARI

DATE OF ORIGIN: 1960s

PLACE OF ORIGIN: Scotland

ANCESTRY: Scottish Fold (short haired variety), domestic and farm cats

OTHER NAMES: Scottish Fold Long-hair (American CFA), Highland Fold (American ACFA)

COLOURS: all colours and patterns including pointed, sepia and mink

COAT LENGTH: Soft and dense, standing away from the body

TYPE OF FUR: Soft and dense, standing away from the body

SIZE: 2.4–6 kg (6–13 lb)

SEAL TABBY POINT COUPARI

The Coupari is one of the names given to the long-haired variety of the Scottish Fold (see page 186). The name is derived from the home of the founding cat in Coupar Angus in Scotland. In the American CFA, the Coupari is called the Scottish Fold Long-hair; while in the American ACFA, it is known as the Highland Fold – despite the fact that Coupar Angus is not in the Scottish Highlands, which causes some mirth among Scottish breeders in particular! Both long- and short-haired varieties are distinguished by the folded ears – but these do not appear until kittens are about three weeks old – but straight (normal) eared kittens are also produced because the folded ear is the product of an incomplete gene and is the result of spontaneous mutation. Consequently both Scottish folds – the short-haired variety – and Couparis – the long haired variety – are still very rare. Cats with 'folded' ears have been known for centuries, but all Couparis and Scottish Folds can trace their ancestry back to Susie, a white farm cat born in 1961 on a farm in Coupar Angus, in the Tayside region of Scotland, northwest of Dundee. Susie was 'discovered' by William and Mollie Ross, who asked the original owners if they could have one of the kittens and proceeded to develop the breed.

Genetic studies by Pat Turner and Peter Dyte in the 1960s discovered that Susie also carried the gene for long hair: this could be carried in short-haired offspring and could appear in later generations. While the short-haired Scottish Fold was to find successful out crosses in British and American Shorthairs (see pages 192–197), long-haired out crosses were absent, until it was discovered that the prick-eared Scottish Vannant had all the same genes for the breed type – except for the folded ears. The Scottish Vannant can thus be successfully mated to both a Scottish Fold and a Coupari, to produce both short- and long-haired cats with folded ears. This avoids the dangers of breeding 'fold-to-fold' which may produce litters with inherited osteodystrophy. Nevertheless, the Coupari and its short-haired cousin still remain quite rare.

In 1983, when the Cat Association of Britain was formed, one of the first new breeds to gain Championship status was the Scottish Fold, and the following year the Coupari was also accepted for competition. Breeders in the UK today are united in the Scottish Breeds Association. In the USA the Coupari is a Championship breed, while in the UK it has medalist titles. Although it is not (as yet) eligible itself for titles, the Scottish Vannant can be shown in the class for new breeds.

AMERICAN CURL

DATE OF ORIGIN: 1981

PLACE OF ORIGIN: USA

ANCESTRY: American household cats

OTHER NAMES: none

COLOURS: all self and tortie colours, all patterns of smoke, shaded and tipped, tabbies and Silver tabbies

BICOLOURS: classic and Van

SELF, TABBY (LYNX) AND TORTIE POINT

COAT LENGTH: medium to long (long-haired variety)

TYPE OF FUR: silky with minimal undercoat, so lying close to body in both long- and short-haired varieties

SIZE: 3—5 kg (7—11 lb)

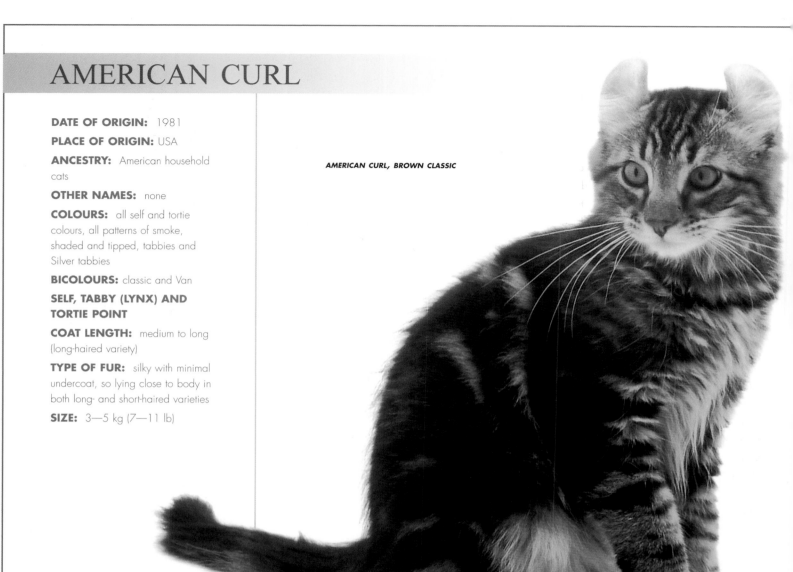

AMERICAN CURL, BROWN CLASSIC

The American Curl breed includes both long- and short-coat types. The short-haired American Curl has taken slightly longer to develop because the original Curls were all long-haired and many short-haired Curls carry the hidden long-hair gene and produce long-haired kittens. The American Curl is best known not for its coat, but for the mutation which causes the ears of these cats to curl backwards, creating its highly distinctive appearance.

The Curl has three grades: cats with their ears just turned back (first degree) are called American Curl Straight Ears and become household pets, those with a 50% curl (second degree) are used for breeding and those with full crescents (third degree) are shown competitively. The kittens are born with normal-looking ears and typically half the litter will develop the curl at about a week old, continuing to develop over several months. In spite of their appearance, even third-degree-curled ears can be swivelled around by the cat like any other normal-eared cat!

The ancestry of the breed is unknown, although in 1981 a stray, black, long-haired kitten, with unusual, curled ears found herself a new home with Grace and Joe Ruga in Lakeland, California. The Rugas named the kitten Shulamith, which means 'peaceful one', after the shepherdess in the Song of Songs, and all Curls – whether long- or short-haired – today trace their origin back to her.

In December 1981, Shulamith had a litter of four kittens, two of which had the same curly ears. The Rugas realised that a new breed could be established because the trait was dominant. The cats were first shown in 1983 in California, and they were soon formally recognised in the US with the first American Curls reaching the UK in 1995.

Nevertheless, the American Curl has established itself as a popular cat, not only for its dramatic face – often described as 'pixie–like', enhanced by walnut-shaped and slightly tilted eyes – but for its lively, friendly and independent spirit. Semi-foreign in build, with moderate muscles, the Curl has sturdy legs, a little bowed at the front, with the hind legs slightly longer in length. This is set off in the long-haired Curl by a magnificently plumed tail, and in the shorthair by a tail that equals the length of the body, wide at the base and tapering to the tip. The show standards for short-haired American Curls differ from their long-haired cousins only in coat length.

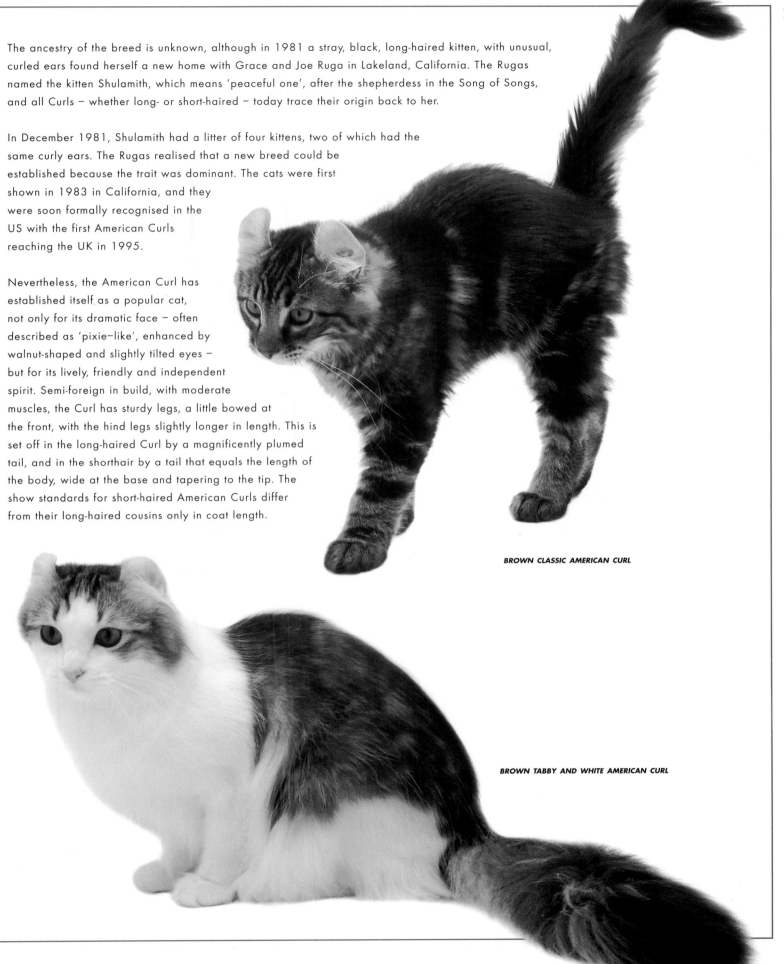

BROWN CLASSIC AMERICAN CURL

BROWN TABBY AND WHITE AMERICAN CURL

SHORT-HAIRED BREEDS

When, thousands of years ago, domestic cats spread from Egypt across the world, new varieties evolved to suit the local climate and terrain. In northern climates, cats developed stocky, cobby bodies and thicker coats, while those cats which spread eastwards across Asia, developed thinner coats and smaller bodies to help them lose excess heat in warmer climates. In the wild, short hair is normal in cats. It is only in the extreme cold of regions such as Siberia, the home of the Siberian Tiger, that longer hair is found on wild cats. Short fur is much easier to keep clean and pest- and tangle-free and is also genetically dominant. There are many types of short-hair coats in cats, ranging from the silky-soft, fine fur of the Rex to the dense coat of the Manx.

THE BURMESE IS A CLASSIC SHORT-HAIRED BREED

THE AMERICAN SHORT-HAIR IS A VERY POPULAR BREED

THE AMERICAN SHORT-HAIR IS GENERALLY LARGER THAN ITS BRITISH/ EUROPEAN AND ORIENTAL COUNTERPARTS.

The Romans were said to have introduced domestic cats to northern Europe some 2,000 years ago, so it is not surprising that when breeding and exhibiting cats at shows became popular in the 19th century, British and European breeders concentrated their attentions on their native cats.

There are three main categories of short-haired cats: British (and European), American, and Foreign (or Oriental). The British Shorthair is a cobby with strong, short legs, a short, dense coat, a broad, round head, round eyes and superb colouring. There are only slight differences between the British and European Shorthairs, but since 1982 they have been recognised as separate breeds. Over the years since it was established as a breed, the European Shorthair has become less cobby than the British type, with a slightly longer body. Both do, however, display the same basic traits of being a strong, hardy cat with a beautiful coat and a calm, affectionate personalit

THE SLEEK LINES OF THE ORIENTAL SHORT-HAIR MAKE THIS A VERY POPULAR BREED.

The pure-bred American Shorthair is a larger and more athletic cat with longer legs and a more oblong-shaped head. Some consider the pure-bred American Shorthair to be closer in body type to its non-pedigree counterpart, but a pure-bred anima – the result of generations of selective breeding – will have a body, coat and colouring that represent the very highest standards of quality.

The Foreign, or Oriental, Shorthair, looks completely different to its occidental cousins. These are slender-bodied cats with long, slim legs, the characteristic wedge-shaped head and long, pointed ears, and the very distinctive, slanting eyes.

At the first cat shows held in the 19th century, short-haired breeds had pride of place as few Siamese cats had been imported. By the end of the century, however, the situation had changed markedly as Long-haired, or Persian, cats had become immensely poplar and begun to outnumber the shorthairs at shows by 4 to 1.

These long-haired cats with the luxurious, slinky coats and the appeal of originating in faraway parts of the world meant that a short-haired kitten has never since fetched the price commanded by a Persian one.

Nevertheless, the native short-haired breeds of Britain, Europe and

THE SIAMESE IS ONE OF THE MOST WIDELY RECOGNISED AND BEST-LOVED OF ALL BREEDS.

North America, have many advantages as domestic companions. They have a hardiness and stamina born of countless generations of life in all climates, and temperamentally, they are ideally suited to family life – being less excitable and easy to groom.

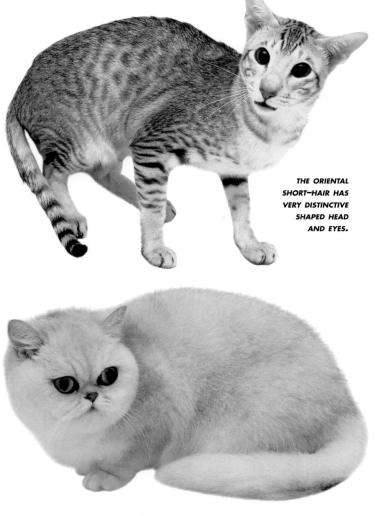

THE ORIENTAL SHORT-HAIR HAS VERY DISTINCTIVE SHAPED HEAD AND EYES.

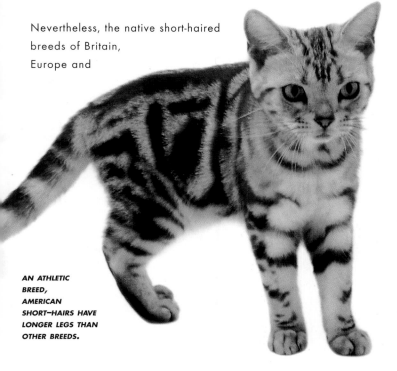

AN ATHLETIC BREED, AMERICAN SHORT-HAIRS HAVE LONGER LEGS THAN OTHER BREEDS.

THE EXOTIC SHORT-HAIR IS A RELATIVELY NEW BREED, AND SHARES CHARACTERISTICS OF BOTH LONG AND SHORT-HAIRED BREEDS.

BRITISH SHORTHAIR

DATE OF ORIGIN: 1880s

PLACE OF ORIGIN: Britain

ANCESTRY: household, farm and street cats

OTHER NAMES: tipped colours were once known as Chinchilla Shorthairs

COLOURS:

SELF (SOLID) COLOURS: white, cream, blue, blue-cream, black, chocolate, lilac and red

TABBY (CLASSIC, MACKEREL, AND SPOTTED – OR BLOTCHED – MARKINGS): silver, brown, red, cream and blue

SPOTTED: red, brown, silver or any other tabby colour

TORTOISESHELL: tortoiseshell, blue-cream tortie, chocolate tortie and lilac tortie.

BICOLOUR: all self and tortie colours with white

SMOKE AND TIPPED: colours as for self and tortie

COLOURPOINT: all self, tortie and tabby colours

COAT LENGTH: short

TYPE OF FUR: dense and springy, 'breaks' over joints

SIZE: 4—8 kg (9—18 lb)

All the European cat breeds suffered during World War II, but some say that the British Shorthair suffered the most. In the immediate post-war years there were very few pedigree stud males left and, as a result, some breeders mated their cats to shorthairs of foreign body type, which nearly led to the cobby build being lost. In the 1950s, breeders reversed the trend by mating to large-built, blue Persians. While this did restore the breed's qualities, it also meant that some kittens had longer, softer coats, and a more Persian head shape.

LILAC TORTIE BRITISH SHORTHAIR

The show standards set for British and European Shorthairs specifies a straight nose – a difficult feat to achieve using Persian ancestry, even when the Persians bred in Europe are not as snub- or 'peke-nosed' as those in America. One rare trait separates the British Shorthair breed from most short-haired cats: about half of all British Shorthairs have Type B blood.

BLUE SPOTTED BRITISH SHORTHAIR

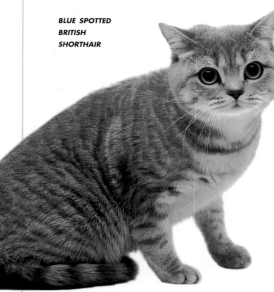

BLACK SMOKE TORTIE BRITISH SHORTHAIR

CINNAMON SELF BRITISH SHORTHAIR

In the early days of the breed, the self colours of the British Shorthair were the most popular, probably because solid-coloured cats, with no markings, were less common in non-pedigree pets. Of the various self colours, the most highly prized was the blue – which is, in fact, a beautiful bluish-grey – and this has remained poplar ever since. As a result the Blue British Shorthair is sometimes accorded solitary breed status as the 'British Blue' and is regarded as the epitome of the breed. As with all British Shorthairs, the ideal is a lovely, rounded face with full cheeks, a cobby body with strong, broad shoulders, a deep chest and strong, short legs.

BLUE/SILVER BRITISH SHORTHAIR

LILAC TORTIE BRITISH SHORTHAIR

The ears are small with rounded tips and set well apart. The nose is short and straight, with the nose pad corresponding to the coat colour. In self-coloured British Shorthairs, the well-rounded eyes are copper, deep orange or deep gold, except in the Blue- and Odd-eyed White. The Orange-Eyed White – which rarely suffers from the congenital

deafness suffered by Blue- and Odd-Eyed Whites – was developed from the Blue-Eyed White, which appeared at the end of the 19th century, but a perfect white coat, with no yellow tinge is very rare.

The cream British Shorthair, recognised since the 1920s, is one of the most difficult to breed in the ideal coat colour: a pale cream shade completely free of any tabby markings. Often the colour is too 'hot' (too red) and there are residual tabby type bars on the tail and markings on the face.

BLUE TORTIE BRITISH SHORTHAIR

WHITE BRITISH SHORTHAIR

BI-COLOURED BRITISH SHORTHAIR

Tortoiseshell cats are not rare, but they are also very difficult to breed to the breed standard, which calls for a mingling of colours without obvious patches, brindling or tabby markings. Both the nose leather and paws pads in torties must correspond with the coat colours. Even under the most 'favourable' circumstances a litter may contain only one tortie and, because the colour and sex of cats is genetically linked, torties are nearly always female – the rare, male tortie will be infertile. Tortie-and-Whites, known as Calicoes in the US, have distinct patches of red and black because, for some as-yet-unknown reason, the bicolour gene affects the red sex-linked gene making the mingled colours of the 'pure' tortie unachievable in tortie-and-whites. The breed standard requires Tortie-and-Whites to have a colour balance in their coats of one-third to one-half white, as in other bicoloured cats.

The British Tabby Shorthair, whether classic, mackerel or spotted (botched) has complete rings on the tail and even bars on the legs. The original tabby was the Brown and is less commonly seen today. Soon after, the Reds made their appearance on the scene. Ginger-reds are common in non-pedigree cats in Britain, but a century of selective breeding means that a pedigree red tabby is a truly magnificent animal, far removed in richness of colour from the common 'ginger toms'. The word 'tabby' is said to be derived from the town of Attabiya, near Baghdad, in Iraq, which was famous for producing a watered silk cloth known as 'tabbi silk', the pattern of which was shared by local cats. On the tabby's forehead is the 'M' mark – said to have been left by the prophet Mohammed when he embraced a cat! Like the self-coloured British Shorthairs, tabbies have the same copper-coloured eyes, except in the Silver Tabby, which has green or hazel eyes.

BLACK BRITISH SHORTHAIR

TORTIE BRITISH SHORTHAIR

BLUE/CREAM BRITISH SHORTHAIR

CREAM COLOURPOINT BRITISH SHORTHA

SELF FAWN BRITISH SHORTHAIR

The Spotted Shorthair has a coat very similar to the mackerel tabby's, but here, the stripes are broken into spots. This very striking pattern was one of the earliest, appearing in the 1880s. While black remains one of the most popular colours, there are Silver versions, which as in other breeds have hazel or green eyes, rather than copper or deep orange. The Smoke, which has a single colour topcoat of either black or blue over a white undercoat, was developed in the late 19th century by crossing Silver Tabby and self British Shorthairs. Two distinct genes were responsible for the smoke coat: one inhibiting coloration in the undercoat, the other emphasising colour along the guard hairs. The effect is magnificent, for when the cat moves, the white undercoat flickers through creating a shimmering, 'smoky' effect.

The British Colourpoint, as well as some other self colours, in British Shorthairs, are the result of out crossings to Foreign, or, Oriental, breeds. British Seal Colourpoint Shorthairs, while having the physical characteristics of other British Shorthairs, share their exotic coat pattern with Siamese, while the gene for the rich brown colour of the Chocolate self originally came from Oriental breeds, first introduced into the Long-hair/Persian breed and then into the British Shorthair.

The British Tipped Shorthair, which was known as the Chinchilla Shorthair until 1978, was developed through matings with Chinchilla Longhairs. In kittens, it is possible to see this long-hair ancestry because it is some months before they develop their adult coats. In some instances, these new coat colours are not accepted outside the UK.

As a breed, all British Shorthairs, whatever their colour or markings, are delightful cats that are intelligent, affectionate and, for want of another expression, 'cuddly' – their plump, round cheeks make tickling them very difficult to resist!

BLACK/CHOCOLATE/LILAC TORTIE BRITISH SHORTHAIR

RED SILVER SPOTTED BRITISH SHORTHAIR

BROWN SPOTTED BRITISH SHORTHAIR

SILVER TABBY BRITISH SHORTHAIR

BLACK TIPPED BRITISH SHORTHAIR

AMERICAN SHORTHAIR

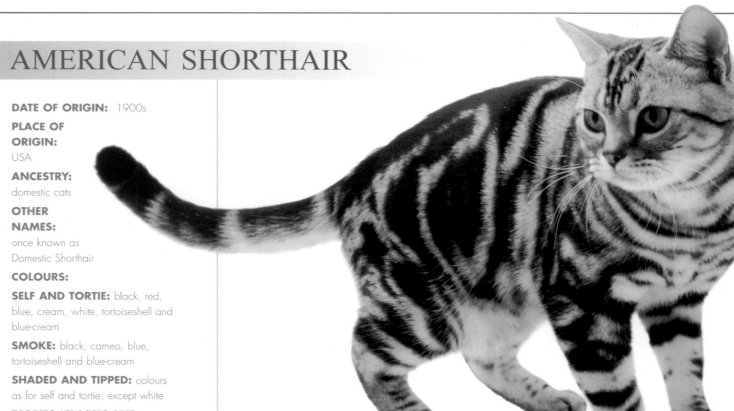

DATE OF ORIGIN: 1900s

PLACE OF ORIGIN: USA

ANCESTRY: domestic cats

OTHER NAMES: once known as Domestic Shorthair

COLOURS:

SELF AND TORTIE: black, red, blue, cream, white, tortoiseshell and blue-cream

SMOKE: black, cameo, blue, tortoiseshell and blue-cream

SHADED AND TIPPED: colours as for self and tortie, except white

TABBIES (CLASSIC AND MACKEREL): brown, red, blue, cream, brown patched, blue patched

TABBY BICOLOUR: all tabby colours with white

SHADED TABBIES: colours and patterns as for standard tabbies

BICOLOUR (STANDARDS AND VANS): as for self and tortie except white

SMOKE, SHADED & TIPPED BICOLOUR: black smoke, cameo smoke, blue smoke, tortoiseshell smoke, shaded cameo, shell cameo with white

SILVER TABBY BICOLOUR: silver tabby, cameo tabby, silver patched tabby with white

COAT LENGTH: short

TYPE OF FUR: thick, quite hard

SIZE: 3.5–kg (8–15 lb)

SILVER TABBY AMERICAN SHORTHAIR

It may be that the first domestic cats reached North America with the Pilgrim Fathers aboard the Mayflower. The non-pedigree cats of America, like their European cousins, certainly earned their keep as efficient pest controllers for over two centuries before a systematic, selective breeding and show programme was developed.

At the earliest cat shows, held in the north-eastern states in the 19th century, the gentle giants of the cat world, the long-haired Maine Coon dominated. However, the tough conditions and working environments of many of the American short-haired cats meant that these were – like the very people themselves – tough, resilient and resourceful. While in the early days of the breed, the lines were strengthened by matings with pedigree British Shorthairs, today the American Shorthair is a very distinctive breed of strong and hardy cats. With more natural predators around in the United States than in Europe, the American Shorthairs evolved into bigger cats than their continental cousins.

The history of the American Shorthair is said to date from around 1900 when a pedigree red tabby male – with the particularly feminine name of 'Belle' – was sent from England to America and was the first short-haired cat to be registered as a pedigree animal by the CFA. So the first American Shorthair was actually a British Shorthair émigré! Others soon followed Belle across the Atlantic to a new world, including a male Silver Tabby delightfully named 'Pretty Correct'. But American breeders were also starting to register their own cats. The first home-grown American Shorthair to be registered was 'Buster Brown', a male Black Smoke, said to have been born on 15 January, 1904.

At first, the breed was called simply the 'Shorthair', but soon it became known as the Domestic Shorthair – a name it is sometimes still called today, although officially it is called the American Shorthair – and bred in a huge range of magnificent colours and markings. Although no longer permitted, for a time any non-pedigree cat that met the standard could be registered, widening the gene pool of the breed. In 1971, one such cat was even declared American Shorthair of the year by the CFA. The CFA breed standard describes the American Shorthair as having 'no part of its anatomy so exaggerated as to foster weakness... The general effect is of the trained athlete'.

The body is solid, powerful and muscular, and less square in shape than the British Shorthair. The legs are of medium length (a little longer than the British), capable of high leaps and heavily muscled to cope with any terrain. The head is large, but slightly longer than it is wide, with full cheeks and large, rounded eyes that are very slightly tilted. The tail is medium length and thick

at the base, and the coat is short and thick, with quite a hard texture to it – at shows, in fact, judges penalise exhibits for having soft, fluffy coats!

The best known American Shorthairs are undoubtedly the Silver Tabbies with their dense black markings on a silver background.

**BROWN CLASSIC TABBY
AMERICAN SHORTHAIR**

In 1965, a Silver Tabby won the United States Cat of the Year award, and prompted the breed name to be changed from 'Domestic Shorthair' to the appropriately proud 'American Shorthair'. While the CFA accepts only blotched and striped tabby patterns – markings that were prevalent among the breed's emigrant ancestors – the TICA accepts spotted and ticked patterns as well.

Apart from their famous hardiness, American Shorthairs are noted for their easy-going temperament, their hunting abilities and their intelligence. Easy to rear and feed, they also make ideal house pets.

**CLASSIC SILVER TABBY
AMERICAN SHORTHAIR**

EXOTIC SHORTHAIR

DATE OF ORIGIN: 1960s

PLACE OF ORIGIN: USA

ANCESTRY: Long-hair and American Shorthair

OTHER NAMES: none

COLOURS: all colours and patterns including sepia, pointed and mink

COAT LENGTH: medium – slightly longer than other shorthairs

TYPE OF FUR: a double coat that is soft and plush, and dense enough to stand slightly away from the body

SIZE: 3—6.5 kg (7—14 lb)

SILVER TIPPED EXOTIC SHORTHAIR

This exotic-looking breed is a 'short-haired long-hair' or, the short-haired version of the Long-hair/Persian (see page 182)! They have the compact body conformation of the Longhairs, along with its flattened, 'teddy-ear' face, but a rather original, dense, double coat that is not quite long and not quite short, but still needs twice-weekly combing to keep it in tiptop condition! The beautiful Exotic Shorthair is both a recently developed breed and one that is still quite rare, in part because many litters contain long-haired kittens.

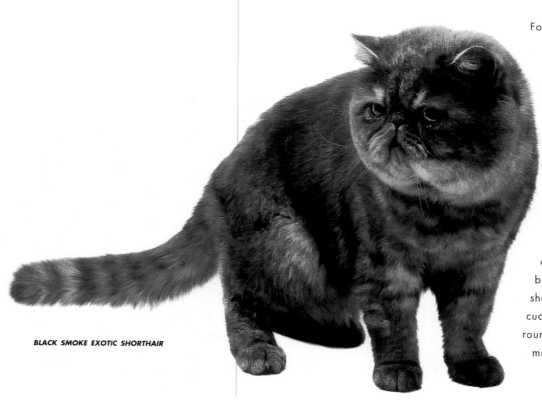

BLACK SMOKE EXOTIC SHORTHAIR

For some years, breeders in North America out crossed American Shorthairs to Long-hair/Persians. In mid 1967, it was decided that a new breed name should be created for cats of mixed Long-hair/Persian and American Shorthair ancestry to leave the American Shorthair breed free of cats with mixed ancestry. Consequently, the parents of an Exotic Shorthair must either be one Long-hair/Persian and one American Shorthair, two Exotic Shorthairs, or one Long-hair/Persian and one Exotic Shorthair. Whatever the original blend, the result is a cat that is round in shape from its ears to its toes, and perfect for cuddling! It's not the soft coat that makes the roundness though – underneath it are strong muscles that give the breed its curves!

Often described as 'chunky', the Exotic Shorthair has a medium to large, cobby body standing on short but firm legs. The head is large and round with full cheeks and a nose that is shorter than that of a British or American Shorthair. Because it has inherited some of the Long-hair/Persian 'flawed' characteristics, such as the overflowing tear ducts, constricted nostrils and dental problems, the British breed standard – in an effort to breed for health rather than appearance – calls for the nose leather of the Exotic Shorthair to be below the edge of the eye.

CREAM EXOTIC SHORTHAIR

with only the body marking varying. While the pointed pattern is a separate group in Longhairs/Persians, in the Exotic it is included in the colours. All points should be evenly matched, with the mask extending over the entire face. In the tortie Exotics, the standard calls for the colours to be balanced and softly intermingled, and for all four feet and the tail to contain both colours. Because tortie patterning is inherently difficult to predict and to breed, some distinct patches of colour are allowed, as are blazes of colour on the face.

CREAM MACKEREL TABBY AND WHITE EXOTIC SHORTHAIR

SELF BLACK EXOTIC SHORTHAIR

Nevertheless, like many hybrids, the Exotic Shorthair is very hardy and combines the best of the parental breed-temperaments, making for an affectionate and relaxed cat.

An even coat is a show standard essential – judges find fault with the merest suggestion of feathery hair on the ears or tail along with any tufting on the toes. Exotic tabbies may be classic, mackerel or spotted – unlike Longhairs/Persians, which are only recognised in the classic pattern. The facial markings of all three patterns are the same

CHARTREUX

DATE OF ORIGIN:
pre-18th century

PLACE OF ORIGIN: France

ANCESTRY: household cats

OTHER NAMES: none

COLOURS: blue self only

COAT LENGTH: blue self only

TYPE OF FUR: dense and glossy

SIZE: 3—7.5 kg (7—17 lb)

It is possibly that the Chartreux's ancestors came from Syria and were taken by ship to France in the Middle Ages. References to the breed date back as far as 1558. They were said to have been bred by the Carthusian monks at the monastery of La Grande Chartreuse in France, which is most well known for its production of Chartreuse, the famous aromatic liqueur. The earliest recorded use of the name Chartreux (spelled with an 'x') was in 1723, when the Universal Dictionary of Commerce in France used this name to describe cats with blue fur. Later, the naturalist Carolus Linneaus (1707–78) recognised the Chartreux as a distinct variety and Georges Louis Leclerc, Comte de Buffon (1707–88) described it as, 'the cat of France' and gave it its own scientific name – Felis catus cartusianorum. A lovely description of the Chartreux comes from the pen of the French writer, Colette (1873–1954), who wrote of her own cat, 'the sun played on her Chartreux coat, mauve and blue like a wood pigeon's neck'.

The Leger sisters from Brittany in northern France were the first fanciers known to have shown Chartreux cats, in Paris in 1931. With a massive body, but with a head that is not so round as the British Blue Shorthair, and a slightly more silvery coat, the Chartreux nearly became extinct after World War II. Today, very few truly pure Chartreux remain in France but the breed was successfully re-established by out crossing survivors with blue Longhairs/Persians (see page 107) and especially, with British Blue Shorthairs (see page 130). For a time FIFé made no distinctions between the Chartreux and British Blue and, in the 1970s, assimilated them into one class under the name 'British Blue'. Today, however, these two breeds are treated as distinct.

BLUE CHARTREUX

The Chartreux is neither cobby nor slender – many cat fanciers describe its conformation as 'primitive', and even as a 'potato on matchsticks' – and its finely boned legs are not thick, although they are short and sturdy and the rounded paws are small in relation to body size. The Chartreux head is a broad trapezoid shape, with a high forehead and rounded-tip ears set high. While the muzzle is narrow, the Chartreux face does not look pointed because of the rounded whisker pads and quite heavy jowls that become more pronounced with age. The nose leather is a delightful, matching dark blue and the eyes are large, round and copper or gold in

colour. To many fanciers of the Chartreux, it is its sweet expression that is irresistible – the Chartreux always seems to have a slight smile! Also intriguing is the naming system for Chartreux cats: each year is assigned a letter – omitting K, Q, W, X, Y and Z – and the cats' names begin with the letter assigned to the year of their birth. Cats born in 2003 will have names beginning with the letter 'U'.

BLUE CHARTREUX

AMERICAN WIREHAIR

DATE OF ORIGIN: 1966

PLACE OF ORIGIN: USA

ANCESTRY: farm cat, American Shorthair

OTHER NAMES: none

COLOURS:

SELF (SOLID) AND TORTIE: black, red, blue, cream, white (blue-, gold- and odd-eyed), tortoiseshell and blue tortie

SMOKE: black, red and blue

SHADED AND TIPPED: shaded silver, shade cameo, chinchilla silver and shell cameo

TABBIES (CLASSIC AND MACKEREL): brown, red, blue and cream

SHADED TABBIES: silver, cameo

BICOLOURS: self and tortie colours with white

COAT LENGTH: medium

TYPE OF FUR: springy, tight and frizzy, a bit like lamb's wool, but needs several days to regain curl after getting wet. Curly whiskers

SIZE: 3.5—7 kg (8—15 lb)

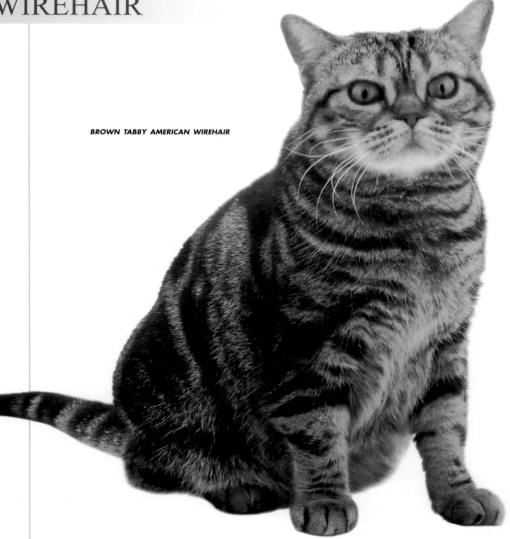

BROWN TABBY AMERICAN WIREHAIR

These rare cats are almost unknown outside their native North America, and are one of the very few cat breeds to have truly originated in the USA. The American Wirehair traces its origins back to 1966, when a litter of litters was born to a pair of farm cats called Bootsie and Fluffy, near Vernon, in upper New York state. One of the kittens, a male, had a sparse, very wiry coat. The owners contacted a local breeder John O'Shea, who took the male kitten and one of the 'normal' females from the litter, and began a breeding programme designed to establish the genetic nature of the unusual coat and, if possible, to establish a new breed.

Following tests by geneticists on samples of the hairs, it was discovered that the cat was indeed a completely new type and that it represented a spontaneous mutation whereby each of the longer hairs was crimped and wiry, and bent into a hook at the end. This wiry hair contrasted with other curly-coated cats such as Rexes, whose coats are quite soft to the touch. The American Wirehair it seemed was even more wiry than the Wire-haired Terrier!

The original wiry-haired kitten, appropriately called Adam, was a red and white male who, when mature, was mated with its 'normal' litter mate – reputedly a brown tabby and white, but more likely a brown 'torbie' (a brown tabby tortie) – and their first litter was born on 7 July, 1967. Of the four kittens born, two females were wire-haired red and whites – like dad. One died young, but the surviving female, called Amy, was mated with Adam and went on to give birth to a number of other wire-haired kittens, among them the delightfully named Barberry Ellen, the first homozygous (true breeding) American Wirehair, born in 1969. Adam was also mated to an unrelated short-haired white cat and their litter produced three further wire-haired kittens, thereby establishing the fact that the wirehair gene is inherited in a dominant manner – provided one parent is wirehaired, the litter will contain wire-haired kittens.

Wire-haired kittens are easy to identify at birth: the whiskers and hairs on their faces and ears, as well as those on their coats, are crimped and stick out at different angles. Longer-haired kittens have lovely ringlets, shorter-haired ones have a more wavy appearance. In both instances, however, the coats develop their adult texture in its first year.

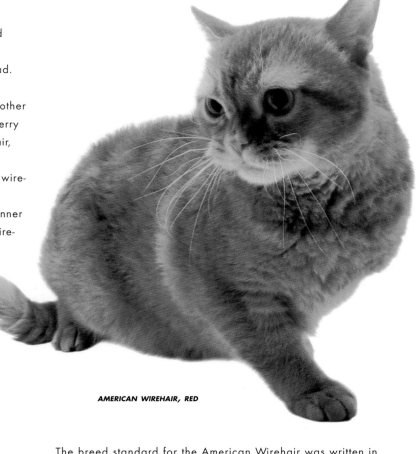

AMERICAN WIREHAIR, RED

The breed standard for the American Wirehair was written in 1967. The CFA requires that all colours, except the silvers, have brilliant golden eyes, although the TICA does not recognise any relationship between eye and coat colour. A rounded head with high cheekbones, a level back and rounded torso, sturdy, medium-length legs with rounded paws and a tapering tail, rounded at the tip but not blunt are defining characteristics of the American Wirehairs conformation. More revealing are the words owners of American Wirehairs use to describe their cats – sinewy, muscular, intelligent and apt to rule the household (and other cats) with 'iron paws', yet at the same time, relaxed, rarely destructive and loving to be handled!

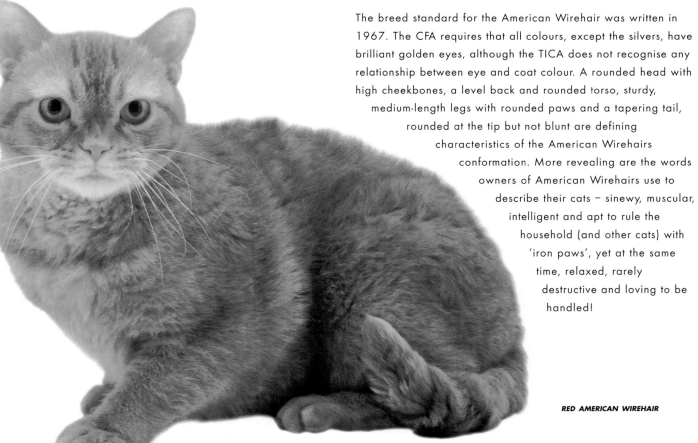

RED AMERICAN WIREHAIR

SNOWSHOE

DATE OF ORIGIN: 1960s

PLACE OF ORIGIN: USA

ANCESTRY: Siamese, American Shorthair

OTHER NAMES: Silver Laces

COLOURS:

MITTED COLOURS: seal, chocolate, lilac and blue

BICOLOURS: mitted colours with white

COAT LENGTH: short

TYPE OF FUR: rich and thick. White feet with Siamese-type points

SIZE: 2.5—5.5 kg (6—12 lb)

Named for its characteristic white mittens, the Snowshoe or 'Silver Laces' combines the pointing of the Siamese (see page 208) with white spotting. These beautiful white 'booties' resemble slightly those found on the long-haired Birman (see page 158), but the Snowshoe has a longer head than is considered desirable in a Birman, probably due to the influence of the short-haired breeds that helped to create it.

SEAL POINT AND WHITE SNOWSHOE

The Snowshoe is the result of efforts on the part of Dorothy Hinds-Daugherty in the 1960s to cross her Siamese with American Shorthairs. At first, other breeders of Siamese cats were suspicious and very cautious of this new hybrid – white toes were a known 'fault' in early Siamese and many feared that the spotting might find its way back into the Siamese bloodlines after many decades of breeding to eradicate it. In fact, the fault may have been inherited from the Siamese's American Shorthair ancestors. Moreover, at the time, the beautiful pointing pattern was the trademark of the Siamese, although today, colour points are recognised in numerous breeds.

The Snowshoe is a moderately sized cat, with what is described as a semi-foreign build – lean yet muscular, somewhere between the muscular cats of northern Europe and the more sinuous cats of Africa and Asia, with a moderately wedge-shaped head, blue eyes and large, pointed ears. It has more oval-shaped paws, with pink and grey paw pads and a long, gently tapering tail. The Snowshoe's coat is short, rich and thick, and lies close to the body.

The mitted pattern is the 'classic' Snowshoe, with the white booties ideally stopping at the ankles on the forelegs and below the hocks on the hind legs. The amount of white must not exceed one-third of the body – except in Seal Bicolour where it must not exceed two-thirds of the total body area – with no isolated white spots, although there may be some white on the face. It is, in fact, the facial pattern of the Snowshoe which determines whether a cat is mitted or bicoloured: an inverted 'V' on the nose up between the eyes means a Snowshoe is a bicolour, while anything less makes it mitted. Kittens are born white and it may take up to two years for the markings to be fully defined, with the coloration darkening as the cat matures. This extremely pretty cat, with a talkative, but soft-voiced nature, remained little known until the 1980s. It was recognised by the TICA in 1983 and though it has deservedly grown in popularity, the Snowshoe still remains rare outside of the US.

BLUE AND WHITE POINT SNOWSHOE

ABYSSINIAN

DATE OF ORIGIN: 1860s

PLACE OF ORIGIN: Ethiopia

ANCESTRY: Ethiopian household and street cats

OTHER NAMES: none

COLOURS: names vary internationally

TABBIES (TICKED): ruddy (usual), red (sorrel), blue, fawn, lilac (lavender), cream, chocolate tortie, cinnamon tortie, blue tortie, lilac tortie and fawn tortie

SILVER TABBIES (TICKED): silver, silver sorrel and silver blue

COAT LENGTH: short

TYPE OF FUR: glossy and dense, ticked fur colour caused by at least four bands of colour on each shaft of hair

SIZE: 4—7.5 kg (9—16 lb)

BLUE/SILVER ABYSSINIAN

BLACK ABYSSINIAN

The strikingly beautiful Abyssinian is one of the world's oldest breeds of cat, and one of the world's most popular. The Abyssinian – and its younger, long-haired version, the Somali (see page 178) – are unique in the feline world in that their coat pattern is based on a single mutant gene, not found in any other pure breed. The gene is known as the Abyssinian and denoted, Ta.

The gene is one of the agouti series of alleles and gives each hair several dark bands of colour, which are evenly dispersed on a lighter background. The result is the strikingly beautiful 'ticked' coat pattern, like that of the African Wild Cat. Some residual tabby markings can be found on the head and sometimes on the tail and legs. This breed also has a unique body shape: long, lean, yet powerful and, while it is definitely foreign in body type, it is far less so than the Siamese (see page 208)

Like many of the older cat breeds, the Abyssinian's origins are obscure. Some fanciers trace it back to the Nile valley, as they share a very similar body type to the cats painted and sculpted in ancient Egyptian art. Abyssinians were first brought to Europe in 1868, when a cat called Zula was brought to England by British soldiers returning from the Abyssinian War. It's likely that Zula, along with other imported cats of unknown origin, but with similar markings, were bred as this was a time of great political, economic, cultural and scientific interest in North Africa. These distinctive cats were known by a variety of different names including the 'Hare cat' or 'Rabbit cat', no doubt because its coat was similar to that of a wild rabbit. In France, even today, the standard Ruddy (as it is called in the USA) or Usual (as it is called in the UK) coat colour – a rich, golden brown ticked with bands of black – is called lièvre, or hare. Genetically, Ruddy/Usual Abyssinians are black cats with the 'ruddiness' due to rufus polygenes. This group of genes modifies the orange colour to produce rich red. They also act on some other pigments to produce the rich colouring of 'show' tabbies and the warm chestnut tone of the Abyssinian.

complete CAT

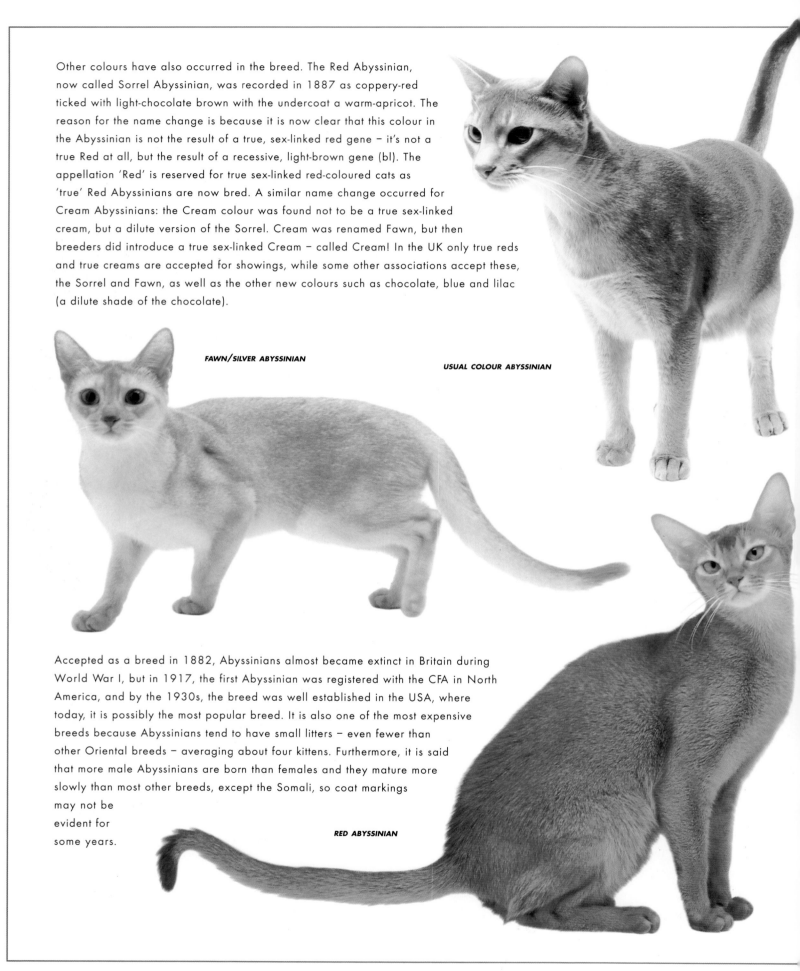

Other colours have also occurred in the breed. The Red Abyssinian, now called Sorrel Abyssinian, was recorded in 1887 as coppery-red ticked with light-chocolate brown with the undercoat a warm-apricot. The reason for the name change is because it is now clear that this colour in the Abyssinian is not the result of a true, sex-linked red gene – it's not a true Red at all, but the result of a recessive, light-brown gene (bl). The appellation 'Red' is reserved for true sex-linked red-coloured cats as 'true' Red Abyssinians are now bred. A similar name change occurred for Cream Abyssinians: the Cream colour was found not to be a true sex-linked cream, but a dilute version of the Sorrel. Cream was renamed Fawn, but then breeders did introduce a true sex-linked Cream – called Cream! In the UK only true reds and true creams are accepted for showings, while some other associations accept these, the Sorrel and Fawn, as well as the other new colours such as chocolate, blue and lilac (a dilute shade of the chocolate).

FAWN/SILVER ABYSSINIAN

USUAL COLOUR ABYSSINIAN

Accepted as a breed in 1882, Abyssinians almost became extinct in Britain during World War I, but in 1917, the first Abyssinian was registered with the CFA in North America, and by the 1930s, the breed was well established in the USA, where today, it is possibly the most popular breed. It is also one of the most expensive breeds because Abyssinians tend to have small litters – even fewer than other Oriental breeds – averaging about four kittens. Furthermore, it is said that more male Abyssinians are born than females and they mature more slowly than most other breeds, except the Somali, so coat markings may not be evident for some years.

RED ABYSSINIAN

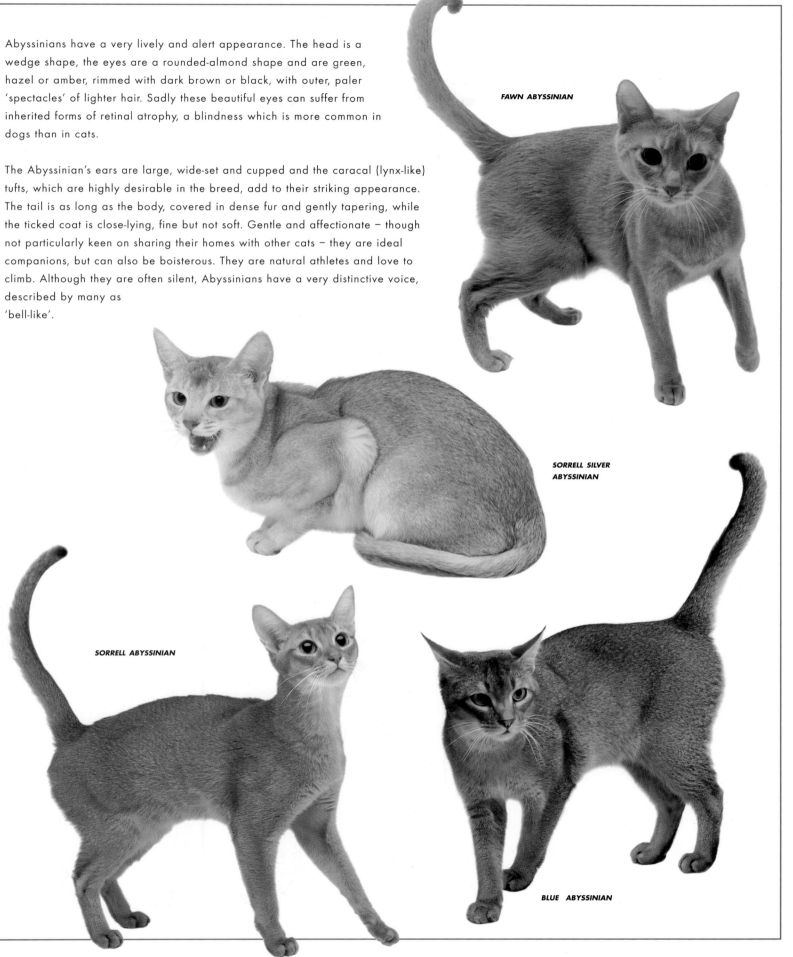

Abyssinians have a very lively and alert appearance. The head is a wedge shape, the eyes are a rounded-almond shape and are green, hazel or amber, rimmed with dark brown or black, with outer, paler 'spectacles' of lighter hair. Sadly these beautiful eyes can suffer from inherited forms of retinal atrophy, a blindness which is more common in dogs than in cats.

The Abyssinian's ears are large, wide-set and cupped and the caracal (lynx-like) tufts, which are highly desirable in the breed, add to their striking appearance. The tail is as long as the body, covered in dense fur and gently tapering, while the ticked coat is close-lying, fine but not soft. Gentle and affectionate – though not particularly keen on sharing their homes with other cats – they are ideal companions, but can also be boisterous. They are natural athletes and love to climb. Although they are often silent, Abyssinians have a very distinctive voice, described by many as 'bell-like'.

FAWN ABYSSINIAN

SORRELL SILVER ABYSSINIAN

SORRELL ABYSSINIAN

BLUE ABYSSINIAN

SIAMESE

DATE OF ORIGIN: pre-1700s

PLACE OF ORIGIN: Thailand

ANCESTRY: household and temple cats

OTHER NAMES: Royal Cat of Siam

COLOURS:

SIAMESE POINT COLOURS: seal, chocolate, blue and lilac

NEWER COLOURPOINT SHORTHAIR POINT COLOURS: (produced by recessive genes) recognised by CFA: red, cream, tortie and tabby versions of all colours

COAT LENGTH: short

TYPE OF FUR: close—ying and fine

SIZE: 2.5—5.5 kg (6—12 lb)

CHOCOLATE POINT SIAMESE

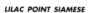
LILAC POINT SIAMESE

To many people, the Siamese cat represents the ultimate in feline beauty and, of all the breeds, it is probably the most instantly recognisable with its points – the coloured ears, mask, 'stockings' and tail – set against a paler body and offset by brilliant, piercing, blue eyes. Siamese kittens, perhaps surprisingly, are white at birth and only develop their markings and colour very gradually! The Siamese is well documented in the art and literature of ancient Siam (now Thailand) and boasts a truly Oriental – and exotic – origin. More than 100 years since it was first introduced to the Western world, the Siamese has remained one of the most popular breeds of both pet and show cat.

There have been many theories as to the origins of the Siamese – including those that say it is related to Egyptian and Manx cats – but it is generally accepted that the Siamese was a variety of cat found in the ancient city of Ayudha, which was founded in 1530 and was Siam's capital until 1767, when the city was invaded by the Burmese. Among the artefacts and manuscripts saved from the city and now housed in the Thai National Library in Bangkok, the most well known – and for many, the most beautiful – is The Cat-Book Poems. Its exact date is unknown but it could have been written any time between 1350 and 1750. This manuscript depicts beautiful, pale-coated, seal-point Siamese cats, while the accompanying verses tell of their black tails, feet and ears, and the characteristic reddish eye glow of their eyes at night.

These pointed cats were not the only type to be found in Ayudha: other native cats recorded in the manuscripts include the Si-Siwat (see page 222) and the Supalak, but it seems that the pointed cats were particularly valued and were kept in temples and in the royal places. In 1884, the King of Siam gave two Siamese cats to the British Consul-General in Bangkok, whose sister took them back to England to show at the Crystal Palace in 1885. But there are records of Siamese cats in Britain at the first true cat show in 1871 – even though they were described as 'an unnatural nightmare kind of cat'!

When the first Siamese cats arrived in Europe, exotic tales accompanied them – or were invented – to explain their squinting eyes and the kink in their tails. It was said that sacred temple cats were put in charge of the Buddha's sacred vase overnight. In order to make sure nothing happened to it, the cats wrapped their tails hard around the vase and stared at it intently, so that their tail got bent and their eyes became crossed! According to another legend, the ladies of the court entrusted their jewels to their cats – rings were slipped onto their tails at night for safe-keeping and the kink developed to stop them falling off. Scientific explanations for both the squint and the kink are based on genetic discoveries. Today, the squint and kink are considered defects and through selective breeding, they have largely been removed from the breed.

In spite of early reactions to the appearance of the Siamese in 1871, they soon became a very popular and desirable breed. They are very difficult to rear as they are not the most robust of cats and are prone to feline enteritis (a potentially fatal virus that damages the gut lining, but which can be vaccinated against) and respiratory problems. But, despite the difficulties, by the end of the 19th century, the Siamese was well established in Britain and had reached America in the 1890s.

CHOCOLATE TABBY SIAMESE

BLUE TABBY POINT SIAMESE

APRICOT POINT SIAMESE

SEAL POINT TABBY SIAMESE

The first standards for the breed were written in 1892. Early writers on the breed stated that there were two kinds of Siamese among the early imported cats, but it was the pale-bodied, pointed kind – called the Royal Cat of Siam – that was most highly prized by fanciers. The other type was described as 'chocolate point' – a rich brown colour on the body – with dark points. In 1896, a blue point was exhibited in Britain by a Mr. Spearman, recently home from Siam, but the cat was disqualified by the judge – none other than the famous painter of cats, Louis Wain! Some reports say that this blue-pointed Siamese was a blue self like the Korat (see page 222) but, nevertheless, a blue-pointed Siamese was registered in the late 19th century. By the 1920s, they were appearing in the US where, in 1932, the CFA recognised them, but they were not officially recognised in Britain until 1936. The lilac-point Siamese is the outcome of combining the blue dilution and chocolate-brown genes, and was recognised in the 1950s in the US, and in the 1960s in Britain.

The quartet of colours – seal, blue, chocolate and lilac-pointed Siamese – are the only varieties regarded as true Siamese by many cat associations. Some purists insist that the only true Siamese is the blue-eyed seal point! Nevertheless, many new colours have been introduced – sometimes classed as Siamese, sometimes as 'Colourpoint Shorthairs'. The first of these colours to become established was the red, followed by tortie points – bred today in seal, blue, chocolate and lilac – and then by cream and tabby point, or lynx point, as it is known in the US. In the 1970s, the discovery of the inhibitor gene (I), responsible for the silver colour in cats, meant that it was possible to breed the Silver Tabby Point Siamese. As a direct result of genetic investigations into cat colours, further varieties were now possible, such as smoke pointed (also known as shadow points), which has

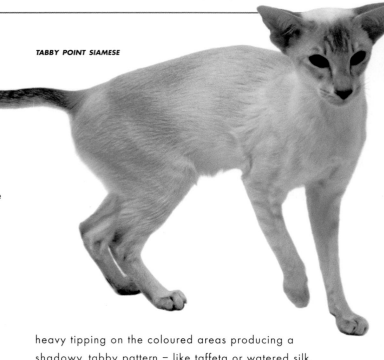

TABBY POINT SIAMESE

heavy tipping on the coloured areas producing a shadowy, tabby pattern – like taffeta or watered silk.

Whatever the colour of their points, all Siamese share the outgoing and vocal characteristics typical of this beautiful breed. Extreme in their looks – their svelte bodies, long heads with slanting eyes and fine muzzles, hind legs longer than their forelegs and long, tapering, kink-free tails – Siamese are also extreme in their character. They are the noisiest, the most boisterous, the most temperamental, the most intelligent and the most demanding cats. But above all, they are the most affectionate cats and, to many fanciers, the most beautiful ever to grace the earth.

In their ancestral home, Siamese cats were never defined solely as those with colour on their points – it was only by chance that the first cats to come from Siam and attract the attention of Western fanciers were pointed.

BLUE TORTIE POINT SIAMESE

CHOCOLATE POINT SIAMESE

BURMESE: AMERICAN AND EUROPEAN

DATE OF ORIGIN: 1930s

PLACE OF ORIGIN: Burma (now Myanmar)

ANCESTRY: Temple cats, Siamese crosses

OTHER NAMES: none, but some colours were previously called Malayans

COLOURS:

SEPIA AMERICAN BURMESE: sable, champagne, blue and platinum

EUROPEAN BURMESE: self and tortie colours – brown, red, chocolate, blue, lilac, cream, brown tortie, chocolate tortie, blue tortie and lilac tortie

COAT LENGTH: short

TYPE OF FUR: sleek and satiny

SIZE: 3.5—6.5 kg (8–14 lb)

Sleek and richly coloured, the muscular, yet compact Burmese have been described as 'bricks wrapped in silk'! While brown Burmese cats have lived in Myanmar for several centuries, the Burmese was the first pedigree breed to be developed entirely in the United States and one of the first breeds to undergo comprehensive genetic studies. Since it was first introduced to the West in 1930 the Burmese has developed into two types – almost two separate breeds – on either side of the Atlantic Ocean, although the European Burmese is descended from American cats imported into Europe after World War II.

European or American, virtually all modern pedigree Burmese can trace their ancestry back to a single female called Wong Mau. She was an attractive walnut-brown cat, with discernible darker points, taken from Rangoon to the US by US Navy psychiatrist, Joseph Thompson. At the time, no similar cats were known 'All-over-brown Siamese' cats had been seen at 19th century cat shows and similar cats were recorded in ancient Thai manuscripts, but these could have been Burmese or Burmese-Siamese hybrids.

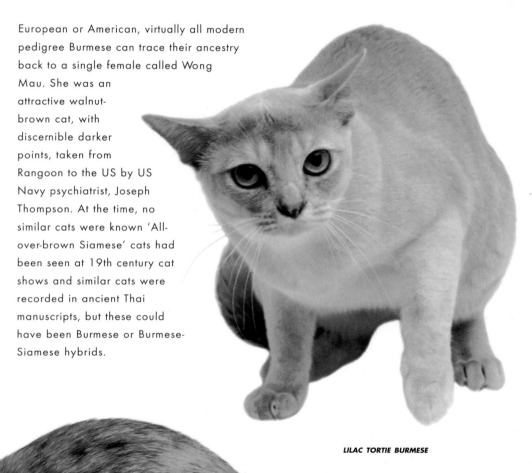

LILAC TORTIE BURMESE

BROWN TORTIE BURMESE

Since there were no other similar cats to mate with Wong Mau, Thompson bred her with a cat of the closest breed – a Siamese – and followed with crosses between the offspring and back to Wong Mau herself. Over the course of several generations, three types of kittens were found in Wong Mau's descendants: those with typical Siamese colouring, those like Wong Mau herself and those which were brown all over – the first true Burmese. Further breeding experiments finally established the existence of the Burmese gene (cb) and all Burmese cats are homozygous for this – they will breed true. Cats like Wong Mau with intermediate colouring have one Burmese gene and one Siamese gene, and such cats are now being deliberately bred as the Tonkinese (see page 226).

The show standards for Burmese in North America and those in Europe – as well as in South Africa, Australia and New Zealand – are different. The European-Burmese standard considers an oriental, moderately wedge-shaped head, oval eyes and long legs as the ideal. In contrast, the American-Burmese standard favours a well rounded head shape with rounded eyes. This look, however, has brought with it an inherited deformity of the skull that can be lethal, often requiring such unfortunate cats to be put to sleep.

In all Burmese, the short, dense glossy coat, which is fine and shiny in texture, is a marked feature and all agree that brown – known in North America as sable – is the primary colour of the breed. There are other colours though, which for some time were classed as Malayans by the CFA.

Such colours are blue, where the coat is a beautiful soft, silver grey, shading slightly to the belly with a distinctive sheen on the rounded parts, chocolate

CHOCOLATE TORTIE BURMESE

(known in the US as champagne) and its dilute form, lilac (or platinum in the US). It is difficult to tell a lilac from a chocolate until kittens are a few weeks old, since both are almost white when born.

CREAM BURMESE

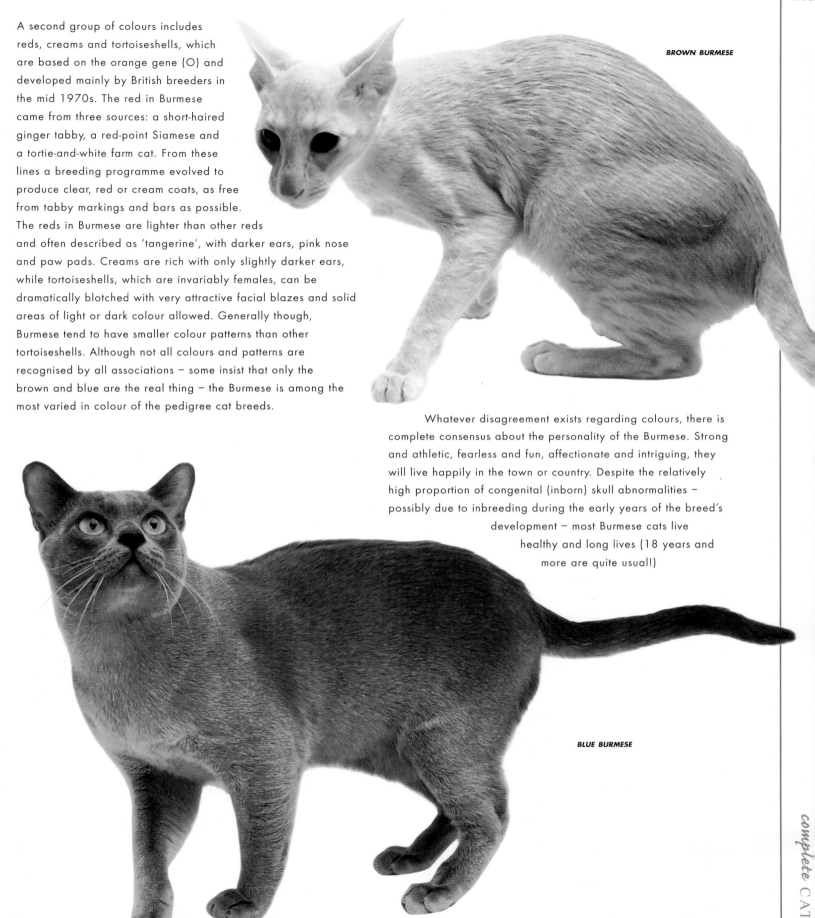

A second group of colours includes reds, creams and tortoiseshells, which are based on the orange gene (O) and developed mainly by British breeders in the mid 1970s. The red in Burmese came from three sources: a short-haired ginger tabby, a red-point Siamese and a tortie-and-white farm cat. From these lines a breeding programme evolved to produce clear, red or cream coats, as free from tabby markings and bars as possible. The reds in Burmese are lighter than other reds and often described as 'tangerine', with darker ears, pink nose and paw pads. Creams are rich with only slightly darker ears, while tortoiseshells, which are invariably females, can be dramatically blotched with very attractive facial blazes and solid areas of light or dark colour allowed. Generally though, Burmese tend to have smaller colour patterns than other tortoiseshells. Although not all colours and patterns are recognised by all associations – some insist that only the brown and blue are the real thing – the Burmese is among the most varied in colour of the pedigree cat breeds.

BROWN BURMESE

Whatever disagreement exists regarding colours, there is complete consensus about the personality of the Burmese. Strong and athletic, fearless and fun, affectionate and intriguing, they will live happily in the town or country. Despite the relatively high proportion of congenital (inborn) skull abnormalities – possibly due to inbreeding during the early years of the breed's development – most Burmese cats live healthy and long lives (18 years and more are quite usual!)

BLUE BURMESE

SAVANNAH

DATE OF ORIGIN: 1990s

PLACE OF ORIGIN: USA

ANCESTRY: African Serval Cats and Bengals

OTHER NAMES: Savana

COLOURS: Varied

COAT LENGTH: short

TYPE OF FUR: varied from coarse to fine

SIZE: Up to 76 cm (30 in) from nose to tip of tail, 8–13 kg (18–29 lb)

Only since 2002 has the F3 (third generation) of this new breed been accepted with experimental status by the TICA only.

The Savannah is a new cat breed – in many instances still in the early 'experimental' stages of development. It was developed as a hybrid of domestic cats and African Serval cats (Felis serval), a long limbed African cat with a tawny coat spotted with black, about 60 cm (24 in) at the shoulder, and about 1.5 m (5 ft) from nose to tail tip. Because the domestic cat and the Serval Cat are two different species, successful matings of this kind are difficult to achieve, so consequently, Savannah cats are still extremely rare. The Serval Cat's gestation period is 74 days; a domestic cat's is around 65 days. The difference in these two periods has led to premature births and stillborn offspring.

In appearance, the Savannah is a small 'replica' of its wild ancestor, but still larger than an average domestic cat. The first three generation of Savannahs, were called F1, F2 and F3 respectively: these offspring had a spotted coat pattern identical to the Serval, but with varied background colours. At the moment the only colour variations that are permitted are gold to orange ground colours with bold, black markings; silver ground with bold black markings, and black smoke. Additionally, the coat textures can vary from the coarser texture of the Serval coat, to the denser, softer and smoother coat of the domestic cat.

Some breeders are using Bengals (see page 235), which are also spotted, in their breeding programmes in order to maintain and enhance the spotted coat pattern, and in the expectation that, with each successive generation, the Savannah will 'shrink' in size, until they are about the same size as the average domestic cat. The first three generations (F1, F2 and F3) of males were expected to be sterile, and the females to be fertile. The rare examples of Savannahs show this new breed to be a very distinctive and beautiful cat: lean and muscular, with long slender legs and small feet with long toes, the Savannah has a tail that is three-quarters the length of the average domestic cat's tail. When alert the Savannah's tail is held curled up and back a little over the rump. The body is long, almost 'Oriental' but much more massive; the neck is sleek, the ears large and round. The slightly oval-slightly almond-shaped eyes are rich yellow, green, golden or a caramel brown and there are black 'tear drops' at the inner eyes.

In character Savannahs are described as 'dog-like' – they do like to be at the centre of activity, but like all cats, they also enjoy climbing and perching in high up places where they can watch the world go by! Although they remain rare, the Savannah is fortunately displaying 'hybrid vigour': a strong and disease-resistant constitution. Coupled with their distinctive good looks, the Savannah seems set to become a firm favourite with cat lovers.

SAVANNAH

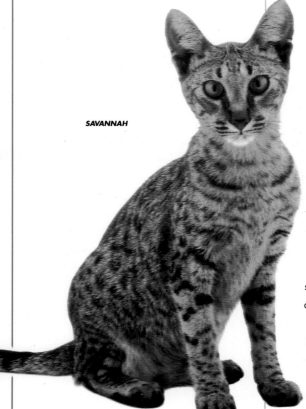

SAVANNAH

CHAUSIE

DATE OF ORIGIN: 1990s

PLACE OF ORIGIN: USA

ANCESTRY: African Jungle Cat (Felis chaus) and domestic cats

OTHER NAMES: none

COLOURS: black, black with silver ticking, golden

COAT LENGTH: short

TYPE OF FUR: close lying

SIZE: 35.5–45.7 cm at the shoulders (14–18 in), 8–13 kg (18–29 lb)

The Chausie is currently not recognised by the CFA, and has provisional acceptance by the TICA.

BROWN TICKED TABBY CHAUSIE

The Chausie is one of the most recent cat breeds – its foundation was registered with the TICA only in July of 1995 – and was originally a hybrid of the African Jungle Cat (Felis chaus) and the domestic cat. The African Jungle Cat is also known as the Swamp or Reed Cat and is native to Egypt and South Asia where, as it names imply, it can be found living in marsh and scrubby grasslands. The Jungle Cat is one of the larger of the small wild cats, and weighs on average between 7 and 16 kg (16–35 lb).

The Chausie is recognised provisionally by the TICA in three colours of their short, close lying coats – all of which are the same as those found in the wild Jungle Cat: black, black with silver ticking, and golden, which ranges from a ruddy colour (similar to the Abyssinian's colour, see page 205) to a light, reddy-fawn. As kittens, Chausies commonly display stripes or spots, but as they mature, these fade to leave a beautiful ticked coat, which ideally has between three and seven 'bars' of colour on each hair. In adult cats, bars or stripes on the legs remain visible.

The head is a moderate wedge shape, with a square muzzle and round whisker pads; the eyes are large and angle slightly towards the lower edge of the moderately large ears.(Ear tufts, like those of its wild ancestor, are highly desirable in a Chausie). Yellow and gold are the preferred eye colours, but hazel is also acceptable. A distinctive feature of the Chausie is its relatively short tail: only three-quarters of the natural tail length of the domestic cat, the Chausie's tail extends to just past the hock (heel) on the hind leg. This feature is due to a recessive gene: artificial 'docking' of the tail is not permitted in the breed.

The Chausie is becoming famous for its speed and athleticism: they are capable of jumping vertically to heights of nearly 2 m (6 ft), and their long hind legs make them capable of quite a speed! With a rectangular-shaped body, a full, broad chest and strong bones, ideally, the Chausie should be twice as long as it is tall. Consequently, this large cat is often twice as tall as the average domestic cat and can be up to three times as heavy!

In spite of their size and recent wild origins, Chausies are sweet-natured and affectionate cats that are also very loyal to their owners. They have been described as 'dog-like' in their behaviour – perhaps because of their loyalty and devotion, and the fact that they are also highly intelligent: they enjoy fetching toys when they are tossed! However, they are certainly cats in their curiosity and their habits of enjoying a climb along the mantelpiece, sitting on shelves, and lying in warm places, such as on top of the computer!

BROWN TICKED TABBY CHAUSIE

complete CAT

BURMILLA (ASIAN GROUP)

LILAC SHADED SILVER
BURMILLA

DATE OF ORIGIN: 1981

PLACE OF ORIGIN: Britain

ANCESTRY: Burmese, Chinchilla Longhair/Persian

OTHER NAMES: Burmilla

COLOURS:

BURMILLA OR SHADED (SOLID, SEPIA): black, chocolate, red, blue, lilac, cream, caramel, apricot, tortoiseshell, chocolate tortie, blue tortie, lilac tortie and caramel tortie

SILVER SHADED: colours and patterns as for shaded

SMOKE (SOLID, SEPIA): as for shaded

SELF (SOLID): bombay (ie. black but not to be confused with the breed of same name, see page 183): chocolate, red, blue, lilac, cream, caramel, apricot, tortoiseshell, chocolate tortie, blue tortie, lilac tortie and sepia colours

TABBY: (all patterns in solid, sepia): brown, chocolate, red, blue, lilac, cream, caramel, apricot, tortoiseshell, chocolate tortie, blue tortie, lilac tortie and caramel tortie

SILVER TABBIES: colours and patterns as for standard tabbies

COAT LENGTH: short

TYPE OF FUR: fine, soft and dense, and close-lying

SIZE: 4—7 kg (9—15 lb)

The Asian Group of cats, also known as the Burmilla, is a Burmese-Chinchilla Longhair/Persian (see page 182) cross and is the result of a chance mating between a Lilac Burmese queen and a Chinchilla tom in London in 1981. Their offspring of four were very attractive, silver-shaded kittens and were the founders of the breed. In 1984 the Burmilla Cat Club was founded and following consultations with the various cat-fancy organisations, a breeding programme was established.

The original litter were of the Burmese type and, initially, the policy was to breed Burmillas to Burmese mates at every other generation in order to enlarge the genetic base. Although the Burmilla shares essentially the same origins as the long-haired Tiffanie (see page 180), in 1989 the beautiful Burmilla was recognised by the GCCF – and, in 1994, by FIFé – as sufficiently distinct in breeding to designate them as a group, rather than a breed, and the Asian Group had the first breed standards that allowed points to be awarded for temperament. Consequently, the Burmilla is set to become increasingly popular not only because of its good looks but also for its extremely good nature, which makes it an ideal household pet.

The most striking features of the Burmilla are their dark 'eyeliner' and the way that their nose pads – which are a lovely terracotta red rather than pink – are also outlined, making these cats look as if they have enjoyed a full beauty and make-up treatment. Their magnificent eyes are half way between round and almond-shaped and a delightful green. Burmillas have strong bodies, with a gently rounded head and quite large ears that are set wide apart and angled slightly outwards. Their legs are a medium length – the hind legs are slightly longer than the forelegs – with oval-shaped paws and black paw pads. A long tail that tapers to a rounded tip is usually carried elegantly, slightly up. Their coats are short and fine, but also very soft and dense, the fur lying close to their bodies.

The Burmilla, or Asian Group, includes shaded and tipped cats, but their coats should not be so lightly tipped that it appears white. Tabby markings are restricted to the 'M' mark on the face, legs and tail, and the 'necklaces' – rings around the neck – must be broken. Ticked tabbies are allowed in both standard and silvered coats in all the Asian colours. Although the intensity of colour may be reduced in silver tabbies, there should always be at least two bands of darker ticking on each hair.

The original self colour of the Burmilla, is the 'Bombay' – a sleek black. This colour name must not be confused with the Bombay breed (see page 217), which stands alone as both a breed and type of cat.

CHOCOLATE SHADED
SILVER BURMILLA

BOMBAY

DATE OF ORIGIN: 1960s

PLACE OF ORIGIN: USA

ANCESTRY: Sable Burmese and black American Shorthairs

OTHER NAMES: none, but often described as 'mini black panthers'

COLOURS:

SELF (SOLID) COLOURS: black

COAT LENGTH: short

TYPE OF FUR: thick and glossy, like patent leather!

SIZE: 2.5—5 kg (6—11 lb)

Named after the Indian city where black leopards, or panthers, are still to be found, the Bombay was the result of American breeder Nikki Horner's attempts in the 1950s to create a 'mini black panther'. By the 1960s, Horner had produced the first of these glossy, black-coated, muscular cats with rounded heads and brilliant copper-coloured eyes. Although Bombays are similar to Burmese, they are not simply black Burmese cats: Bombays were produced by a mating with a black American Shorthair (see page 196) and a sable (brown) Burmese (see page 211).

SELF BLACK BOMBAY

The resulting offspring, having only one Burmese gene (cb) were black, but had the silky, short coat of the breed. Because the sepia-pointing gene of the Burmese is recessive, sable kittens with sepia pointing, still sometimes appear in Bombay litters and all Bombay kittens have tabby markings at birth! The full luxurious depth and colour of the Bombay can take up to two years to develop fully.

As a breed, the Bombay was slow to be recognised, but in 1976, it was accepted for championship status by the CFA and, since then, the Bombay has changed its appearance from that of its Burmese ancestors. The Burmese heritage meant that some Bombay lines suffered the congenital skull deformities and breeding to avoid this has meant that the Bombay's head is now closer to that of the American Shorthair (see page 196). The face is a moderate wedge-shape, and the nose leather, paw pads and eye rims are solid black (or a very, very dark brown). The largish ears have rounded tips and tilt forwards very slightly, giving the Bombay the impression that it is always listening intently to what you are saying! The long tail is carried proudly, the back is straight and the body muscular – and surprisingly heavy. Bombays have rather voracious appetites and while they can grow into quite large adults, they never lose their natural gracefulness.

Highly affectionate, the Bombay, like the Burmese, is best described as a 'heat seeking' cat – it adores the warmth and consequently will sit happily for hours (or days if given the opportunity) on someone's lap, having their coats stroked to maintain the sheen and texture.

BLACK BOMBAY

complete CAT

HAVANA

DATE OF ORIGIN: 1952

PLACE OF ORIGIN: USA
and Britain

ANCESTRY: chocolate–point
Siamese and Russian Blue

OTHER NAMES: none, but
see text

COLOURS: chocolate brown is
standard, but frost (lilac) cats occur

COAT LENGTH: very short

TYPE OF FUR: dense and glossy,
close-lying and no markings

SIZE: 2.5—4.5 kg (6—10 lb)

The poets of ancient Siam (Thailand) treasured all-brown cats. Considered to be of great beauty, they protected their owners from evil. Such cats were among the first Siamese to arrive in the West in the 19th century. It now appears likely that there were in fact, several distinct genetic types among these cats including what we would now call Burmese (see page 211) and Tonkinese (see page 226), as well as self chocolates. In the early 20th century, the Siamese Cat Club in Britain ruled that it would only encourage the breeding of the blue-eyed Siamese cats that are typical of the breed today and the few all-browns remained in obscurity until the 1950s.

Two breeders in Britain began working to breed solid-brown cats with the chocolate colouring of Siamese rather than the sable colour of the newly imported Burmese. At this time, the only recognised foreign breeds – other than Siamese – were the Russian Blue (see page 220) and the Abyssinian (see page 205). The first kitten of the new colour was born in 1952 and was the result of a cross between a Seal Point Siamese (carrying the chocolate-brown gene) and a short-haired black cat (itself produced by crossing a seal point with a black cat). This became the foundation of the new breed of elegant and graceful cats that was originally registered in Britain as Chestnut Brown Foreign Shorthair in 1958.

HAVANA KITTEN

Around the same time, a pair of Chestnut Brown Foreign Shorthairs were taken to the United States to establish the breed in America, and here they were registered as Havanas – named not after the Cuban city, but after the breed of rabbits of the same colour! In 1959, the breed was recognised in the US, but was called officially 'Havana Brown'. British 'Chestnuts' continued to be imported into the US and registered as Havana Browns until 1973, when the CFA accepted the Oriental Shorthair breed (see page 232) and, from then on, these imports were registered as Chestnut Oriental Shorthairs. Just to confuse things even more, the Oriental Shorthair colour that is called 'chestnut' in the US is now confusingly called 'Havana' in Britain!

The Havana Brown thus developed as a uniquely North American breed and the standards for judging are different to those in the UK. In the US, breeders prohibited the use of Siamese in the breeding programme and consequently the American cat is a much sturdier animal with a more rounded face and slightly longer fur. In Britain, on the other hand, the emphasis was towards a more Siamese-type body and, consequently, British Havanas are much more vocal than their American counterparts!

In either case, standing high on its legs, with a head slightly longer than it is wide and a distinct 'stop' on the nose just between the oval, chartreuse-green-coloured eyes, the Havana is indeed the rich, dark colour of a very expensive cigar!

Because Russian Blues were used in the breeding programme to create the Havana, the recessive dilute-blue gene was introduced which has led to the occasional appearance of delicately coloured Lilac (Lavender) Havana cats.

COLOUR HAVANA

RUSSIAN BLUE

DATE OF ORIGIN: pre-1800s

PLACE OF ORIGIN: believed to be the Russian port of Archangel

ANCESTRY: domestic cats

OTHER NAMES: Archangel Cat, Maltese Cat, Spanish Blue, Russian Shorthair, Foreign Blue

COLOURS: blue, (black and white have been developed and accepted in UK, but not in the USA or by FIFé)

COAT LENGTH: short

TYPE OF FUR: Double coat with dense undercoat, the plush fur is reminiscent of seal fur

SIZE: 3—5.5 kg (7—12 lb)

Exotic origins – always attractive in a cat breed – coupled with the most desirable of all the self colours, blue, makes the Russian Blue one of the most magnificent cats. The Blue is the original self colour of the breed and, some say, the only genuine Russian, although black and white forms have been developed recently. The Russians are said to have originated in the White Sea port of Archangel, from where sailors took them to western Europe in the 1860s.

Although Harrison Weir mentions the cats by name in his book Our Cats (1893), the Russian Blues were also known by a variety of names: the Archangel Cat, the Spanish Blue and the Maltese Cat. However, from 1917 – the date of the Russian Revolution – until 1948, they were known officially as Foreign Blues.

In their early years, at cat shows in Britain, all short-haired blue cats were shown in one class whatever their body-type. Consequently, the Russian Blues competed in the same group as British Shorthairs. The British type – cobby and round headed – invariably won in this class and interest in the finer-boned and narrower-headed Russian breed declined. In 1912, separate classes for British and Russians Blues – still called Foreigns at this time – were established and interest in the Russians flourished once more.

Like many European breeds, the Russian Blues suffered greatly during World War II and, in fact, came dangerously close to extinction. In the late 1940s and early 1950s though, breeders in Scandinavia began developing the breed, crossing a blue cat from Finland with a Siamese carrying the dilution (d) gene which is responsible for the blue colouring. At the same time in Britain, Russian Blue breeders were out crossing two blue-point Siamese and produced cats with a much more pronounced Oriental/Foreign body-type.

More recently, breeders have been working to re-create the original features of the breed by crossings with British Blues (see page 192).

RUSSIAN BLUE

The Russian Blue bred true for centuries because the gene responsible for the colour dilution is recessive, never masking any other colours. The newer Russian Blacks and Russian Whites are therefore regarded by many purists as controversial and they are not officially recognised in North America or by FIFé. Most controversial of all are Blue-Pointed Russians, the result of the earlier Siamese out crosses.

The most vivid features of the Russian Blue are its wonderfully thick, lustrous coat and its wonderful emerald-green eyes. The soft, dense double coat, ideal for insulating the body from the icy blasts of a Russian winter, is unique in its feel. The British breed standard describes the coat as 'the truest criterion of the Russian'. The original blue colour is an even blue with a silvery sheen that gives the Russian's coat a luminous appearance. Many breeders claim that the less frequently a Russian is brushed, the more radiant the coat becomes! This is because the coat is 'upstanding' and care must be taken not to polish and flatten it, although the coat of a Russian Blue in tiptop condition will spring up regardless of which

way you brush it! The eye colour is more recent in origin: the first Russians exhibited at the Crystal Palace show in England in 1871 had yellow eyes and it was not until 1933 that the breed standards called for them to be as 'vividly green as possible'.

The Russian is a well-muscled cat, but its body is never cobby or heavy. The long legs make for an elegance that belies their sturdiness. The head is a moderate wedge shape and longer from ears to eyes than from eyes to nose, with prominent whisker pads and large, pointed ears wide-set on the head. Those remarkable eyes are large, almond-shaped and wide-set on the head. Nose and paw pads match the body colour, while the tail tapers to a rounded tip.

Quiet voiced and very non-destructive cats, Russians make ideal house pets, although they can be very offhand with strangers – in most instances they disdainfully ignore them! The reason for this behaviour is that they save all their affection for their owners and each other!

RUSSIAN BLUE

complete CAT

KORAT

DATE OF ORIGIN: pre-1700s

PLACE OF ORIGIN: Thailand

ANCESTRY: household cats

OTHER NAMES: Si-Sawat

COLOURS: blue

COAT LENGTH: short

TYPE OF FUR: flat and silky, lacks full undercoat

SIZE: 2.5—5 kg (6—11 lb)

Similar in size and colour to Russian Blues (see page 220) the Korat was known in its native Thailand for centuries as Si-Sawat, which means 'lucky'. Thought to bring prosperity to their owners, they were often given as wedding gifts while, in the rural areas, the 'storm coloured' Korats are reputed to have power over the weather – to encourage rain to fall, farmers were said to pour water over the cats! In the 19th century the Si-Sawat was renamed the Korat by King Rama V, after the remote, high plateau region in north-eastern Siam (now Thailand) where they were believed to have originated.

In the ancient Thai manuscript, The Cat-Book Poems, dating from the Ayutthaya period (1350–1767) these muscular, curved-bodied cats had silver-blue coats described as having 'roots like clouds and tips like silver', and eyes that shine 'like dewdrops on a lotus leaf'.

These manuscripts also show that the Korat today not only has the same beautiful coat texture and colour, but also the same, semi-cobby build evident in Korats centuries ago. In this respect, the Korat is pretty unique since other native Thai breeds, also represented in these manuscripts, have subsequently been developed by western breeders into cats far-removed in looks from their ancestors.

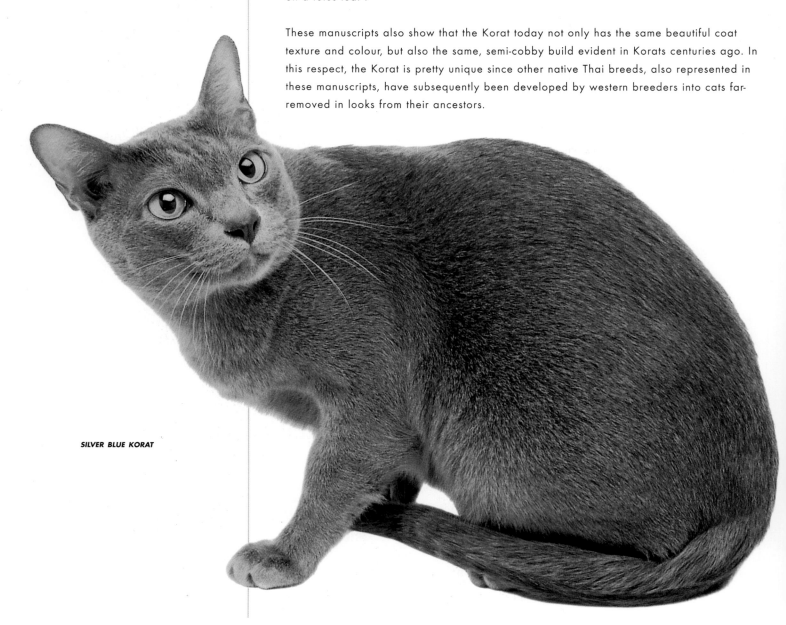

SILVER BLUE KORAT

The first Korats reached Britain about the same time as the Siamese in the late 19th century. In 1896, a Korat was entered in the Siamese class at a National Cat Club show in England, but was disqualified on account of its colour. Some say this cat was a blue-point Siamese, others say it was an all-blue Siamese, but Korats were not registered until 1959, when a pair named Darra and Nara were brought from Bangkok to the United States by Mrs Jean Johnson. The pair were soon joined by more of these delightful cats and, in 1965, a breed club was formed to promote them. By 1969, all the major North American (and Australian and South African) associations recognised the breed. The Korat reached Europe later in 1972, when they were exported from the US to Britain. At first there was some opposition from fanciers who initially felt that the Korat was not especially different from other blue short-haired cats, but by 1975 the breed was recognised in the UK.

Nevertheless, the Korat remains rare – even in its native Thailand. This is because Korat clubs insist that the breed be maintained as a natural breed, so out crossing with other breeds is forbidden. Consequently, all Korats should have an ancestry that can be traced back to the original cats of Thailand as depicted in the ancient art and literature of the country.

The Korat has a delightful heart-shaped head and remarkable, oversized, round, peridot-green eyes, giving it a rather innocent expression – belying the fact that they are notoriously pushy, demanding, stubborn and intent on having their own way! The paws are oval and compact, with dark-blue pads with five toes in front and four at the back. Because of their tropical origins, the Korat lacks a full undercoat and, therefore, must be protected from cold weather. Rarely, some cats suffer from neuromuscular disorders called GM1 and GM2, the presence of which needs to be established by blood tests.

SILVER BLUE KORAT

SINGAPURA

DATE OF ORIGIN: 1975

PLACE OF ORIGIN: Singapore and the USA

ANCESTRY: disputed

OTHER NAMES: none

COLOURS:

TICKED TABBIES: sepia agouti

COAT LENGTH: short

TYPE OF FUR: sleek

SIZE: 2—4 kg (4—9 lb)

The Singapura is the smallest breed of cat in the world – the average cat weighs in at a mere 2.7 kg (6 lb) – and it is also one of the most recent breeds. It takes its name from the Malaysian name for the city of Singapore, which means 'lion-city'. The official mascot of Singapore is a Singapura cat called Kucinta, and there is also a statue of one of the cats on the Singapore River. The original cats of Singapore were nocturnal, feral cats that lived largely in and around the sewers, scavenging for food at night. These cats were known locally as 'Drain Cats'.

In 1975, two American breeders, Hal and Tommy Meadows, brought cats from Singapore to the United States to originate a breeding programme. All of the cats registered today as Singapuras originate from the Meadows' breeding programme. The Singapura achieved formal championship recognition in 1988, although neither FIFé nor the GCCF recognise it because there are still doubts surrounding the breeds origins. While feral cats from Southeast Asia have been the basis of other breeds such as the Wild Abyssinian, the Meadows were also prominent breeders of both

BROWN TICKED SINGAPURA

Burmese and Abyssinians and some maintain that these were used in the Singapura's breeding programme, making the feral cats the 'inspiration' for the breed, rather than being the genetic founders of the breed.

This view hinges on the fact that the only colour in which the Singapura is bred is Sepia Agouti – a distinctive ticked tabby with at least two bands of ticking on each hair. Genetically, it is a sable ticked tabby, which is the result of combining the Burmese allele with the agouti (tabby) pattern, first known in the Abyssinian (see page 205).

If the Singapura's colour and pattern are derived from Burmese and Abyssinian genes, its size and quiet, retiring temperament are characteristics of its cautious feral ancestors, which attracted little attention to themselves and developed only to a size that can be maintained on a very meagre diet.

The small body of the Singapura is carried on strong, but not stocky legs. The paws are small and oval in shape with brown paw pads and dark hairs between the toes. The head is rounded, with a straight nose and a rather broad, blunt muzzle. Ears are wide and deeply cupped, set slightly outwards – giving the impression that the cat is always listening out for anything sneaking up on them. The almond-shaped eyes are hazel, green or yellow and beautifully outlined in black. From the inner corner of the eyes and running to the whisker pads are dark marks called 'cheetah lines', which are evident even in young kittens.

The Singapura is an extremely rare breed, even in the USA where it was developed, and there are still only some 2,000 Singapuras, making them one of the most valuable breeds.

BROWN TICKED TABBY SINGAPURA

TONKINESE

DATE OF ORIGIN: 1960s

PLACE OF ORIGIN: USA and Canada

ANCESTRY: Burmese and Siamese

OTHER NAMES: once known as the Golden Siamese

COLOURS:

SELF (SOLID) COLOURS AND TORTIE MINK: brown (called natural mink in US), chocolate (honey mink in US), blue (blue mink in US), lilac (champagne mink in US), red, cream (both not universally recognised in the US), brown tortie, chocolate tortie, blue tortie, and l ilac tortie

TABBIES (ALL PATTERNS): colours as for self and torties

COAT LENGTH: medium-short

TYPE OF FUR: soft, thick and close-lying, with a natural sheen – often described as being like a 'mink coat'

SIZE: 2.5—5.5 kg (6—12 lb)

'Tonkinese' is the new name for an old breed – the ancient 'Copper Cat' of Siam (Thailand). The coppery-brown cats of ancient Siam were known as the Supalak, or Thong Daeng and were illustrated in the manuscript called The Cat-Book Poems created by artists and poets in the old capital of Ayudha between 1350 and 1767. The Supalak are now considered to be the ancestors of the Burmese (see page 211) and also the Havana (see page 218) and the Tonkinese itself is a cross between the Burmese and Siamese.

It may be that the all-brown chocolate Siamese first seen in Britain in the 1880s were Tonk-type Burmese-Siamese hybrids. The first documented Tonkinese seen in the West was the lovely Wong Mau, the founding mother of the American Burmese breed (see page 211) imported from Rangoon in the 1930s. Wong Mau's natural hybrid characteristics were bred out of her offspring and it wasn't until the 1950s that breeders started to try and recreate the 'blend' through new breeding programmes. The modern Tonkinese was the first breed to originate in Canada, where they were developed in the 1960s. Despite its recent arrival, the Tonkinese has already proven to be one of the most popular breeds.

Tonks carry one Siamese (cs) gene and one Burmese (cb) gene and its physical features represent a beautiful blend of its two parent breeds – less angular and sleek than the Siamese, but strong and quite heavy, like the Burmese, with a personality that has the lively and affectionate nature of all Oriental breeds.

APRICOT POINT TONKINESE

BLUE TONKINESE

RED TONKINESE KITTEN

A Siamese-Burmese cross produces all-Tonkinese kittens, but mating two Tonks will produce on average, two Tonk kittens and two other kittens – one with Burmese and one with Siamese colourings. Because of the slight differences in the European Burmese and the American Burmese, European Tonks tend to be slightly more angular than their North American counterparts.

The Tonkinese was first recognised by the Canadian Cat Association and given championship status in 1984. Not surprisingly, soon after, these attractive and friendly cats were accepted by all the major registries. There is, however, considerable variation in the colours accepted and even in the names of colours!

The colour known in the US as 'Natural', is known everywhere else as Brown. It is a light brown, halfway between the Burmese 'sable' colouring and the Siamese 'seal' colouring with darker seal points merging gently into the body colour. The eye colour in Naturals is blue-green. The Lilac – known in the US as Champagne – is a pale, dove grey with a pinkish-coloured cast, with the points a darker shade of the same colour. For Lilacs, the eye colour ranges from light blue to green, but show standards regard any tinge of yellow as unacceptable. In all Tonks the upper edges of the eyes are oval, while the lower edges are rounded.

Red and Cream Tonks may show slight tabby markings – these are very difficult to eliminate in all breeds in these colours – but both Red and Cream Tonks, while recognised in UK standards, are not universally recognised in the US. In Torties and Tabby Tonks, the pointing is much less apparent because it is overlaid with the coat patterns, but the masks and legs should still be darker than the body. The Tonkinese varieties are known as 'Mink' because the Tonk's coats are so remarkably soft and dense and have an exceptional sheen. This coat can take up to two years to develop to its full beauty.

LILAC MINK TONKINESE

CHAMPAGNE MINK TONKINESE

BROWN TORTIE TONKINESE

LILAC TORTIE TONKINESE

EGYPTIAN MAU

DATE OF ORIGIN: 1950s

PLACE OF ORIGIN: Egypt and Italy

ANCESTRY: Egyptian street cats, Italian domestic cats

OTHER NAMES: none

COLOURS:

SELF (SOLID) COLOURS: black does occur, but not universally accepted

TABBY (SPOTTED): bronze

SILVER TABBY (SPOTTED): silver (pewter in US)

SMOKE: black

COAT LENGTH: short

TYPE OF FUR: soft and dense

SIZE: 2.25—5 kg (5—11 lb)

BRONZE EGYPTIAN MAU

SILVER EGYPTIAN MAU

The spotted tabby pattern can be found on a number of breeds of cats, but only one makes any serious claim to be a natural spotted breed rather than the deliberate creation of modern-day breeders. The Egyptian Mau is one breed that closely resembles its ancient ancestors – the common ancestors of all domestic cats. Many examples in ancient Egyptian art depict cats with a colour and coat pattern of spotted tabbies. 'Mau' is an appropriate name for the breed – in Egyptian it means 'cat'!

The Egyptian Mau was introduced to the United States in the early 1950s by Russian émigré, Nathalie Troubetskoy who, while in Cairo, Egypt, was captivated by the spotted markings of the street cats which roamed the city. Troubetskoy took a silver-spotted female home with her to Italy where she was mated with a local smoke-spotted tom. The results were bronze-spotted kittens. In 1953, the first pair of Maus, called Gepa and Ludol, reached the US, but it would be another 15 years before the first cat association, the CFF, gave the Mau official recognition and another 10 years before the Mau was recognised in Britain.

The Mau is a svelte cat, medium sized and well muscled, it is neither cobby nor foreign. The face likewise, is neither rounded nor wedge shaped and the nose is the same width from tip to brow. The 'M' mark is apparent on the forehead, along with an intricate pattern of spots, which have been likened by many fanciers to a scarab beetle. The unusually large, green eyes, which change colour from dark to pale green as the cat matures, are accentuated by very distinctive 'mascara lines'. These wishbone-shaped lines run underneath the eyes from the outer edges of each eye, a bit like Cleopatra's eye make-up as seen in the movies! The most striking parts of their appearance, however, are the spots along the spine running in symmetrical lines and merging into the dorsal stripe at the beginning of the tail, where the spots turn into bands. Although show judges prefer the spots on the flanks to be round and evenly distributed, more often they are random – but no less lovely! The legs too are banded.

The recognised colours in the breed are silver (black spots on a silver agouti background), bronze (chocolate spots on a bronze agouti background) and smoke (black spots on grey, with a silver undercoat). Mau smokes differ from smokes in other breeds because instead of being selfs with no tabby markings, they are distinctly tabbies. The silvery-white undercoat shows just enough to provide contrast and no more. In all colours, gooseberry-green eyes are preferred.

Although they appear to have a worried look – largely due to their large, rounded eyes and their tendency to 'talk to themselves' in a variety of melodious 'chortles' – Maus are very friendly cats, although they can be annoyingly aloof at times!

SILVER EGYPTIAN MAU

BLACK SILVER SPOTTED EGYPTIAN MAU

OCICAT

DATE OF ORIGIN: 1964

PLACE OF ORIGIN: USA

ANCESTRY: Siamese, Abyssinian, American Shorthair

OTHER NAMES: Oci

COLOURS:

SPOTTED TABBIES: tawny (CFA Designation), brown, chocolate, cinnamon, blue, lavender/lilac and fawn

SILVER TABBIES (SPOTTED): as for standard tabbies

SMOKES: as for tabbies

SELF (SOLID) COLOURS: as for tabbies

COAT LENGTH: short

TYPE OF FUR: soft, fine and sleek

SIZE: 2.5—7 kg (6—15 lb)

SILVER OCICAT

A relatively new breed, the delightfully named and fine-looking Ocicat, is the result of a chance mating between a male Chocolate Point Siamese and a female hybrid – an Abyssinian Seal Point Siamese. The offspring, born in 1964 in Michigan, USA, looked Abyssinian, but when one was bred to a Siamese, the litter included not only Abyssinian-pointed Siamese, but a spotted kitten, called Tonga. At first, this spotted cat was called an 'Accicat' – to describe the accidental ancestry – and then later 'Ocelette' – to describe its similarity to the ocelot.

Tonga was neutered and became a much-loved pet, but owner, Virginia Daly, then repeated the mating, producing Dalai Talua, the foundation female of the breed. Tom Brown helped to continue the Ocicat's development, introducing American Shorthairs. In 1966, the Ocicat received its first official recognition from TICA.

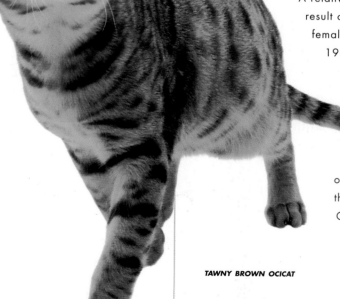

TAWNY BROWN OCICAT

CHOCOLATE OCICAT

both with golden-yellow eyes. More recently though, silver Ocicats have been developed – the genes coming from American-Shorthair out crosses during the development of the breed. All the silver colours have a white ground, which does much to show off the magnificent markings.

The wedge-shaped head with a broad muzzle makes for a pointed face, enhanced by large, almond-shaped and slightly tilted eyes. Like the Egyptian Mau (see page 228) the Ocicat's eyes – which, according to show standards, must not be blue – are enhanced by dark rims, surrounded by lighter 'spectacles' and wishbone-shaped 'mascara lines' on the temples and cheeks. The tail is long and slender and, like the legs, is banded. But right at the tip is where the coat is most truly shown.

While breed standards called for a cat of 'wild' appearance, the Ocicat is graceful, playful and very sociable – as sweet natured as any cat one could ever wish for!

A rather large breed – they are muscular and surprisingly solidly built cats – an Ocicat averages about 6 kg (13 lb) when fully grown (males are much larger than females). Most outstanding is the Ocicat's rich, 'jungle-like' coat pattern of distinctive spots, the distribution of which should follow the classic tabby pattern, swirling around the centre of their fine flanks.

Originally, these spots were either chestnut-brown on a cream background, or light chocolate on cream,

CHOCOLATE SILVER SPOTTED OCICAT

ORIENTAL SHORTHAIR

DATE OF ORIGIN: 1950s

PLACE OF ORIGIN: Britain

ANCESTRY: Siamese, Korat, Longhairs/Persians, Shorthairs

OTHER NAMES: in Britain, they were previously known as Foreign Shorthairs

COLOURS:

SELF (SOLID) AND TORTIE COLOURS: black, havana (chestnut brown in the US), cinnamon, red, blue, lilac, fawn, cream, caramel, apricot, 'Foreign White' (in UK), oriental white (US), black tortie, chocolate tortie, cinnamon tortie, blue tortie, lilac tortie, fawn tortie and caramel tortie .

SHADED, SMOKE, TIPPED: colours as for self colours and torties, except white

TABBY (ALL PATTERNS) AND SILVER TABBIES (ALL PATTERNS): colours as for self colours and torties

COAT LENGTH: short

TYPE OF FUR: close-lying, fine and very glossy

SIZE: 4—6.5 kg (9—14 lb)

BLACK ORIENTAL SHORTHAIR

In spite of the name – and their beautiful exotic looks – Oriental Shorthairs, which were formerly known as 'Foreign Shorthairs' in the UK, do not necessarily come from the East! The name, in fact, refers to breeds that have a slender physique, a pointed head and slanted eyes. In other words, these Oriental Shorthairs are Siamese cats, but without the colourpoint markings. In the ancient manuscript, The Cat-Book Poems, the ancestors of modern brown and blue breeds, as well as black, white, black and white bicolour (called the Singhasep) and shaded silvers were all depicted. Even today in Thailand, it is estimated that in the Bangkok area, only some 20% of 'Siamese' cats are pointed, and the rest are self or selfs-with-white.

After the Siamese Cat Club of Britain ruled that it would only encourage the breeding of the blue-eyed pointed Siamese, self cats with yellow or green eyes were excluded from the Siamese classes at shows. While this marked a period of initial decline in the excluded cats, it also marked the beginnings of a new chapter in the history of the separate breed of cats now known as Oriental Shorthairs.

BLUE ORIENTAL SHORTHAIR

CHOCOLATE TORTIE SHORTHAIR

CARAMEL CLASSIC TABBY ORIENTAL SHORTHAIR

The Oriental Shorthair encompasses all cats with the 'Siamese' (i.e. Oriental or Foreign) body shape that are not pointed. Technically, whether self coloured, bicolour, tortoiseshell, tabbies, tipped, smoked or shaded, these cats are all one breed, sharing the elegant, lithe and sinuous body shape, the long expressive tail and narrow, wedge-shaped head.

In Britain, each colour was referred to as an individual breed, collectively called Foreign Shorthairs, while in the US, they were known as Oriental Shorthairs and judged as one breed. In 1991, to avoid confusion, Britain agreed to call them Oriental Shorthairs too. Nevertheless, there are still differences of opinion, especially regarding colour names!

With the exclusion of all but the blue-eyed pointed Siamese from the show class, interest in the breed as a whole declined, except for all-black and all-blue cats of similar

body shape which were being bred in Germany until the outbreak of World War II. It was only after the war that a breeding programme in Britain was planned, the aim of which was to breed all-brown cats with a Foreign/Oriental body shape. The real progress in breeding the modern Orientals began in 1962, when a ten-year programme began to create a breed of true-breeding, blue-eyed, white Oriental cats. These blue-eyed whites were totally different in appearance and character to

APRICOT SILVER SPOTTED ORIENTAL SHORTHAIR

white cats of other breeds and, significantly, did not suffer any of the problems of deafness associated with the colour. UK show standards require White Orientals to have blue eyes, while in the US and elsewhere, green eyes are also permitted. Because of this difference in standards, in Britain, blue-eyed whites are designated 'Foreign White' while in the US and elsewhere, blue- or green-eyed whites are called 'Oriental Whites'.

TORTIE SMOKE SHORTHAIR

CINNAMON ORIENTAL SHORTHAIR

CARAMEL SILVER SHADED ORIENTAL SHORTHAIR

Because the white coat of the breed is dominant and masks any underlying colour genes and because to 'fix' the blue eyes and body shape of the Oriental back crosses to pointed Siamese were required, some of the kittens bred in the early Foreign White litters were non-white. Some didn't simply have coloured points, but were coloured all over, and the first of these were solid reds, solid blacks and spotted tabbies. Oriental Spotted Tabbies were once called Maus – but this name was often confused with the Egyptian Mau (see page 228) bred in the US and they were subsequently renamed.

Also apparent was one kitten with an obviously Siamese body and a rich chestnut colouring. This colour was first called Havana but was recognised as Chestnut Brown. In 1970 it reverted to being called Havana – but in the US it is still called Chestnut Brown to distinguish it from the separate breed of brown cats called Havana! Siring this chestnut-coloured cat with a lilac-point Siamese, gave the potential to produce cats both of its own rich-brown colour and of lilac – called Lavender in the US!

Other selfs soon followed: the magnificently striking Black Orientals are indeed jet-black, from the tips to the roots of their coats and in their eye rims and paw pads. There are also pale browns, such as Cinnamon and Caramel. The former is a light brown, best described as the colour of milk chocolate, while the latter is often described, equally deliciously, as café au lait. New, gorgeous colours and patterns continue to be produced so that today there are more than 50 recognised.

CHOCOLATE SILVER SPOTTED ORIENTAL SHORTHAIR

CINNAMON SELF ORIENTAL SHORTHAIR

RED ORIENTAL SHORTHAIR

LILAC ORIENTAL SHORTHAIR

BENGAL

DATE OF ORIGIN: 1983

PLACE OF ORIGIN: USA

ANCESTRY: Asian Leopard Cat, Egyptian Mau, Indian street and household cats

OTHER NAMES: once called Leopardettes

COLOURS:

TABBIES (SPOTTED AND MARBLED): brown, charcoal and snow

COAT LENGTH: medium-short

TYPE OF FUR: soft and dense

SIZE: 5.5—10 kg (12—22 lb)

Still a rare breed, the Bengal combines the wonderful wild colours and markings of the Asian Leopard Cat with the dependable, trusting nature of the domestic cat. The Asian Leopard Cat is a small wild cat weighing only about 4.5 kg (10 lb) that inhabits the forests of Southern Asia. In the 1960s, there was concern about the possible extinction of the Asian Leopard Cat, which led Jean Sugden (later Mill) of California, in 1963, to attempt to conserve the breed by mating it with domestic cats. Other wild cats such as ocelots and margays have often found their ways into homes where they have bred successfully with household cats and, in most cases, their offspring have displayed the same temperaments as their wild parent. Ten years later, Dr. Willard Centerwall at the University of California continued the breeding programme while investigating the Asian Leopard Cat's natural immunity to feline leukaemia. From these beginnings, the beautiful Bengal was developed.

Dr. Centerwall gave eight of his hybrids to Jean Mill and the first Bengal, called Millwood Finally Found, was registered in 1983.

BROWN/BLACK SPOTTED BENGAL

BROWN MARBLED BENGAL

While early crosses to non-pedigrees introduced some 'undesirable' genes for colour dilution and long hair, later crossings to Indian street cats and Egyptian Maus introduced genes for spotting, the Siamese coat pattern and blue eyes, resulting in the extraordinarily beautiful 'Snow' shades. While breed registries are controlled to avoid unexpected occurrences, Bengal breeders were delighted with the happy accident of introducing pointed lines from non-pedigree cats to create really stunning colours, which are described as a 'pearl dusting' on the coat.

SNOW-SPOTTED/AOC EYE BENGAL

SEAL MINK MARBLE BENGAL

SNOW-SPOTTED BENGAL

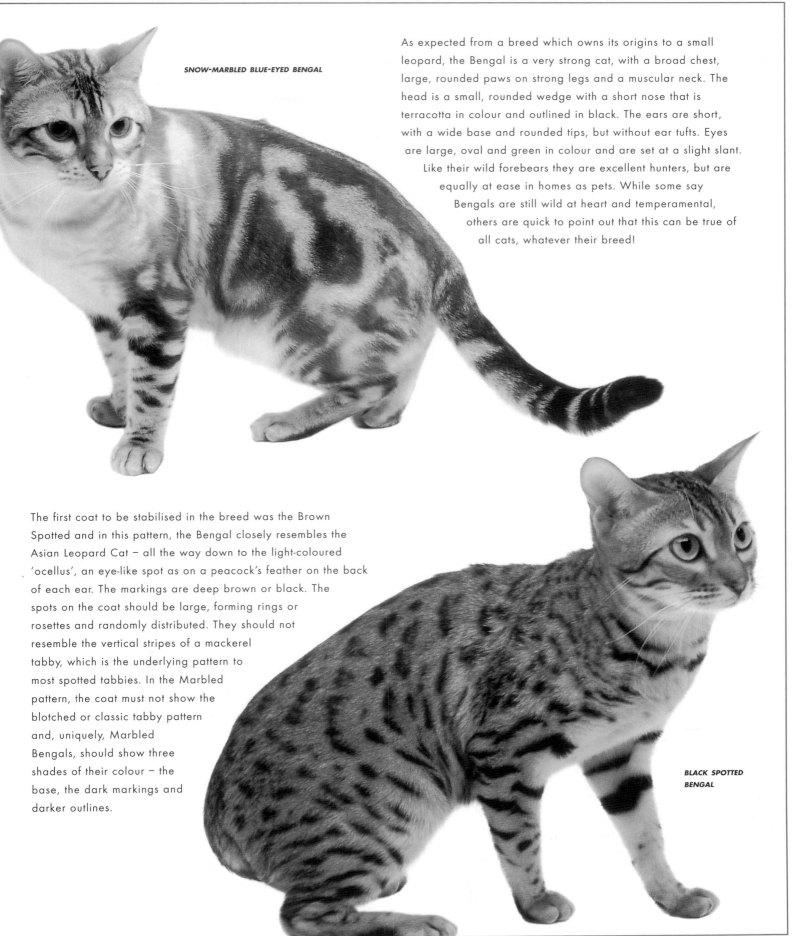

SNOW-MARBLED BLUE-EYED BENGAL

As expected from a breed which owns its origins to a small leopard, the Bengal is a very strong cat, with a broad chest, large, rounded paws on strong legs and a muscular neck. The head is a small, rounded wedge with a short nose that is terracotta in colour and outlined in black. The ears are short, with a wide base and rounded tips, but without ear tufts. Eyes are large, oval and green in colour and are set at a slight slant. Like their wild forebears they are excellent hunters, but are equally at ease in homes as pets. While some say Bengals are still wild at heart and temperamental, others are quick to point out that this can be true of all cats, whatever their breed!

The first coat to be stabilised in the breed was the Brown Spotted and in this pattern, the Bengal closely resembles the Asian Leopard Cat – all the way down to the light-coloured 'ocellus', an eye-like spot as on a peacock's feather on the back of each ear. The markings are deep brown or black. The spots on the coat should be large, forming rings or rosettes and randomly distributed. They should not resemble the vertical stripes of a mackerel tabby, which is the underlying pattern to most spotted tabbies. In the Marbled pattern, the coat must not show the blotched or classic tabby pattern and, uniquely, Marbled Bengals, should show three shades of their colour – the base, the dark markings and darker outlines.

BLACK SPOTTED BENGAL

MANX

DATE OF ORIGIN: pre-1700s

PLACE OF ORIGIN:
Isle of Man, UK

ANCESTRY: household cats

OTHER NAMES: none

COLOURS: Most recognised
colours are permitted (see also
British Shorthairs, page 192)

COAT LENGTH: short, double
coat, with thick undercoat and
slightly longer overcoat

TYPE OF FUR: coarse but glossy

SIZE: 3.5—5.5 kg (8—12 lb)

RED TABBY MANX

There are numerous colourful tales about the origins of the famous tail-less cats from the Isle of
Man, which lies between the east coast of Ireland and the west coast of Britain. According to
legends, they were the last cats to get aboard the Ark and Noah accidentally slammed the
door on their tails! Other say Irish invaders took the tails to decorate their war helmets and
later mothers bit off their kittens' tails so they couldn't be taken. Some say the Manx cat came
aboard Phoenician trading ships 1000 years ago, all the way from Japan – where there are
also tail-less cats – and others still, say that they swam ashore from a wrecked ship of the
Spanish Armada.

In truth, the isolation of the island allowed an incomplete, dominant gene to become
established. The original mutation is thought to have happened some 400 years ago.
Spontaneous mutations, such as 'tail-lessness', do occur from time to time in all feline
populations but, in large populations, such mutations usually disappear. However, in isolated
groups such as the Manx and the Japanese Bobtail, such mutations can survive.
Despite being tail-less, the Manx does not suffer from any loss of balance, and is
quite good at climbing trees – when the mood takes it!

Manx cats are quite rare; litters are quite small – often only two kittens are born – and this is
another result of the Manx gene. Homozygous Manx – those inheriting the Manx gene from
both parents – often die in the womb at an early stage of development. The Manx known to
cat shows today is heterozygous – it has one gene for tail-lessness and one for a normal tail –
but even these show a higher proportion of stillborn and early deaths than most other breeds
because the Manx gene can cause malformations in other parts of the body apart from the
tail. Spina bifida is quite common and there is often fusion of the bones in the lower spine.

Any cat that is heterozygous can never breed true and, consequently, a number of normal-tailed kittens are likely to be born in any Manx litter. Manx kittens show degrees of variation and these have been divided into four groups for clarity:

'Rumpies', are the true 'exhibition' Manx. They are completely tail-less and have a dimple at the base of the spine; 'Rumpy-Risers' have a small number of tail vertebrae forming a small knob; 'Stumpies' (or sometimes 'Stubbies') have a definite tail stump that is normally moveable and has a curve or kink; 'Longies' have an almost-normal, but truncated tail, which makes them a little difficult to distinguish from 'normal-tailed' cats.

Nevertheless, they are all Manx cats since breeders normally mate Manx with Manx-bred, normal-tailed cats rather than with British or American Shorthairs.

While the missing tail is the most obvious visible characteristic, Manx cats also combine short front legs with longer back legs giving them their equally distinctive 'bunny-hop' gait, known as the 'Manx hop'. Consequently, the Manx's movement is completely unlike the lithe, sinuous movement of other cats. Contributing further to their 'rounded' look, are a round head, full cheeks and a lovely, double coat that shows a well-defined difference between the soft downy under hair and glossier, but coarser, top coat.

In Britain, the GCCF recognises the Manx in any colour or pattern, while in North America, the CFA excludes varieties that show the effects of chocolate-brown or Siamese genes. While Rumpies alone are show cats, Rumpy-Risers, Stumpies and Longies all make excellent pets with delightful personalities.

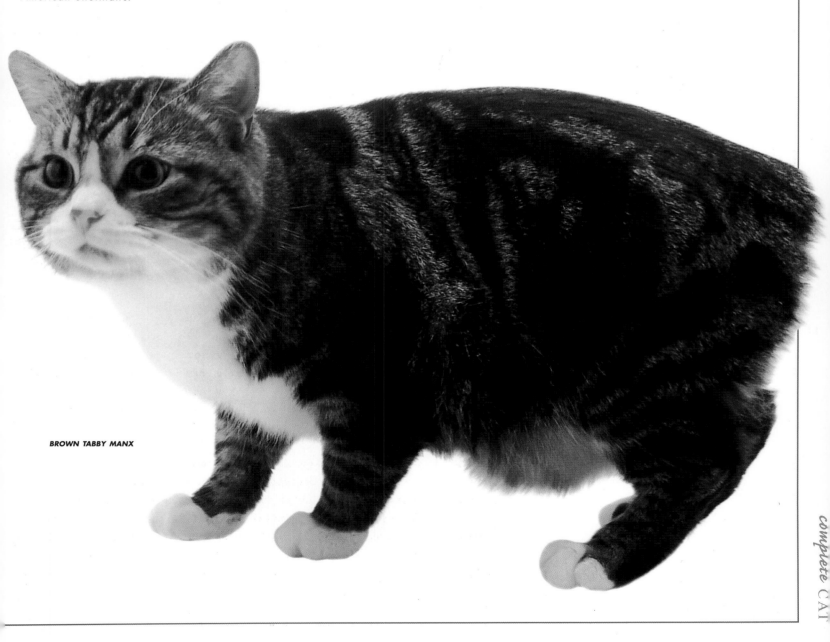

BROWN TABBY MANX

AMERICAN BOBTAIL

DATE OF ORIGIN: 1960s

PLACE OF ORIGIN: USA

ANCESTRY: uncertain

OTHER NAMES: none

COLOURS: All colours and patterns, including sepia, pointed and mink

COAT LENGTH: short, but long enough to stand away from body

TYPE OF FUR: slightly shaggy in appearance but does not matt easily

SIZE: 3–7 kg (7–15 lb)

Until recently, there were few tail-less or bobtailed breeds. But both the Manx cat (see page 238) and the Japanese Bobtail have existed for centuries, the latter featuring in ancient prints and paintings as well as on the facade of the Gotokuji Temple in Tokyo, its paw upraised as a symbol of good fortune. More recently, the Kurile Island Bobtail, which hails from a chain of islands running from the easternmost point of the Russian Federation to the tip of Japan's Hokkaido Island, has emerged as a new breed, although it is the product of a recessive gene that is believed to have occurred about 200 years ago.

The American Bobtail is among the first of these new bobtailed breeds. Its origins are obscure – the Bobcat, one of North America's native wild cats, is the only tail-less cat to live on the continent but its part in the parentage of the American Bobtail is unconfirmed. It could also be that Manx (see page 238) and/or Japanese-Bobtail genes may be present since cats of both breeds were popular among breeders in the US. Manx cats appear in early US breed registers and the Japanese Bobtails were first shown in the US in 1963, with the first breeding cats arriving in 1968.

**BLUE LYNX POINT
AMERICAN BOBTAIL**

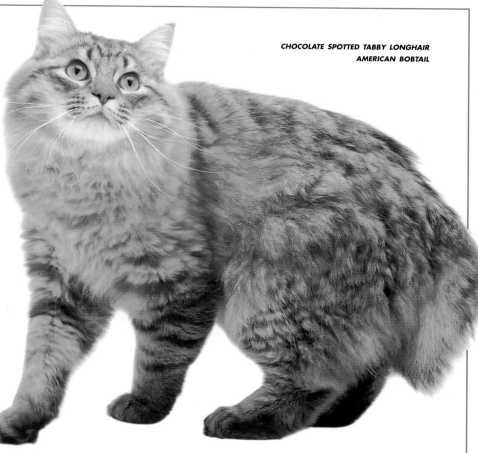

CHOCOLATE SPOTTED TABBY LONGHAIR AMERICAN BOBTAIL

The American Bobtail can only be traced as far back as a random-bred, bob-tailed tabby kitten found on an American-Indian reservation in Arizona, which was adopted and taken home to Iowa by John and Brenda Sanders in the early 1960s. Early breeding work was aiming at producing bob-tailed cats with a pattern like that of the Snowshoe (see page 204), but the cats became unhealthy. Subsequently, breeder Reaha Evans reintroduced more colours and patterns to strengthen the health of the breed which, in 1989, was recognised by the TICA.

There are both long-haired and short-haired American Bobtails, but because the longhair gene is recessive, there are fewer examples of this already rare breed. The short-haired variety, in fact, has a coat whose hairs are long enough to stand away from the body and give the cat a somewhat wild, shaggy appearance. Substantially muscled, the American Bobtail is a semi-cobby cat, with heavy legs and large, rounded paws. Unlike the Rumpie Manx, in the American Bobtail a tail must be present, but should ideally stop short, just above the hock.

SEAL LYNX POINT AMERICAN BOBTAIL

PIXIEBOB

DATE OF ORIGIN: 1980s

PLACE OF ORIGIN: USA

ANCESTRY: domestic cats, possible native North American Bobcat

OTHER NAMES: none

COLOURS:

TABBIES (SPOTTED AND ROSETTE): brown

COAT LENGTH: short, but long enough to appear shaggy

TYPE OF FUR: thick and dense

SIZE: 4—8 kg (9—18 lb)

In the past 20 years or so there has been increased interest among breeders in developing new cat breeds by mating domestic cats with wild cat species. In most cases, the offspring inherit the wild temperaments of their ancestors but, in some instances, breeders have made successful crosses with cats such as Geoffroy's Ocelot (Felis geoffroyi), a wild cat of the South American upland forests and scrub. Found from Bolivia to Patagonia, the Geoffroy's Ocelot is grey with small, black spots and weighs 2–3 kg (4 1/2–8 lb). When mated with domestic cats, their offspring is a tame cat with the beautiful and exotically spotted coat of the wild cat. Crossing with wild cats such as this, introduces coat patterns not before seen in domestic cats, such as the ocelot-like rosette or ring-shaped spots. Sometimes such cats are called Feral Domestic Hybrid cats, but this is something of a misnomer since the term feral is correctly applied to domestic cats that have 'gone native' and reverted to the wild.

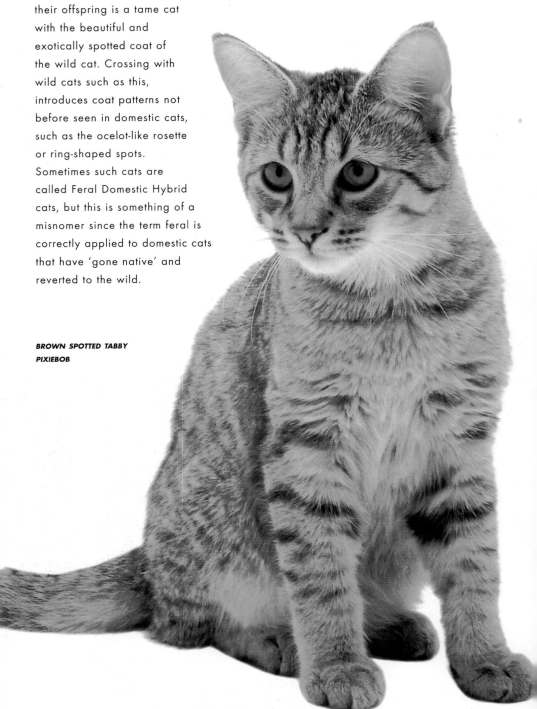

BROWN SPOTTED TABBY PIXIEBOB

North American breeders have, for some time, been interested in developing a cat that resembles the native tail-less wild cat, the bobcat. There have been instances of natural matings between wild cats and domestic cats and the origins of the delightful Pixiebob are thought to be the result of such an encounter, although DNA profiles have yet to provide sufficient data to substantiate these origins. In fact, most such kittens have been acquired by breeders from farmers who would otherwise have culled such offspring Two such 'bobcat-to-domestic cat' mated cats were acquired by Carol Ann Brewer in 1985 in Washington State – suitably in bobcat territory! These were then bred to produce Pixie, the founding cat of the breed. Although not known outside of the USA, the Pixiebob was 'allowed' by the TICA in 1995.

In spite of the beautiful wild looks, Pixiebobs are described as having the temperament of a faithful dog! They become very attached to their owners and their homes, and do not readily accept changes to either. Many owners say that they are happiest being the single cat. Their wild looks are enhanced by their wide, round eyes and very strong facial markings – 'mascara' lines on the cheeks and light coloured 'spectacles' around the eyes. Although not essential, caracal, or lynx-like tips on their ears are desirable. But overall, the wild looks of the Pixiebob are in someway mellowed by the delightful, creamy-whiteness of the lips and chin.

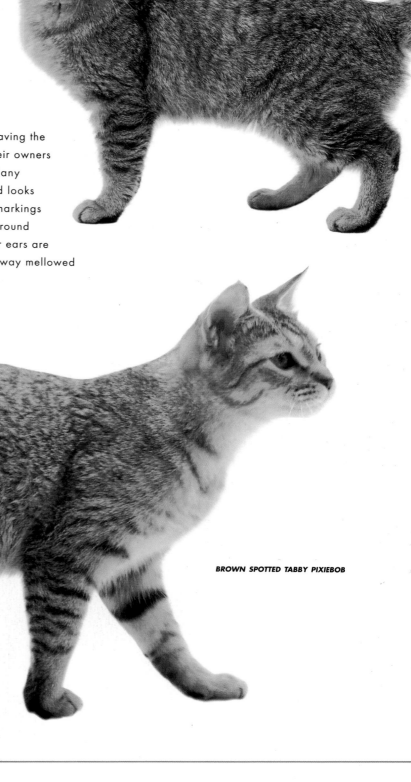

BROWN TICKED TABBY PIXIEBOB

BROWN SPOTTED TABBY PIXIEBOB

CORNISH REX

DATE OF ORIGIN: 1950s

PLACE OF ORIGIN: Cornwall, Britain

ANCESTRY: farm cats

OTHER NAMES: none

COLOURS: all colours and patterns including sepia and mink

COAT LENGTH: very short

TYPE OF FUR: guard hairs are absent, so coat is short, plush and 'rippled'

SIZE: 2.5—4.5 kg (6—10 lb)

BROWN MACKEREL TABBY CORNISH REX

Various rex breeds with short, curly coats have occurred from time to time as a result of spontaneous mutations. They have occurred in Britain, Germany and the US. The degree of curl in rex cats varies from the 'marcel-wave' curl of the Cornish Rex to the 'swirly curls' of the Devon Rex and the 'tufty' curls of the delightfully named La Perm – an American breed developed in Oregon in 1982, which does indeed look like it has a 'permanent-wave' hairdo! In spite of their apparent similarities, these rex cats are distinct breeds: mating a Devon Rex with a Cornish Rex will result in kittens with a straight coat, although they will be a little different in texture to that of a 'normal' shorthair.

In 1950, a curly-coated male kitten, called Kallibunker, was born to a farm cat in Cornwall, England. Kallibunker's owner, Nina Ennismore, recognised this curly coat as similar to the rex mutation found in rabbits. By back crossing Kallibunker to his mother, more rex kittens were produced, proving that the rex gene was recessive. In 1957, two of Kallibunker's descendants were sent to the US to found the breed there. Crosses with Oriental Shorthairs and Siamese in the US were called 'Si-rex', while other descendants of Kallibunker were crossed with British Shorthairs and Burmese in Britain.

BLACK SMOKE CORNISH REX

BLUE CREAM TORTIE CORNISH REX

What both British- and American-bred Cornish Rexes have in common is the fabulous curly coat. In the Cornish Rex, the guard hairs are absent, making the coat soft, short and plush. The waves of curls – which some say look like instant Chinese noodles! – are most evident over the gently arching back and the rump. Because rex cats have finer coats than other short-haired breeds (and the Cornish is completely lacking in guard hairs) they are very sensitive to changes in temperature and need to be kept cosy and warm at all times – just like any other cat, but with an extra special dollop of TLC!

The Cornish Rex has been bred in Britain with a moderately Oriental body type, a wedge-shaped head and with what has been described as a 'Roman nose' – straight down from the curved forehead. The ears are quite large and cupped, and are set high on the head, while the small- to medium-sized, well-muscled body is carried high on long and very slender legs – with the hind legs longer than the forelegs. They are famous for jumping and will spend many happy hours leaping from their owner's shoulders onto furniture and back again! British cats are less delicate than their North American counterparts – these have a shape that is a little more like a greyhound, with a more 'tucked up' torso.

BLUE AND WHITE CORNISH REX

CREAM SMOKE CORNISH REX

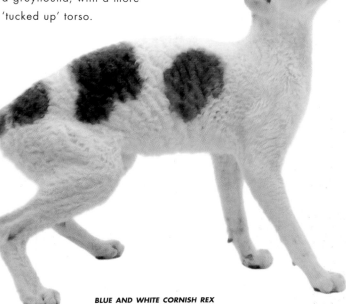

BLUE AND WHITE CORNISH REX

DEVON REX

DATE OF ORIGIN: 1960

PLACE OF ORIGIN:
Devon, Britain

ANCESTRY: feral and
household cats

OTHER NAMES: Poodle cats

COLOURS: all colours and
patterns including pointed

COAT LENGTH: very short

TYPE OF FUR: although Devon
Rex have all three types of
hair, they are severely
distorted, making
the coat curly.

SIZE:
2.5—4 kg
(6—9 lb)

**CHOCOLATE TORTIE WITH SILVER
DARKER POINTS DEVON REX**

In 1960, near a disused tin-mine
near Buckfastleigh, Devon,
England, Beryl Cox found a curly-
coated feral cat. A young tortie-
and-white stray being cared for by a
neighbour mated with this feral cat
and, in the resulting litter, was a curly-
coated, Black Smoke kitten, named
appropriately, Kirlee. The parents of Kirlee
were undoubtedly related because the gene
for the curly coat is recessive.

Because of the earlier publicity surrounding
the curly Cornish Rex, which had appeared
some 10 years earlier, Beryl Cox was
encouraged to breed Kirlee into the Cornish
line. To her surprise − and despite several
amorous encounters − no curly kittens were born.
Only then was it realised that, despite Devon and Cornwall being so
close, the two rex cats from these counties carried completely
unrelated mutations that would have to be established by separate
breeding programmes.

**CREAM SMOKE DEVON
REX**

WHITE BLUE-EYED DEVON REX

**CHOCOLATE SILVER TABBY
WITH DARKER POINTS
DEVON REX**

While the Cornish Rex and Devon Rex both have curly coats, there are significant differences in the breeds. The Devon Rex has an unmistakable head shape that is unique in pedigree cats and is based on the head shape of Kirlee. It's a short wedge-shaped head, with a well defined 'stop' to the nose, large, oval-shaped eyes and prominent whisker pads from which sprout coarsely textured, 'crinkled' whiskers. Furthermore, the Devon Rex has quite enormous ears that are very wide at the base and taper to rounded tips. The effect is a rather pixie or elfin-like face! Facial appearances can be deceptive, however, because the Devon Rex's body, although slender, is solid, hard and muscular! Their broad chests combined with slender legs – the hind legs are longer than the forelegs – can give them the appearance of being bowlegged, like a feline 'bulldog'!

Unlike the waves of the Cornish Rex coat, the Devon Rex coat is a masterpiece of short, soft rippling and swirling curls and wide out crossings have made for a huge variety of patterns and colours. Most fanciers agree that the curly coat of the Devon Rex will show a Smoke shading far better than any straight-haired cat breed.

BLACK, SMOKE AND WHITE DEVON REX

TORTIE DEVON REX

BLACK SMOKE DEVON REX

DEVON REX

BROWN TABBY DEVON REX

CHOCOLATE SMOKE DEVON REX

SPHYNX

DATE OF ORIGIN: 1966

PLACE OF ORIGIN: Ontario, Canada, USA and Europe

ANCESTRY: non-pedigree Longhair/Persian

OTHER NAMES: once called Canadian

COLOURS: all colours and patterns, including pointed, sepia and mink

COAT LENGTH: no fur

TYPE OF FUR: Skin is soft and suede-like

SIZE: 3.5—7 kg (8—15 lb)

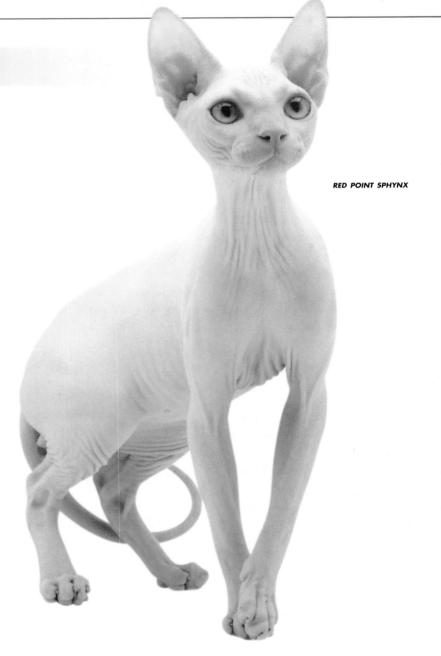

RED POINT SPHYNX

RED MINK AND WHITE SPHYNX

For many people the Sphynx is missing the one vital and attractive feature shared by all cats, whatever their pedigree – a furry coat. More or less bald cats, like curly-coated rex cats, have appeared from time to time in various parts of the world.

There is some evidence that the Aztecs encouraged hairless cats in their domestic breeds – which may have been destined for human consumption – and for a short time in the 1880s, the Mexican Hairless, was popular.

The 'hairlessness' of the Sphynx is due to a gene. The effects of this gene are incomplete, however, as the Sphynx is not completely hairless – they do have a soft 'peach fuzz' of downy hair. Very thin, very short hairs grow on the ears, muzzle, tail, and feet – and in tom cats, on the testicles. Each hair follicle has an oil producing gland but, with no real hair as such to absorb it, instead of being combed, Sphynx require a daily rub down with a chamois leather to keep their 'coat' and suede-like skin in tiptop condition.

The first Sphynx – called Prune – was born in 1966, but his line died out. In 1978, a long-haired cat with a hairless kitten were rescued in Toronto, Canada. The 'mutant' kitten was neutered so it could not pass on this 'malformation' but, when the mother had subsequent litters, further hairless kittens were born. Two such kittens were exported to England, where one was mated to a Devon Rex. The result – hairless kittens! That implied that this hairless gene was not only recessive, but dominant over the Devon Rex gene. Further out crossings to Devon Rex were carried out by Vicki and Peter Markstein in New York with their Sphynx, called E.T., but the breed is still rare.

The Sphynx is recognised as a breed only by the TICA as many other organisations still fear there may be potential health risks associated with it. In Britain, Sphynx are registered with the GCCF to make sure that the dominant gene for hairlessness isn't carried into Devon Rex lines.

The influence of the Devon Rex can be seen in the Sphynx's similar 'elfin-like' face with its large eyes and big ears. Their bodies are round and well muscled, with a powerful neck and firm legs. Coat colours and patterns are discernible in the vestigial coat and the underlying skin. In show cats, the 'natural' absence of a coat is vital and any evidence of deliberate hair removal is severely penalised.

While many people find the appearance of the Sphynx 'un-catlike' – they rely on their owners for extra physical protection since their lack of hair makes them very vulnerable both to the cold and to sunlight – in many other respects, the Sphynx is as much a cat as any other. They are affectionate and devoted companions, warm and soft and delightfully playful.

LILAC SPHYNX

BLUE TORTIE AND WHITE SPHYNX

HOUSEHOLD/RANDOM-BRED CAT

DATE OF ORIGIN: continuous since domestication, 4000 years ago

PLACE OF ORIGIN: worldwide

ANCESTRY: the mighty hunters, the wild cats of the plains and jungles!

OTHER NAMES: Pussycat, Kitty–Cat, Moggie, Tiddles, Fluffikins, Ginger, Stripey…

COLOURS: all patterns and colours and, like snowflakes, no two are ever alike!

COAT LENGTH: short, medium and long

TYPE OF FUR: infinitely strokeable

SIZE: from petite to fat cat: Himmy, a famous Australian cat weighed in at a mighty 20.8 kg (46 lb). Because his weight made walking difficult, his owners wheeled him around in a wheelbarrow until he was put on a strict diet and exercise regime.

With no clubs to promote them or extol their virtues, random-bred cats are nonetheless, the most popular cats worldwide! Random-bred cats live in palaces and small apartments, and are the adored companions of presidents and monarchs, pensioners and children. Sometimes these cats are sociable – they may like other cats and even dogs – other times they are not. Some are talkative, others are silent scrutinisers of the world. Some are 'well-behaved' and others are downright naughty. Some will eat almost anything, others demand a strict gourmet diet!

ODD-EYE COLOUR

Whatever their colour, pattern, size or temperament, cats like these have been immortalised in poems, prose, musicals and opera. They have been painted, sculpted and photographed, and have been the stars of movies, cartoons and television adverts.

SMOKE TABBY HOUSEHOLD

From home to home and country to country, random-bred cats vary in colour, pattern and size, but each one is still related to the wild cats of America, Europe, Asia and Africa and most random-bred cats will demonstrate this ancestry. Watch them slink as silently as the night through the long grass in the garden! See how they stalk such mighty prey as butterflies! Marvel at their agility as they climb the trees in your neighbours' gardens! Wonder at their mighty roars at night when the big tom from down the road enters their kingdom! And when they're not busy being tigers, you'll find them asleep, curled up or stretched out, in a warm, sunny place – or in the clean laundry basket!

Pedigree puss or alley cat, in essence, all cats are the same: beautiful, demanding, affectionate, and mysterious creatures deserving of our love and attention to their health and well-being. As the American author Mark Twain wrote,

'A HOUSE WITHOUT A CAT, AND A WELL-FED, WELL-PETTED, AND PROPERLY REVERED CAT, MAY BE THE PERFECT HOUSE, PERHAPS, BUT HOW CAN IT PROVE ITS TITLE?'

GLOSSARY

ACA: American Cat Association, North America's oldest governing body

ACFA: American Cat Fancier's Association

Agouti: The colour between a tabby's stripes

Allele: Any of the genes found at a particular position on a chromosome, which produce alternative physical outcomes. The genes for agouti and non-agouti, and the genes for long or short hair are alleles

Alter: US term for neuter

Awn hairs: Short, coarse hairs lying underneath the cat's top coat

Back crossing: Mating a cat back to one of its parents

Barring: Striped pattern found in tabbies, but considered faults in self (solid coloured) cats

Bicolour: A patched coat of white and anothe colour

Blaze: A marking down the centre of the forehead

Bloodline: A 'family' or line of cats related by ancestry or pedigree

Blue: Colouring ranging from pale, blue-grey to dark, slate-grey

Breed: A group of cats with similar, defined physical characteristics and related ancestry

Brindling: Scattered 'wrong', or coloured hairs in the coat

Calico: US term for tortoiseshell-and-white patterned cats

Cameo: Coats with red or cream tipping

Carpal pads: Pads found above the front feet to help absorb impact on landing

CFA: Cat Fancier's Association, America's largest cat association, also encompassing Canada and Japan

Champagne: US term for the chocolate colour in Burmese (see page 211) and lilac colour in Tonkinese (see page 226)

Chinchilla: Colouring where the outermost tips of the hairs are black, or another colour, with the rest of the hair white or pale

Chocolate: Medium- to pale-brown colour. In Siamese, it's paler than seal

Cobby: One of the body types of the cat – short, compact with broad shoulders and rump, short tail and rounded head

Conformation: Also called 'type' – refers to body size, shape and characteristics of a breed

Cross: Imprecise term for mating two cats and implying that they are distinctly different in colour and/or breed. The term can also be used to describe the offspring of such a mating

Dilute: A paler version of a basic colour such as blue, lilac or cream

Domestic: US term for cats of non-foreign body types, the equivalent of the term 'American' as in American Shorthair (see page 196)

Dominant characteristic: A genetic characteristic passed on to kittens by parents

Double coat: Short, soft undercoat with longer oute coat

Down hairs: Short, soft, secondary hairs

Feral: A domesticated animal that has reverted to, or been born, in the wild. Feral cats are the same species as domestic cats, unlike true wild cats.

FIFé: Fédération International Féline

Flehmen: The facial gesture seen when a cat' Jacobson's organ, in the roof of it mouth, is stimulated

Frost point: US term for lilac (lavender) point

GLOSSARY (CONTINUED)

GCCF: Governing Council of the Cat Fancy, the governing body of cat shows in Britain

Guard hairs: Long hairs forming the outer coat

Haw: US term for the nictitating membrane, or 'third eyelid'

Heterozygous: Having one pair of dissimilar alleles – one from each parent – for a particular characteristic

Himalayan patterning: Darker colour at extremities of body, often affected by tem perature

Hock: The ankle of a cat's hind leg

Homozygous: Having an identical pair of alleles for a particular characteristic

Honey mink: Intermediate brown colour of Tonkinese (see page 226), corresponding to chocolate in other breeds

Hybrid: The offspring of a cross between parents that are genetically dissimilar – especially between two different species or breeds

In-breeding: Mating closely related cats such as parents to offspring, or brothers to sisters

Jacobson's organ (Vomeronasal organ): A sense organ in the roof of the mouth in cats that responds to chemical stimuli

Kink: Bend in the tail, found in Siamese (see page 208) and other Oriental/Foreign cats

Lavender: US term for lilac

Lilac: Pale, pinkish-grey colour, known in US as lavender

Litter: Kittens born in a single birth

Longhair: Long-haired cats, called Persian cats in the US (see page 182)

Lynx point: US term for tabby point

Mask: The darker coloured areas of the face as seen in Siamese and Himalayan (Colourpoint Longhairs)

Masking (epistasis): The effect that some genes have to conceal or 'mask' the presence of other genes

Mittens: White fur on front feet, as in the Snowshoe (see page 204)

Moggie: Slang word for mongrel, random-bred cat – of mixed or unknown parentage

Moult: Shedding of fur, usually a seasonal occurrence, but common in Longhairs/Persians when stroked

Mutation: Genetic change causing a difference in appearance from parents

Muzzle: The nose and jaws

Natural mink: The darkest colour of the Tonkinese, corresponding to seal-point Siamese and brown (sable in US) Burmese

Nictitating membrane: The 'third eyelid'. Also called a haw in the US

Nose leather: The skin of the nose pad

Odd-eyed: Having eyes of different colours, usually one blue and one orange/copper

Oriental: A term used interchangeably with 'Foreign', refers to body type, especially the extreme body type of the Oriental Shorthair (see page 222)

Pads: Cushions without fur on underside of cats' feet

Papillae: Tiny hooks on cats' tongues which give it its roughness

Pedigree: The line of descent of a pure-bred animal, or the document recording it

Pewter: The British term for Shaded Silver

Pinna: The ear flap

Platinum: The US term for a lilac (lavender) Burmese (see page 211)

Points: The extremities of a cat's body – the head, ears, tail and feet – which are coloured in Siamese (see page 208) and other breeds

Polydactyl: Having more than the usual number of toes

Queen: An un-neutered female cat, especially one kept for breeding

Rangy: A cat with long slender legs

Recessive gene: A gene passed from generation to generation, but not always with visible results

Recognition: The acceptance of a new breed, colour or coat pattern of cat by an association, under each association's rules

Roman: Describes a nose with a high, prominent bridge seen in some Siamese

Sable: US term for brown, the darkest coat colour, in Burmese (see page 211)

Scarab marking: 'M' shaped mark on forehead of tabbies

Seal: The dark-brown colour found at the points of the darkest variety of Siamese

Selective breeding: Breeding by planned mating between individual cats with certain characteristics, which breeders wish to perpetuate or enhance

Self: (in US called solid) having a coat of a single, uniform colour

Shaded: Colouring where the tips of the hairs are coloured, the rest being white or pale, the tipping being part way between the chinchilla and the smoke

Show standard: A description of the 'ideal' cat of a particular breed against which actual cats are judged

Silver: Term applied to shaded silver and silver tabby, both tipped colourings

Smoke: Where most of the hairs are coloured but the roots are white or pal

Solid: US term for self-coloured cats

Spotting: White patches in the coat

Stifle: Cat's knee joint on hind leg

Stop: An abrupt change in the slope of the nose profile

Tabby: A coat marking which can be striped, spotted, blotched or full agouti

Tabby Tortoiseshell: A tortoiseshell cat with tabby rather than self (solid) black patching, also called patched tabby or torbie

TICA: The Independent Cat Association (USA)

Ticking: Bands of colour on each hair, seen characteristically on the Abyssinian's coat (see page 205)

Tipped: The ends of the hairs have coloured tips. The degree of colour or tipping decides whether a cat is a chinchilla, shaded or smoke.

Tom: Un-neutered male cat

Torbie: A tortoiseshell tabby cat

Tortie: Shortened term for Tortoiseshell

True breeding: Homozygous for traits being considered. Such a cat, if mated with a similar cat, will produce offspring like itself which, if in bred, will produce more offspring with exactly the same traits

Type: Overall size and shape of a cat

Van pattern: Bicolour, in which most of body is white, with colouring restricted to extremities

Variety: Strictly, a subdivision of a breed, such as particular colour form. However, sometimes the term is used interchangeably with the term 'breed'

Vibrissae: Whiskers

Wedge shape: The shape of Siamese and other Oriental/Foreign cats' heads

INDEX

A

Abscess 148
Abyssinian 205-207
Afflictions
- ears 126
o deafness 128
o haematoma 127
o infections 128
o mites 126
o sunburn 127
- eyes 129
o blindness 131
o cataract 131
o conjunctivitis 131
o cornea, scratched 130
o entropion 131
o foreign bodies 130
o glaucoma 131
o haw problems 130
o tear ducts, blocked 130
- mouth 133
o abscess 134
o anaemia 134
o gingivitis 134
o mouth ulcers 134
o ranula 134
o rodent ulcer 134
o tartar 133
- nose 132
- skin and coat 122
o acne 125
o alopecia 124
o dermatitis 125
o excema 125
o harvest mites 124
o lice 123
o maggots 124
o mange 124
o ringworm 123
o stud tail 125
o ticks 123
Angora 161
- Turkish 162-163

B

Balance 22
Balinese 164
bandages 139
Bengal 233-237
Birman 158-160
Bleeding 152
Bobtail, American 240-241
Bombay 217
Bones, broken 152
Burmese 211-213
Burmilla 216
Burns 149

C

Charteux 200-201
Chausie 215
Children 81
Choking 151
Christianity 11
Claws 25
Communication 39
Coupari 187
Crossbreds 15
Crosspeds 17
Curl, American 188-189

D

Diana 9
Dinictis 7
Disease, respiratory 90
Drowning 152

E

Equipment 60
- basket, carrying 60
- bed 72
- dishes 61
- food 61
- grooming 69
- indoor cat 67
- litter tray 66
- outdoor cat 67
- toys 74
Egypt, ancient 7, 8, Bast 8

F

Feeding 63, 101
Felidae 7
Felis
- Catus 7
- Domesticus 7
- Sylvestris libica 7
Fitness 108
Fleas 93
Forest cat,
- Norwegian 172-173
- Siberian 174-175

G

Gender 52
Grooming 104

H

Handling 80
Havana 218-219
Herodotus 8
Himalayan 168-169
Household 250
Hygiene 103

I

Identification 95
Islam 11

K

Kittens 50, 97,
- caring for 99
Korat 222-223

L

Leukaemia 89
Longhair,
- colourpoint 168-169
- oriental 161

M

Machairodus 7
Mafdet 8
Maine coon 170-171
Maintenance, self 43
Manx 238-239
Mau, Egyptian 228-229
Medication 136
Miacis 7
Moggie 54, 250

N

Neutering 96
Nursing 140

O

Ocicat 230-231

P

Panleucopenia 88
Pedigree 54
Persian 182-185
Pixiebob 242-243
Poisoning 150
Problems
- gastric and bowel 146
- mobility 144
- respiratory 145
- urinary 145
Purebreds 156

R

Ra 8
Ragdoll 176-177
Random-bred 250
Resuscitating 153
Rex,
- Cornish 244-245
- Devon 246-247
Russian blue 220-221

S

Safety 75
Savannah 214
Scent marking 35
Scottish fold 186
Senses 28
- hearing 33
- seeing 25
- smelling 34
- tasting 32
- touching 30
Shorthair 15
- American 196-197
- British 192-195
- Exotic 198-199
- Oriental 232-234
Siamese 16, 208-210
Singapura 224-225
Sleep 47
Snowshoe 204
Social life 36
Somali 17, 178-179
Sources 57
Spyinx 15, 248-249
Stings and bits 148
Symptoms 143

T

Tabby 15
Teeth 25
Tiffannie 180-181
Tonkinese 226-227
Training 111
Turkish van 166-167

V

Vaccinations 86
Vet 85
Vital signs, monitoring 135

W

Wildcat, African 7
Wirehair, American 202-203
Witches 12
Worms 91

BIBLIOGRAPHY

George MacBeth and Martin Booth (eds), **The Book of Cats** (Penguin, 1979)

Grace Pond (ed), **The Complete Cat Encyclopedia** (Heinemann, 1972)

Grace Pond and Muriel Calder, **The Longhaired Cat** (B.T Batsford, 1974)

Alison Ashford and Grace Pond, **Abyssinian and Turkish Cats** (J.Gifford, 1972)

Mary Dunnill, **The Siamese Cat Owners' Encyclopedia** (Pelham Books, 1974)

Michael W. Fox, **Understanding Your Cat** (Bantam Books, 1977)

Howard Loxton, **Cats:From Family Pets to Pedigrees** (Sundial, 1979)

Michael Wright and Sally Walters, **The Book of the Cat** (Pan Books, 1990)

Collins Gem Cats (Harper-Collins, 1999)

Dr. Bruce Fogle, **Cats** (Dorling Kindersley, 2000)

ADDRESSES

Governing Council of the Associated Cat Clubs
of South Africa
c/o Mrs. M. Simpson,
45 Edison Drive, Meadowridge 7800,
South Africa

Co-ordinating Cat Council of Australia
(CCCofA)
Box No 4317 GPO,
Sydney,
NSW 2001,
Australia

New Zealand Cat Fancy Inc
PO Box 3167,
Richmond, Nelson,
New Zealand

Fédération Internationale Féline (FIFé)
Boerhaavelaan 23, NO-5644 BB Eindhoven,
Netherlands

UK

Royal Society for the Prevention of Cruelty to
Animals (RSPCA)
The Manor House,
Horsham, Sussex,
RH12 1HG

Cats Protection League
29 Church Street,
Slough,
Berkshire,
SL1 1PW

Governing Council of the Cat Fancy (GCCF)
4–6 Penel Orlieu,
Bridgwater,
Somerset,
TA6 3PG

Cat Association of Britain (CA)
Mill House,
Letcombe Regis,
Oxfordshire
OX12 9JD

USA

American Society for the Prevention of Cruelty to
Animals (ASPCA)
441 East 92nd St.,
New York,
NY 10028

American Cat Association (ACA)
8101 Katherine Drive,
Panorama City,
CA 91402

American Cat Fancier's Association (ACFA)
PO Box 203,
Point Lookout,
MO 65726

Cat Fancier's Federation (CFF)
9509 Montgomery Road,
Cinncinatti,
OH 45242

CREDITS

With thanks to:

Vic Swift at the British Library, London and to all the cat owners, breed clubs and societies who kindly shared their knowledge and information on the internet.

Find out more about the different breeds, clubs and societies and about caring for your cats by looking on the internet. If you are considering a cat as a pet make sure you are fully committed to it's care before you take one home: a cat or any other animal – is for life.